PENGUIN BOOKS

THE LURE OF THE LAW

Richard W. Moll, a former Dean of Admissions at several of the nation's most selective colleges, is the author of *Playing the Selective College Admissions Game* and *The Public Ivys: A Guide to America's Best Public Undergraduate Colleges and Universities*. Moll has also written for *Harper's, Saturday Review, The College Board Review, The New York Times, The Washington Post*, etc. *The Lure of the Law: Why People Become Lawyers, and What the Profession Does to Them* was written after Richard Moll was hired by a major New York law firm to help change its conservative image. Moll lectures at high schools, colleges and universities, Bar Associations, and academic seminars throughout the nation.

D0031876

THE LURE
of
THE LAW

RICHARD W. MOLL

PENGUIN BOOKS

PENGUIN BOOKS
Published by the Penguin Group
Viking Penguin, a division of Penguin Books USA Inc.,
375 Hudson Street, New York, New York 10014, U.S.A.
Penguin Books Ltd, 27 Wrights Lane, London W8 5TZ, England
Penguin Books Australia Ltd, Ringwood, Victoria, Australia
Penguin Books Canada Ltd, 2801 John Street,
Markham, Ontario, Canada L3R 1B4
Penguin Books (N.Z.) Ltd, 182–190 Wairau Road,
Auckland 10, New Zealand

Penguin Books Ltd, Registered Offices:
Harmondsworth, Middlesex, England

First published in the United States of America by
Viking Penguin, a division of Penguin Books USA Inc., 1990
Published in Penguin Books 1991

1   3   5   7   9   10   8   6   4   2

Grateful acknowledgment is made for permission to reprint excerpts from
the following copyrighted works:
"The Whorehouse Theory of Law" by Florynce Kennedy. By permission
of the author.
"Imagine . . . a time without . . . lawyers" by Lionel Casson, *Smithsonian*,
October 1987. By permission of the author.
"In Defense of Lawyers" by Myron M. Moskovitz. By permission of the
author.

THE LIBRARY OF CONGRESS HAS CATALOGUED THE HARDCOVER AS FOLLOWS:
Moll, Richard W.
The lure of the law / Richard W. Moll.
p.   cm.
ISBN 0-670-81969-7 (hc.)
ISBN 0 14 01.0556 5 (pbk.)
1. Practice of law—United States—Anecdotes.   2. Law—United
States—Anecdotes.   I. Title.
KF300.Z9M57   1990
349.73′023—dc20   89–40332
[347.30023]

Printed in the United States of America

This book is dedicated to the memory of
C. Anthony Friedrich, a twenty-eight-year-old Harvard
Law alumnus and second-year associate with
Arnold & Porter of Washington, D.C. He was
killed on October 21, 1989, in an airplane crash
in Honduras while completing a pro bono fact-finding
mission for the International Human Rights
Law Group.

May Tony Friedrich's conscience and courage
live with those in the law.

■

CONTENTS

■

V. STEPPING OUT:
A View of Lawyers by Nonpracticing Lawyers 163

VI. CONCLUSION 213

PREFACE

This book is an anecdotal, nonscientific survey of who is lured to the law and why, and what attorneys think of their quality of life once in the profession. A few observers, close to the law or to lawyers, have also been invited to comment.

Personal—sometimes very personal—profiles comprise the bulk of the book. The people who appear represent a variety of specializations, styles, ages, and positions but are, obviously, an incomplete representation of everyone in the law. Because basic themes keep reemerging from very different spokespeople, however, I am satisfied that the "mix" gives us the overall view that would have emerged from a larger sampling, had I drawn on an even wider range of geographically and sociologically varied sources. There is a great deal of attention paid to New York City and "the large firm" because this combination is so often cited as the goal by top law students nationwide. To provide balance to this big-city tilt, a "pod" of lawyers from Maine is also given scrutiny, although a national spectrum of place and size is represented overall.

Some of the subjects profiled use their real names—a few of them quite well known—while others have been given pseudonyms at their request. In all cases, conversations are authentic, with alterations made for brevity or clarity.

I can only hope that I have quoted and/or represented these serious, intriguing, often colorful individuals and their opinions about lawyers and the law—usually deeply felt—adequately and fairly.

Finally, let me express thanks to the partners, associates, and staff of one "Wall Street law firm" for my introduction to and intrigue with what lawyers do, and what the law does to lawyers.

THE LURE
of
THE LAW

ONE

■

THE IMAGE

■   ■   ■

The image of "the law" . . . Is the profession under a
cloud? . . . Has it always been? . . . Is the poor image
justified? . . . What are attorneys doing to
improve it?

Considering the pervasive negative views of "the law,"
why do so many people want to be attorneys?

■

AT INTERMISSION OF A MODERN DANCE CONCERT IN Berkeley, I started talking with the thirtyish woman seated next to me. She appeared both professional and athletic.

"Yes, you guessed it, I am a sometime marathoner . . . that is, when there is time. I'm a surgeon first, a runner second. But there is more to running for me than staying in shape. It is my primary source of entertainment. For example, there is a fellow about my age whom I almost always see running on weekends— we seem to chart about the same course at about the same time in the Embarcadero area of San Francisco. I've noticed him because, one, he's a sensational-looking guy, and, two, I can almost feel his fury when I pass him, time after time. Last Sunday, with my curiosity getting the best of me, I decided to brazenly pull up alongside him and say hello. He wasn't certain he wanted to talk, but he recognized me immediately. He grunted a little and then stared straight ahead. He was so obnoxious that I couldn't resist telling him what I had been thinking over the weeks of watching his reaction to 'the competition.'

" 'You must be a lawyer,' I said as softly and empathetically as possible. '*Better* than that: I was just made partner at my firm,' he snapped back.

"I *knew* it!—and I sped on by him as he cursed. The guy just couldn't bear to lose. I knew he had to be a lawyer . . ."

The lady hardly speaks just for herself. *Lawyer* in America has come to connote egoism and rabid competitiveness coupled with greed, a seeming detachment from issues of right and wrong, and yes—one who is very bright and hardworking but, so often, dull.

A new phenomenon? No. Theodore Dreiser said in his 1912 novel *The Financier*: "Lawyers in the main were intellectual mercenaries to be bought and sold in any cause. . . . Life was at best a dark, inhuman, unkind unsympathetic struggle built on cruelties . . . and lawyers were the most despicable representatives of the whole unsatisfactory mess."

Shakespeare talked about the dark side of lawyers much earlier. In *King Henry VI, Part II*: "The first thing we do, let's kill all the lawyers." A professor added a postscript in sending me this quote: "As so often, Shakespeare stated a verity that has lasted through the centuries." Indeed, the line has even been quoted in *Peanuts*.

(. . . So why do so many responsible, respectable, thinking people want to be lawyers? . . .)

Jokes mocking lawyers are in vogue:

Judge to accused: "Would you like a lawyer to represent you?"
Accused: "No thanks, your honor. I've decided to tell the truth."

Why are they starting to use lawyers instead of rats for laboratory experiments? First, there are more of them. And second, there are some things that rats just won't *do*.

But even joking about lawyers is not new. H. L. Mencken quipped, "A peasant between two lawyers is like a fish between two cats."

In 1987 Russell Baker, columnist-humorist of *The New York Times*, lamented the conservative religionist Jerry Falwell's going after *Hustler* magazine's Larry Flynt after Flynt's crude savaging of the Reverend and his mother. Falwell's mandate to his lawyer: "Get him!"

I don't say America would be better off Red than rolling on the floor with laughter at outhouse incest, but it's a close call. . . . On the other hand, neither is it inspirational to see Mr. Falwell seeking legal redress in the form of cash. . . . This passion for converting all problems in human relations into lawsuits is another illustration of decay in the American character. . . . Seeing Mr. Flynt's scabrous outhouse humor, a man of sound character has two choices. He can treat Mr. Flynt as a figure beneath contempt, and ignore him. Or, he can horsewhip him through the streets. The horsewhipping of editors by outraged citizens was a fine American tradition in the 19th century, and ought to be revived today to save the country from the blight of lawsuits. . . . More horsewhips, I say. Fewer lawyers.

■

The lawyers, we think, are in waiting to commandeer *any* dispute, worthy or not. And at a very high price . . .

(. . . So why do so many responsible, respectable, thinking people want to be lawyers? . . .)

A few years ago, this writer, with a background in image development and public relations related to college and university admissions, was invited to join "New York's oldest law firm" to analyze how its conservative reputation might be relaxed and to revitalize its recruitment of new lawyers from the top law schools. "A good job description and an enlightened, quite overdue concept," agreed many who had observed the prominent firm over the years. But alas, the firm just couldn't get off the dime with the new campaign. Why? The partners—each knowing the answer to all problems, well beyond the law—could not agree among themselves if the image *really* needed alteration (it seems the decision to hire an outsider was made by a skillful team of "young turk" partners without full support of most of the firm's old boys), nor what the altered image might ideally be. More important, there were such deep-seated, time-worn, and time-consuming rivalries within the firm among departments, not to mention among individual lawyers, that what little time was spent talking with one another rarely let them get beyond the tree-issues to look at the forest. The scarcest commodity within the firm was, quite simply, time. As soon as their suburban trains pulled into Manhattan, the lawyers were fully absorbed in their daylong private telephone orgies regarding the big cases; seemingly moments later, the evening trains were ready to pull out of the stations again, and the mundane talk of firm and individual welfare was postponed until another day. Intertwined in it all was the frustration (and consequent diminished effectiveness) of the young associates, yearning to be led and trained, and the obvious sacrifice of human potential—the lack of time to develop other interests and talents, time to care for family and friends, time to contribute to the common good beyond law—a sacrifice known to almost all the attorneys, old or young, corporate lawyers or litigators, millionaires or just the well-to-do working up. After some months of observing the dark-suited, paisley-tied (male and female variety), professional, grown-up mice on the treadmill, I whispered to myself . . .

(. . . So why do so many responsible, respectable, thinking people want to be lawyers? . . .)

Indeed, some *inside* the law question the honor of it all. A few grow superimaginative to make their embittered point. Florynce Kennedy, a lawyer and feminist, explains her "Whorehouse Theory of Law":

Ours is a prostitute society. The system of justice, and most especially the legal profession, is a whorehouse serving those best able to afford the luxuries of justice offered to preferred customers. The lawyer, in these terms, is analogous to a prostitute. The difference between the two is simple. The prostitute is honest—the buck is her aim. The lawyer is dishonest—he claims that justice, service to mankind is his primary purpose. The lawyer's deception of the people springs from his actual money-making role; he represents the client who puts the highest fee on the table. . . . As a law student, he is taught not only to park his humanity, but to think only in terms of money, power, and "the law." It follows that many lawyers wish to be in the pay of the business and government "houses." That is their highest aim—to be in a house where the richest johns come. . . . The more delinquent the business or government client, the greater the employment opportunity for lawyers. Some of the two-bit-whore lawyers have spent lives of great disappointment because they have not been recruited and raised to "call girl" status in the major Wall Street firm or the MICE—Military-Industrial-Complex-Establishments. . . . People ask me whether, as a lawyer, I am not, in my own terms, a whore (especially since I'm a woman). The answer is, "of course." I have described my practice as a hustle ever since I discovered that the practice of law had much more to do with money-making than justice. I try to tell it like it is. But whether the hustler in a small, private practice tells it straight or not, this lawyer tends to be a less virulent prostitute than the one at a major law firm that services the MICE. . . . Since the role of almost every lawyer is to perpetuate oppression in a corrupt, unjust Society of Whorehouses, it seems to leave very little alternative to the law students or young practitioners. They don't want to be whores, and they can't survive as virgins. . . .

*(. . . So why do so many responsible, respectable, thinking
people want to be lawyers? . . .)*

There are plenty of those who think Florynce Kennedy is on
target in describing lawyers and the law, but *The National Law
Journal,* in an August 1986 poll entitled "What America *Really*
Thinks About Lawyers," reported a more moderate, though hardly
positive, view among the general public:

> On the subject of which professionals, among 10 choices, deserve
> the most respect, only 5 percent in the sample chose lawyers.
> Members of the clergy scored highest in this category (30 per-
> cent), followed by doctors (28 percent) and teachers (19 percent).
> . . . Nevertheless, when the respondents were asked which profes-
> sion they would recommend to a son or daughter, law was cited
> by 12 percent, ahead of teaching (8 percent) and the clergy (3
> percent), but medicine (24 percent) led all responses. . . . Re-
> sponses to "Of the following phrases, which most closely rep-
> resents your view of the most negative aspect of lawyers?": they
> are too interested in money (32%), they manipulate the legal
> system without any concern for right or wrong (22%), they file
> too many unnecessary lawsuits (20%), they are too interested
> in representing corporations, not people (12%), they are just
> "hired guns" (8%) (and "don't know," 6%).

There is a history to all this. The classicist Lionel Casson
says that although life without lawyers may seem inconceivable,

> . . . It is clear in records going back to before 1500 B.C., and
> for centuries thereafter in Mesopotamia and Egypt, that there
> was no such thing as a lawyer. Parties to disputes had to plead
> their own cases. The courtroom was generally the yard of a
> temple. . . . People happily got along without lawyers right down
> to the middle of the fifth century B.C. Then, in the city of Athens,
> the seeds of fateful change were sown. It happened when learned
> men, interested in higher education, introduced a new subject
> into the curriculum. It was called oratory, and dealt with, among
> other things, logic and the art of persuasion. . . . In the suits
> that Demosthenes brought against his trustees, suits in which he
> represented himself, he was, no question about it, a lawyer in

our sense of the term. . . . The final step to full-fledged professional lawyering did not come about, though, until Rome moved to the forefront of history. Law was Rome's forte, even as literature was Greece's. . . . During the second century B.C., the vital step was taken: in certain circumstances an *advocatus* was allowed to speak on behalf of his client in court. By the end of the first century B.C. they were doing this so regularly that they now were called *causidici* (speakers of cases). A professional lawyer class, which performed a gamut of services for clients and represented them in court as well, had come into being. . . . But lo, the *causidicus* soon earned cynical distrust in Rome: "The most saleable item in the public market is lawyers' crookedness," the historian Tacitus wrote. "Pretend you purposely murdered your mother; they'll promise their extensive special delvings in the law will get you off—if they think you have money," said another contemporary. And from a satirist, "What does a man need to be a lawyer?—Cheating, lying, brass, shouting and shoving." The feeling that lawyers could buy their verdicts instead of winning them was widespread enough for Martial to quip to someone who was making plans to go to court to contest repayment of a loan: "With a judge to pay off and a lawyer to pay, Settle the debt's my advice—much cheaper that way."

Alas, it seems, the raw image of lawyering is hundreds and hundreds of years old, not born yesterday.

(. . . So why do so many responsible, respectable, thinking people want to be lawyers? . . .)

Myron Moskovitz, a rather outspoken professor of law and a habitual community servant in California, feels the pendulum of the lawyers' image swings back and forth in reaction to unpredictable current events. It is even positive now and then. In a paper presented to "Introduction to Law" classes in the San Francisco area, he says:

Back in the mid-1960s, when I began my career in the law, lawyers were generally held in rather high esteem. There were many lawyers in the forefront of the civil rights movement, the consumer rights movement, and the antipoverty program. Law was seen as a noble profession, and idealistic young people flooded our law schools with applications. In the 1970s, however, as the momentum of these movements began to wane, the public's perception of lawyers began to change too. The turning point was no doubt the Watergate affair, where lawyers Nixon, Mitchell, Dean, et al., displayed traits (greed, mendacity, etc.) which much of the public now associates with attorneys.

I really don't think that either of these views accurately describes most lawyers. Most are neither saints nor sinners, just ordinary professional people who put in a full day's work trying to help their clients and to make a decent living.

But it seems that the public's attitude towards lawyers is now at a low ebb. The Chief Justice of the Supreme Court has said that attorneys are "too litigious"—too eager to sue, rather than seek other means of resolving disputes. The president of Harvard says that the legal profession is draining away our best young minds into an endeavor that is of little use to us, as it produces no output which we can see and touch.

People believe that lawyers charge too much, prey on the misfortunes of others, lie, file spurious claims and technical defenses that prevent a just result, serve mainly the rich, create disputes that people could resolve themselves, and simply don't produce anything useful.

Professor Moskovitz doesn't dismiss the charges, although he feels they are grievously overstated and speak more to individual excesses than to the profession as a whole.

The negative attitudes, I believe, stem from a lack of understanding of how most lawyers actually spend their workdays, and more important, a lack of perspective on two essential functions that lawyers play in our society: one, resolving disputes, and two, diffusing power to such an extent that, in America today, the individual has the greatest amount of power ever seen by any civilization.

Moskovitz speaks right up in defense of the legal profession. He starts gesturing emphatically.

Most lawyers spend most of their time helping clients prevent or resolve disputes, trying their best to *avoid* costly litigation.

The call we hear for the creation of new ways to resolve disputes, by "mediators" and "conciliators" instead of quick-to-sue lawyers, is ironic. We already have mediators and conciliators: they are the lawyers themselves.

Disputes are inevitable in a dynamic society with changing mores and a vibrant economy. Divorce has become socially more acceptable, so more marriages break up. More Americans own more cars, so there are more cars on the road to run into each other. New high-tech industries arise suddenly to replace other businesses, and they in turn are driven out by foreign competition, leading to business quarrels about defective goods, broken promises, and unpaid debts. As a relatively wealthy society, we have more money to spend—the more business transactions we have, the more likely it is that disputes will arise.

Movement inevitably involves friction, and friction inevitably means disputes. The more dynamic the society, the more disputes will occur. We happen to have in America today the most dynamic society in the history of the world. Our citizens are just more often put in situations where disputes are more likely to arise.

Here in America, unlike India or Japan where there are severely lower ratios of lawyers to populace, most people are willing to take on the employer, the landlord, the big shot, or even the government itself—and the legal system enables them to do so. Some may think this means we are too litigious, but personally, I think it is wonderful. We exalt the individual not through more rhetoric, but through giving him or her some real power. When the little guy feels that he has been treated unfairly, he need not sit and suffer; he can (and will) sue. The consequences of this are remarkable. With this much power in the individual, we have a diffusion of power unknown to any other civilization. Some lowly wage-earner can hire a storefront sole-practitioner lawyer and sue the biggest corporation in the country. In another country or in another time, such audacity would be unthinkable: both the lawyer and the client would face social, economic, political, and even physical reprisals for such a challenge.

The best insurance against autocracy is to diffuse power as much as possible throughout society. This is exactly what lawyers in America do!

This flag-waving kind of talk has won the day among at least one large delegation in our country—the lawyers themselves, and the hordes of young people (and not-so-young people) who want in. That number is increasing. The 175 American Bar Association–approved law schools normally enroll approximately 126,000 students and hand out at least 37,000 new law degrees per year. Although there was a decline in law school applications recently for a few years running, the tide has definitely turned back up. Why? The twist of current events once again, it would seem: controversial appointments to the Supreme Court dramatically debated on television; public intrigue with the legal ramifications and revelations of such recent happenings as the hostage crises, the Iran-Contra hearings, and the sleuthing to uncover international drug rings; and nervousness regarding entering the investment world after the "Black Monday" crash of October 1987. And one more element: even Harvard Law School has suggested that the smash hit, Emmy-winning television show "L.A. Law" is (possibly . . . partly) responsible for the same kind of rush to the law that "Perry Mason" and "The Paper Chase" prompted in earlier eras. So prelaw numbers are climbing. Law is in.

But, there are such negative reports from behind the law professionals' curtain . . .

Consider the young people who nail what seems to be the most sought-after post on graduation from law school: "associate" at the big firm in the big city. New York City ("the international capital of law") is usually the number-one prize for the highest-ranking students nationwide, with Washington, D.C., a respectable second choice. Associates breathlessly join up, often after a lavish summer of recruitment spent at the firm between the second and third year of law school. They know the "summer camp" was a ruse, and that they'll be given dog work as a test—a long test of perhaps as many as nine or ten years at the most prestigious firm—to see which small percentage of the entering class will make partner. They begin, just after law school, making $80,000-plus at some firms in Manhattan and the other kingpin cities.

But what else do they get . . . or not get?

During this writer's recent stay at a "white-shoe" Wall Street law firm, memories of the old college fraternity kept resurfacing: the "actives" (partners) were in total control, or so they thought, and the "pledges" (young associates) were subjected to servitude—being assigned the grunt jobs, training "to know and respect the organization," faking respect (in most cases) for their elders, and being shielded from meaningful action—decision-making, image-making, recruiting others for a healthy future, and financial management. (Why had we smart youngsters put up with that mockery of our dignity and intelligence in college, and why did we move in public silence until the ordeal was over?) Inside my law firm, the associates—top-of-the-class graduates from the best law schools nationwide—moved quietly in fear of the partners. Conversations between the two groups were muted, associates' honest points of view were muted, and few risky positions were stated because of ". . . what this might do to my chances of making partner."

Associates complained privately to me, the "safe" administrator, about inadequate or nonexistent supervision—or the contrary, the abuse or overuse of the associate's time by a dominant partner whom other partners were reluctant to correct; the uncertain or mysterious context of a specific project; the rare opportunity to follow a project—even a piece of it—from beginning to end; inadequate intellectual challenge in jobs assigned; lack of communications within the firm regarding priorities for billing and for job performance evaluation; low self-esteem resulting from little feedback regarding the quality of one's work; and a cold, stiff, impersonal working environment.

Law-related "trade" publications (there are so many—how do new lawyers know where to start?) often do reports and polls and analyses of associate well-being in the nation's major firms. In a May 1986 *National Law Journal* study, the findings were rather bleak:

> What intrigues us is that large firms appear to think that money is the only answer [to associate dissatisfaction].... But associates don't leave the practice of law at large firms for monetary reasons as often as they do for other reasons, which generally can be lumped under the heading of "quality of life." . . . What we have discovered is that [the associates] themselves often are as perplexed as anyone about why they feel dissatisfied, disillusioned or unfulfilled. But, the fact remains that they *are*. We find

■

it quite difficult to feel sorry for big-firm associates. They knew, or at least should have known, what they were facing—and are getting paid even more than they expected to face it. But we are concerned about the apparent lack of concern on the part of the partners—those who run the firms—about why associates feel the way they do.

A montage of quotes from *NLJ*'s interviews with several mid-level associates (three to five years of experience) at prominent Manhattan firms:

I can never recall working on a case where I thought the interest I was advancing would result in any harm. But do I think genuine social benefits will flow from victory in my cases?—precious few. . . . As a practical matter, I hope I'm always perfecting my skills. . . . But what is a lawyer with a social conscience doing here? . . . Money is probably the first thing that comes to mind. The other considerations are the prestige and social acceptance that work very strongly, first in law school and then when you enter practice. . . . The damn thing about the money, though, is that we get paid too much. You begin to live a lifestyle your salary can sustain, and like other vices, you become addicted to that lifestyle.

■ ■ ■

I think possibly the worst thing in terms of day-to-day existence in the firm is that you're really in no man's land. So many partners and senior associates look at you as just junior to them and you can be anywhere from second-to-sixth year, it doesn't make any difference. You're going to be doing work which can be, not demeaning, but work you can do with one eye tied behind your back.

■ ■ ■

The lows here are always doing the grunt work. The lows are spending late nights distributing documents, pushing stuff through word processing . . . sticking around till 3 in the morning, making your own coffee, and having each of the four copying machines break down and hand-feeding documents one at a time. . . . The high moments are times when a suggestion gets taken seriously. . . . I think that just the fact that you think you are someone special makes you agonize over where you are and whether you're living up to your potential.

Joel Henning, who publishes a highly regarded trade newsletter from Chicago called *The Lawyer Hiring and Training Report*, confirms the impression of the highly paid but deeply dissatisfied large-firm associate. He blames the partners at most firms who ". . . have failed miserably in their task of building from the bottom because they have not trained their associates well or done what's necessary to encourage the best among them to remain."

Henning quotes firm associates he has interviewed who want to leave or already have departed: "I feel like I'm floating in outer space with no lifeline." "I never get to attend or listen in on important meetings and phone calls." "The only time I get feedback is when I screw up. I never get positive feedback or constructive criticism." "I'm afraid that I'm committing malpractice." "I am never permitted enough time to do a decent job."

(. . . So why do so many responsible, respectable, thinking people want to be lawyers? . . .)

One remembers, with Professor Moskovitz, that late-sixties, early-seventies generation of young people who abandoned their political demonstrations to report to law school in hopes of realizing a more ordered change to society. Those young people are often seen marching to the same drummer as their elders now. But is there a remnant of the commitment to public-interest law that we heard so much about just a few decades ago? Currently, only three percent of law school graduates immediately enter the field of public-interest law, where salaries are dreadfully low when compared to escalating wages at the private firms, corporations, and even in government. But many lawyers, young and old, voice interest and/or commitment to pro bono (free) legal work as part of their professional and/or personal duty. What is the extent of pro bono activity today among lawyers?

Disappointing, at best. "When it comes to pro bono publico work," reports the *ABA Journal* (November 1985), "lawyers aren't living up to their own expectations. Three-fourths think all lawyers have an obligation to do pro bono, but only 60 percent have actually *ever* provided services. Even worse, only one in four wants to get more involved in pro bono work. Their excuse, of course, is 'not enough time.' . . . Women are much more committed to pro bono than men—in theory, at least—87 percent think lawyers should contribute. In practice, however, there isn't a significant difference between women's and men's contributions."

By June 1988, *Time* magazine reported further shrinkage. "These are not good days for pro bono. The American Bar Association reports that only 17.7% of the nation's 659,000 private attorneys perform this task. . . . 'It's the biggest pro bono crunch we've ever seen,' says Steven Nissen, Executive Director [of Private Counsel, a Los Angeles group that receives about one thousand calls a day for legal assistance]. The trend toward giant law firms that operate like corporations gets much of the blame. Goaded by a bottom-line mentality, devoting nearly every moment to revenue-earning work, firms that once routinely set pro bono goals for their members now often just issue watery memos of encouragement. In the money-mad 1980s, the thinking goes, plenty of lawyers do well. Fewer do good. . . ."

(. . . So why do so many responsible, respectable, thinking people want to be lawyers? . . .)

Although the legal world still belongs very much to the men, women are growing in number and influence. The American Bar Association estimated in 1987 that approximately 103,000 women had been admitted to the bar and were practicing law. And currently, approximately forty percent of the nation's law students are women. But as recently as November 1986, the *ABA Journal* reported that forty-five percent of America's lawyers recorded that the firms in which they worked did not have female attorneys.

Granted, we can point to Justice Sandra Day O'Connor, to Barbara Black, the first woman dean of an Ivy law school (Columbia), and to a few other women who have distinguished themselves in the field of law. The list is short—and yet one must note that seventy-five percent of the female lawyers graduated from law school *after* 1970.

Clearly, women are now an important component of the law profession. That presents not only new opportunities, but a more intense consideration of some old issues as well.

"No doubt about it," records the June 1988 *ABA Journal,* "women have presented law firms with a unique set of challenges. Membership in discriminatory clubs, gender bias in the courts, parental leave, mentoring, part-time work arrangements, even on-site day-care, are some of the issues they've raised. And they're not just 'women's' issues—they promise to make the profession more rewarding for men as well. . . . But is it true that a 'glass ceiling' keeps the majority of women from enjoying the rights and privileges of being a lawyer?"

The real issue seems to be childbearing. As Columbia dean Barbara Black has said, "The most important problem is combining family and career, which will not go away. We can't wish it out of existence."

Women who make partner are disproportionately unmarried or divorced, and childless. That was the conclusion of two days of hearings on women and the profession conducted by the ABA in Philadelphia. "Men don't have to make that choice. They can have a family and partnership," said one participant.

"As long as women are expected to do the lion's share of the childrearing and household duties, having a family *and* the brass ring will continue to be harder—much harder—for them than for their male counterparts," concludes the ABA report.

But more subtle problems remain—related to sexism, pure and simple. In the November 1986 *ABA Journal* poll, almost half of the country's lawyers (47.4 percent) reported that they'd heard a male lawyer in their firm make a sexist remark recently, and 73.7 percent said they'd heard a male lawyer from *another* firm make a sexist remark.

(. . . So why do so many responsible, respectable, thinking women want to be lawyers? . . .)

The image of the law profession may fall something short of positive, the work to be done (at least by the young) may fall something short of positive, and the working environment and the expectation of time spent on the job may fall something short of positive . . . but clearly, the *money* is positive.

Annually in July, there is a glossy report in *The American Lawyer*—the slickest, least academic, and most read of the law "journals"—revealing what all the law world wants to know:

■

which one hundred firms in the nation made the most money, and how much, in the preceding year. Steve Brill, the outspoken and flamboyant president and editor-in-chief of the publication, always captures the year in a lead article with easy language. In the 1988 edition:

> Whatever the October crash might have done to their clients, as a general matter it didn't hurt big-time corporate lawyers in 1987. . . . Indeed, for most of the law's heavy hitters, business has been so good that law is fast becoming not just a source of wealth for the few but one of the country's largest sources of high incomes. Consider this: according to *Forbes,* the average salary and bonus compensation in 1987 for the 800 chief executives of the country's largest corporations was $762,253. But at the 15 firms in the AM LAW 100 with the highest profits per partner, there were 1,318 partners with average incomes of $739,000.

In Brill's "Revenue per Lawyer, City by City" chart, the astounding number for New York's Wachtell, Lipton, Rosen & Katz was $985,000 (next in line in New York City was Cravath, Swaine & Moore at $560,000 per lawyer). In Boston, the high revenue per lawyer was $285,000 at Ropes & Gray; in Chicago, $350,000 at Kirkland & Ellis; in Cleveland, $285,000 at Jones, Day, Reavis & Pogue; in Houston, $365,000 at Vinson & Elkins; in Los Angeles, $415,000 at Latham & Watkins; in Philadelphia, $275,000 at Wold, Block, Schorr and Solis-Cohen; in San Francisco, $310,000 at McCutchen, Doyle, Brown & Enersen; and in Washington, D.C., $305,000 at Covington & Burling. (Each lawyer, of course, does not get *paid* this kind of money, due to the costs and overhead of the firm, but according to Brill, ". . . revenue per lawyer remains the key to all law firm success. . . . The firms that are best in revenue per lawyer—which is really the ultimate measure of how much business the firm has, how hard its lawyers work to service it, and how much they can get for their work in the marketplace—are usually best in profits per partner.")

According to Brill, "the top profits per *partner*, city by city" (for 1987): in New York, $1,405,000 at Wachtell, Lipton, Rosen & Katz (two other New York City firms were over the million-dollar mark); in Chicago, $670,000 at Kirkland & Ellis; in Cleveland, $280,000 at Jones, Day, Reavis & Pogue; in Houston, $440,000 at Vinson & Elkins; in Los Angeles, $625,000 at Latham & Watkins; in Philadelphia, $290,000 at Morgan, Lewis & Bockus; in San Francisco, $325,000 at Brobeck, Phleger & Harrison; and in Washington, D.C., $340,000 at Akin, Gump, Strauss, Hauer & Feld.

Meanwhile, the lowly new associates, most of whom came directly to the firms from law school, aren't doing so badly. According to the *New York Law Journal,* the average starting pay in the fall of 1988 was $37,000 (up from $24,000 in 1983) for a group whose average age is twenty-six. In New York, some beginners at major firms started at $76,000 in 1988.

> (. . . So is that *why so many responsible, respectable, thinking people want to be lawyers? . . .)*

No one within law seems willing to quarrel with the importance of big money as a primary lure to the profession, at least today. That part of the lawyers' image is on target, insiders and outsiders agree.

But there are other aspects of the lawyers' image that many within the profession lament, and they are begging their own to change their ways. So often, those in high places who chastise fellow lawyers (often at professional meetings or in professional journals) seem, by faulting the imagery so little, to admit silently that it is accurate. Consider this article in *The National Law Journal* (August 18, 1986) by Benjamin Civiletti, former U.S. attorney general, now with a private firm in Washington, D.C.:

> . . . We should not simply accept the fact that the public holds such little esteem for us and do nothing about it. In fact, there is a great deal that we can and ought to do. And, in the process, we can make the practice of law more satisfying and more fun. Instead of worrying about our image, we should focus on two concepts—one, the full performance of our duty to practice our profession in the interest of the public, and two, the practice of our profession consistent with personal values and satisfaction. If we are faithful to these fundamentals, we will be better law-

yers, citizens, and humans, and our standing will grow accordingly.

Civiletti urges particularly against excessive fees ("Excessive fees or other indicia of greed are not in the public interest") and undue delay ("a major culprit in the cost spiral"), and for more pro bono work ("Unfortunately, far too many lawyers, including some of the more noteworthy and otherwise successful and respected ones, willfully ignore this important obligation of the profession").

Even the White House feels the attorneys' image is worth addressing in sharp language. In a 1986 commencement address at the Indiana University School of Law in Indianapolis, Mitchell E. Daniels, Jr., President Reagan's assistant for political and intergovernmental affairs, said:

Polls have consistently shown that ours is the only major Western nation in which the legal system is viewed with decidedly less respect than other institutions. Why? . . . First, there is our sheer number and our pervasiveness. The statistics are almost numbing: The U.S. has more than 90 percent of the world's lawyers, five times as many per capita as Western Europe, 36 times as many as Japan. The overall total has doubled in the last 15 years. . . . In looking at these numbers, Americans sense a sort of Say's Law at work, in which supply is creating its own demand. Many people believe lawyers recommend more work than is needed and send more disputes to court than is necessary. . . . As the gathering revolution against the nation's tort system suggests, they see us less and less as public servants, more and more as croupiers, adding nothing to the plot but always claiming the house's take. Increasingly, the public sees us not as a profession but as just another profit-driven industry, locked in zero-sum competition with its own economic ambitions. . . . Some think we are running a kind of lottery in which traditional values of personal responsibility are replaced by the luck of the draw and the ingenuity of counsel.

So, as you await the results of the bar exam, the American people are conducting a bar examination of their own. Will we as lawyers use our privileged positions to extend our influence, or resist the urge to make ourselves indispensable? Will we display more of the statesmanship, selflessness, and disregard for monetary advantage associated with public service and professional responsibility? Will we "stay our hand" and support the empowerment of average people? Will we support and assist the free flow of market forces and democratic processes whether or not they produce results that we in our wisdom would prefer?

... A career without potential for success for financial reward would be bleak; but a career for profit without honor, without the potential for reform and for the expression of high ideals, would be barren and undeserving of talent like that embodied by this class.

Will the youngsters and the older newcomers change the order of things? The speeches and the mandates are compelling indeed, but what is the "reward" in America, *beyond* wealth, for change within the law? And where are the role models? The image of the law is more down than up, the barometers for change stagnant.

(... So why do so many responsible, respectable, thinking people want to be lawyers? ...)

TWO

·

STEPPING IN:

The Lure of Law School

■   ■   ■

What attracts people to the law? Is the attraction academic or social? . . . Does a "bent toward law" develop early? And what do the latecomers have in mind? . . . Do those who aspire to be lawyers understand what lawyers really do?

More often than not, practicing attorneys are fuzzy about why they entered law—or maybe they're just embarrassed, looking back, at how naïve or shallow their reasons were for aspiring to the profession.

But the prelaw youngsters have it all figured out: "Even though the profession suffers from something of a bad image (created probably by a few), lawyers usually gain respect, are thought to be bright, are secure, are positioned to exert power, and often become rich."

"To see that justice is done" surfaces quite infrequently these days when discussing professional goals with those still in school. Older or "nontraditional" would-be lawyers, however, speak a more sensitive language. Unfortunately, they are usually less well placed and one wonders if high idealism can overcome a late start in allowing their influence to be felt in an Establishment profession.

■

WHO GOES TO LAW SCHOOL TODAY, AND WHY? A sampling of quotes from a tour through midwestern and southern universities and law schools provides broad hints:

A University of Miami law professor: "Law schools get a lot of students today who would have preferred to go to business school, but didn't want to take the risk. We land many of the brightest, but they're very security-conscious."

Another Miami law professor: "Things are about the same as they always have been. It was just groovy for our students to talk in the early 1970s about saving the world as lawyers. Now it is groovy for young lawyers to talk about being entrepreneurial. But they are basically the same people and they'll probably act out their lives similarly too."

A Vanderbilt Law second-year (2L) student: "Why do I want a law career? Where else could I be paid to read voraciously, speak clearly, solve problems, tackle intellectual puzzles, and change lives? Well, I *think* that's what will happen . . ."

A Kentucky Law third-year (3L) student: "Law school seems like getting a master's degree in liberal arts. That's why I came here, and I love it."

A 2L at Duke Law: "Why law? As a black woman, I want to feel a greater sense of control. I want to be at the core of potential societal change. Law provides that, plus status and money."

Another 2L Duke woman (at the same table): "That's interesting. My father is a lawyer and has done his best to discourage me from entering the field. Curiously, I like watching what he does better than he likes doing it."

A third Duke 2L: "Most of the top students in my college senior class (Dartmouth) decided on business school or medical school.

■

Although the image of lawyers today is poor, a number were attracted to law by the good salaries and the tradition, including social position. If you add in the security factor versus, say, the risks of investment banking, then you clearly have the supreme yuppies heading off to law school. But what's wrong with yuppiedom? Even though I'm blond and wear pearls, I notice people gravitate toward me because I'm a law student. There is a certain built-in respect."

The dean of the Ohio State law school: "Law students are quite different from a decade ago. They have lost their sense of outrage."

The Duke undergraduate prelaw adviser (also, chairman of the prelaw advisers' national council): "Fifteen years ago, students came to me with this priority list of questions: Where can I get in? While in law school, where can I get good clinical experience and public-interest internships? After law school, where can I work where it will make a difference to society? . . . From the late seventies through today, the priority list of undergraduates' questions has changed considerably: Where can I get in? Can I get financial aid? How do the school's graduates fare in picking off the top-paying jobs? Am I going to recoup my educational investment and live well soon? . . . Among our students at Duke, seventeen percent of whom go to law school, the entrepreneurial spirit is rampant. Security is in, only outdone by pragmatism."

A Kentucky Law 1L: "I think I want to become an attorney. But white-collar crime seems to be the new image of the law profession. As a result, all my friends and my parents' friends jumped down my throat for wanting to go to law school."

A Vanderbilt Law 3L: "The promise of Big Bucks is important here. The only overriding element is a sense of competition. Ethics and principles rarely figure in . . ."

The notion of "heading for law" seems to surface early. By the time young people must pick a college, many have already picked law as a career goal. But "soft" reasons are almost always cited. One often hears generic responses to "Why law?" when

■

quizzing any age group, college students through practicing attorneys:

A Yale Law 1L: "Everyone said that law school is the natural extension of liberal arts, and that you can use the degree for anything."

A Duke prelaw undergraduate: "Well, since I was a little kid, people have told me that I speak well and would be a lawyer someday. Then I was a whiz in high school debating, so law just seemed a natural."

An Ohio State 2L: "I didn't want to be a doctor, so being a lawyer was the only other respectable option, or so my parents led me to believe."

A Northwestern undergraduate: "Law has always meant brains, money, security, and respect. That was enough to get me to law school, since I've always been a good student."

The *ABA Journal* (September 1986) reported on the reasons practicing attorneys recall for being attracted to law school: fifty-eight percent said they studied law because "the subject interested them" and fifty-one percent said they did so in anticipation that "their work as lawyers would be interesting." But there were less abstract reasons listed as well. Forty-six percent said they chose law because of "income potential"; and forty-three percent listed the "prestige of a legal career." Less than a quarter, twenty-two percent, of the practicing attorneys surveyed said they had been interested in making law a profession because "they wanted to see justice done"; only twenty-three percent indicated they "had a desire to change society."

What is the profile of the person attracted early to the law?

Alexander Astin heads the Higher Education Research Institute at UCLA. He publishes annually, in cooperation with the American Council of Education, an attitudinal survey of America's entering college freshmen. In a recent analysis of the freshmen who cited law as a career goal, he found the prelaw students to . . .

differ substantially from students in general. They come often from highly educated and affluent families, are better prepared academically than most of their college freshman peers, and are more self-confident. A high percentage enroll in selective private colleges and major in one of the social sciences. Prelaw students tend to have a strong political orientation, with the women more likely to identify themselves as liberal and men more likely to identify themselves as conservative. In addition, they give high priority to such goals as keeping up-to-date with political affairs and influencing the political structure. Like students in general, prelaw students have become more conservative over the past decade or so. Indeed, this trend to the right is more pronounced among prelaw students, especially the men, than among all freshmen. Their attitudes manifest an interesting mix: Though they tend to be conservative on such questions as government intervention, academic standards, and legal issues, they are fairly liberal on such issues as equality of the sexes and student rights. They are strongly oriented toward material and power goals: making money, becoming an authority, winning recognition, succeeding in business . . . and less inclined to be concerned about social issues and problems.

In choosing law, do young people really know what they're doing? . . . what a career in law is all about? . . . what lawyers *do?*

At Duke University, the prelaw advising office, jammed with students waiting for private counsel, is also jammed with shelves of free brochures and booklets regarding law school and the law profession. The centerpiece of this literature, a thick 280-page tome entitled *Pre-law Handbook for Duke Students* by prelaw adviser Gerald L. Wilson and former assistant attorney general of North Carolina Harry H. Harkins, Jr., contains at least a brief comment on every conceivable topic regarding law as a career and how to prepare for it. Three small sections seem particularly noteworthy in informing undergraduates of what they're getting into, minus the romance.

The Disciplined Mind

. . . Law students tend to become more concerned with matters of proper procedure and exhibit an increased tendency to reason by analogy. There seems to be substantial validity to the well-known saying that a legal education sharpens a mind by narrowing it. . . . This may trouble those accustomed to approaching issues from a broader perspective. . . . Legal questions are less often matters of what is right or wrong than they are questions of what a particular code of law has to say about a particular situation. Ambitious social reformers or those who consider themselves "free-thinkers" may be frustrated by this; the law deals not with what *should* be, but what *is*. Hence, the legal mind is a disciplined one and the range of actions that a lawyer can take is often quite limited. Lawyers tend to see themselves as technicians more than anything else. . . . The uninitiated may be distressed to find that the personal side of a case, the emotions of the people involved, may be of little concern to the attorney, and may in fact even be viewed as an unwelcome intrusion into his or her work.

A Word of Caution

Paul Hoffman cautions the ambitious young lawyer attracted by the glamour of Wall Street: "There is something about the practice of corporate law which seems to drive men out of it. Not just the associate who never makes partner, but those at or near the top of the profession. Consider the cycle: A lawyer joins a firm at the age of 25 and spends the next five to ten years striving to make partner; for the next 10 to 25 years he's a junior partner, moving up, making money; then at about age 50, the children grown and gone, his home in the suburbs paid for, he surveys his situation, finds his work repetitive and routine, and wonders if he really wants to spend the rest of his life drafting indentures." . . . Such a description is not meant to dissuade anyone from pursuing a legal career, nor is it meant to dissuade one from joining a large firm. Such organizations provide opportunities to work with well-known attorneys on major cases for major clients and carry great prestige. Yet it is important to notice that they too have their drawbacks. The practice of law can be a satisfying and profitable profession if undertaken for the proper reasons. What must be remembered is that each of the various opportunities available to the individual attorney has its pros and cons, its advantages and disadvantages. The lawyer who can most accurately identify these in terms of his or her own personality will be able to avoid many of the stumbling blocks which may trouble less fortunate colleagues.

A Final Word: Goodbye to Perry Mason

It is important for the prospective young lawyer to realize that the days of Perry Mason are gone, if in fact they ever did exist. Although the law provides a huge range of opportunities, few careers contain the glamour which is often associated with an F. Lee Bailey or Melvin Belli. In actuality, many attorneys never enter a courtroom. In terms of specific activities or resulting prestige and financial rewards, the term "lawyer" may be no more of a specific designation than that of "businessman." The term indicates little more than the fact that the person to whom it applies may have the opportunity of either working for the government or for themselves, for big firms or for small ones, as prosecutors, defenders, or perhaps both. Maybe they will join a corporation, whether in its legal department or as a general executive, or perhaps, as other opportunities arise (i.e., in business, government, charitable foundations, etc.) they will abandon legal work altogether. Academic law is another field which the talented young lawyer may consider. Within any sphere, public or private, the individual should have the chance to pursue that area of the law which interests him most. Bound by few traditional stereotypes, the prospective lawyer should basically view his future career not as one which will mold him, but as one which he himself can mold, in accordance with his own interests, abilities and desires.

It is not surprising that the young rely largely on hearsay among friends, coincidental role models, and the popular media to form opinions about professional imagery. But this may be *particularly* true among the young people heading toward law. A job placement officer at Harvard Law School said, "You know, these kids are brilliant, but often socially immature. Most of them have been, all the way along, the brightest in the class and as such, a little outside the mainstream. This means that they can resolve almost any intellectual problem, but perhaps not all normal life situations as well as others. Like any group of young people—and possibly more so—they're swayed by rumors and the desire to belong to the group. They may not be as mature as everyone presupposes in picking the right profession, not to mention the right firm or first law assignment."

One would expect adults or "nontraditional" prelaw candidates who are willing to risk a great deal to start a new career late in life, on the other hand, to have a better handle on what the profession is all about, who should be in it, and whether professional imagery is on target or not.

In San Francisco, Golden Gate University Law School sponsors an "Introduction to Law" course for latecomers. Who are these supposedly more mature individuals and why are they lured to the law? A sampling of the "Introduction to Law" class of adults and their leader follows.

■ ■ ■

"I just could not function well in an adversarial role."

BETTY MARVEL

Betty Marvel's eyes dance. She just can't help it. But one wonders why, given the long road she has traveled. There obviously is some special spirit at work here. . . .

Ms. Marvel, the diminutive black dean of the Golden Gate University Law School in San Francisco, has the challenge and/or opportunity to make thirty or so mature adults, diverse as they could be, understand what the law and law school are all about. It is a novel, surprisingly intense three-week evening course called "Introduction to Law," featuring a parade of professors and attorneys from different academic disciplines and specialized careers within the law. The students are all serious about interrupting current lives and careers to risk a new adventure, and are paying a hefty price to find out what it might be all about. They are multiethnic, evenly split between men and women, range from their

■

mid-twenties to early fifties, and arrive at this downtown campus nightly by every means of transportation, including bicycle, city bus, and in one case, a new steel-gray Jaguar.

Dean Betty Marvel is not quite the Jaguar type. Her old VW has obviously missed a checkup or two and has never ventured close to the corner car wash. But Betty is a single parent supporting an adolescent and has chosen the teacher's rather than the attorney's salary.

"I just could not function well in an adversarial role. And lawyers today are so abrasive, so self-serving. It doesn't *have* to be that way, but it has become that way. Don't get me wrong: The law is basic and important and I feel good being a part of it. But I've had to find the segment of the profession that fits me. And I have found it. It is *very* exciting to attempt training lawyers not just in the law, but to think through elevating the profession as well. God, who ever would have thought that Betty Marvel would be doing *this*?"

Well, certainly not her father, a painting contractor in Queens, New York. Betty's mother had always taken care of accounting matters for her husband's small painting business. When she died, the daughter was an obvious successor. Betty was sent off to Central Commercial High School in Manhattan to learn the trade. But it was soon apparent to her that bookkeeping would just not be enough. She tried it, as an adjunct to her high school studies. Assigned to the intense and grimy garment district in midtown New York, Betty found she was less interested in making the columns add up than in improving the working conditions for all those who sewed and hauled.

"The poor women were paid piecemeal! It was shoddy. I couldn't understand if they were treated so badly *just* because they were minority and female, or if this was typical of our society. It was an eye-opener, and it was puzzling. And something else was wrong. The women had picked up an 'acquisition mentality.' The more they sewed, the more they knew they could *buy*. I didn't like what they were put through, but I liked their values even less. Suddenly it seemed to me that there had to be higher callings than keeping books inside that milieu. Society had big problems, and someone had to dig in."

■

This woman speaks with extraordinary energy. No prodding was needed for the story to continue.

"My father was not pleased. I told him I wanted to go to college, to CCNY (it was really the only one I knew anything about). He was upset that I was abandoning the family business, but we worked it out. And I decided to live at home as I started school.

It seemed to me at the time, in my utter naïveté, that being a psychiatrist was surely the only way to get at individuals' suffering. But my psychology professors seemed not to care at all about minorities. CCNY was ethnocentric and very, very comfortable. But it didn't take long to think through the dynamics of changing society. Where was the power? It seemed to me that lawyers and doctors topped the list in respect, authority, and brainpower. Since I seemed good at *theory*, I quietly decided that law was my new goal."

The lively speaker giggles in remembering her "stage" of "looking like Angela" as the law school years began.

"I decided to try for the top; but Harvard and Columbia decided, in turn, that I wasn't quite up to their standards. So off I went to Rutgers Law, a little black lady with a huge Afro. This was in 1972, when I was also involved in quite a few political demonstrations. At the time, only ten percent of the law students at Rutgers were women—that has changed a lot now—and the percentage of minorities was even lower. But here I was in Newark, of all places, discovering that my law school was Establishment as could be!

"I wasted no time trying to save the world from inside Rutgers by starting a 'prisoners' rights' program. But law school itself began to seem like a waste of time compared to direct social action. The professors weren't addressing social ills! Did they not care, or was it just not part of the program? I found most of the people there arrogant, very arrogant, and I mean professors *and* students. Disenchantment set in regarding the policies and the people. No individualism seemed to be apparent, not to mention encouraged, and the competition was wicked."

Betty gulps some plain tonic water, and sighs.

"I finished, but it was an ordeal. After one interview—at the

Legal Aid Society in New York—I was not certain I really wanted to dig in. Some friends chipped in to give me the graduation gift of a super-saver flight to California, a gift of much-needed R and R from a group who were very proud of me, but a little worried about me, too."

Dean Marvel pours out her smile with those eyes darting once again.

". . . And here I am—still! I never took the return flight home. For a while—seven months at least—I wandered and wondered, '*What* am I going to do?' Law school had really discouraged me from 'law as career.' It was aggressive intellectual gamesmanship, and I wanted something more humane. Then, out of the blue, a new kind of institution out here—New College—founded with social relevance in mind, needed a dean for their legal education program. I was there for seven years. Not only did New College change *my* life—but their graduates change hundreds of other lives in turn.

"And now I've moved up the ladder to a more prestigious institution and, once again, one with a social conscience serving a big troubled city. You see, I still believe law is the best vehicle for change. Now I'm in the right place and am involved in the law for the right reasons. And a *mentor* to others! The money is lousy, but the mission is right."

With the baby-sitter's deadline approaching, Betty Marvel is off, running with a smile. The VW didn't start at first, but soon she sputtered off.

∎ ∎ ∎

"I don't want to do anything anyone else has done.
And by the way, money is very important to me."

NATALIE SMOTHERS

"What adjectives best describe lawyers in their fifties? They're disgruntled, paranoid, glib but articulate, they talk incessantly about money, and they're often alcoholics. Oddly, I find all these qualities interesting, inviting. And that's why I'm 'lured to the law.' "

The speaker has a tight face, a stiff demeanor. She is a fortyish blonde with a rumpled bow tight around her neck and a mix-and-match outfit of black and gray. (Every evening of class for three weeks Natalie wore black, white, and gray, relieved now and then by a touch of khaki.)

"I can tell you at the outset that I speak in black-and-white terms, with no shades of gray. Also, I'm *detached*—an essential characteristic for the good lawyer, don't you think?"

Natalie is bright and she knows it. Following the "Introduction to Law" exam at the course's conclusion, the professor Xeroxed and circulated Natalie's paper to show the class "a good model to strive for when you get to law school." But Natalie has never had the courage to apply her brainpower to a challenging task and stick with it. She is a complex of strong intellectuality and perhaps stronger self-doubt.

"*Why* didn't I find the perfect job after college? That's one reason I'm in therapy now. Has it worked? It's eighty-five dollars an hour, but I'm still here, aren't I? Listen to this: I worked for the phone company, was a computer programmer, made jewelry and took booths at places like the Renaissance Fair and Dickens Fair, sold bronze and copper kitchen utensils, had a fabric store, sold rattan furniture, did silk screening, and finally, in 1982, bought a tiny travel agency with money borrowed from my parents. And one of my big hobbies is swimming in the near-ice-cold Pacific with other zany Dolphin Club members."

Natalie chastises me for being an aggressive interviewer. But she holds back nothing.

"I have *no* friends from high school or college. And my list of 'don't likes' is long: I don't like people except in the abstract— the exception would be some of my older lawyer friends who are also my best travel clients; I don't like the trees and forests, the trout, the rains or the farmers around the little town of [fifteen thousand] in Oregon where I was raised. Dad, by the way, is an architect and Mom is an artist who works with Dad. He's the *only* architect in our town. He did set my sights high for education, and my first choice of college was Stanford. They didn't take me because of all their damn quotas, including on women. One guy they took from my class flunked out—I was so glad!"

An adjustment of her tight neck ruffle, and Natalie continues, looking me straight in the eye with a stern glare. Her father is often mentioned as the autobiography continues.

"Dad *thought* he recognized things intellectual, conservative as he is. Language was the intellectual exercise that always intrigued me. I picked Greek up in a minute. Manipulating words, analyzing word structure—all that appeals to me, and I'm good at it."

Natalie summarizes without the least glint of a smile.

"What will I be doing in several years? Hopefully, I'll sell the travel business, I'll make a success of law school. The skills learned there will be good for me. Then, I don't know. But I don't want to do *anything* anyone else has done. And by the way, money is very important to me." She twists and looks down.

"But I'm still depressed. I need nine hours' sleep each night. And I'm rather shy. But deep down, I know I'd make a good judge—immediately."

■ ■ ■

New Beginnings: "The up side of the law is compassion."

MICHAEL AND MEG BARTON

The Bartons stood out in the "Introduction to Law" course student body. First, they were a middle-aged *couple*—obviously, a happy, communicating couple. They arrived together, always walked to seats in the front row so nothing would be missed, carried leather briefcases, raised their hands and participated thoughtfully, and appeared very "well set." ("Why do *they* need second careers?" seemed to be quietly on everyone's mind.)

Indeed, Michael and Meg are "well set" and always have been. But the tried-and-true suburban route to personal and professional success, even though realized, has not proved to be quite enough. It is time for new turns.

Meg, at forty-three, seems the more eager and determined of the two to try law. She just missed that generation of young women who, on leaving prestigious private colleges, head straight to the professional job market rather than "start a family." With her children now almost "out of the nest," she wants to make up for lost time.

■

Meg and her twin sister started at a private day school on Long Island; but she reports not finding her own identity until her Skidmore College years. She was encouraged to undertake all those worthwhile educational and cultural ventures that "substantial" families are good at locating—including, in her case, an internship in Washington as part of the "Kennedy cult."

Between trips to visit her mother, who ran a boutique in Fort Lauderdale, Meg tried a number of jobs: market research for a pulp-and-paper company, editing with a major publisher, selling high fashion in a San Francisco shop, and going to school to "learn a trade"—interior design school, real estate school.

"I started to learn a trade *so* many times, and never finished. But, looking back, it was all fluff stuff. What could a *female* do professionally? I kept asking myself. I just didn't have the confidence of the 'new woman.' In fact, I had serious reservations about my abilities to handle anything truly professional. And when Michael said 'Come back home' during one of my work or study flings, I'd go running. I was always prepared, it seems, to undertake something significant beyond the home and the family. But I didn't follow through. Now, with the kids pulling out of the house to college, I've no excuse. Law seems right, and I'm probably going to bite."

Michael listens to Meg's story without interrupting. He is an ardent listener—in fact, he gives the impression that he is hearing his wife's story for the first time. And he's good at nodding his head approvingly.

Michael's story begins on the same "right" side of the tracks. But he fought privilege rather than use it wisely. He has become something of a self-made man as a result.

"Dad, a Dartmouth graduate, was very successful in the corporate world. But his success somehow didn't rub off on me. I did poorly in a New Jersey public high school, then was yanked off to prep school where my moderate success was hardly good enough to get me into the Ivy League. I entered Saint Lawrence and majored in being a jock—flunked out quickly and my parents cut off my funds. I worked in a bank to make ends meet, then joined the army where I met success after disciplined work for the first time ever. Through my then-fiancée's family connections, I entered a small Wall Street brokerage and became part of the 'pack.' I sensed at the time it was a dumb way to make a living—all that research just to qualify as a securities salesman. But I worked hard during the day, went to school every night. I wore my failure to finish college on my sleeve. That low self-esteem was, looking back, a strong motivator to 'prove myself' in the sophisticated financial marketplace. And lo, I eventually became a member of the New York Stock Exchange and a lead player in a major firm."

Now Meg is doing the nodding. Each is totally wrapped up in the other's tale. Michael proceeds at his leisurely pace, but with certain experience as a storyteller.

"Something very big happened just recently. After eighteen months of night school, every night after work, I finally earned my bachelor of science in economics."

There is a huge, uncontrolled smile, and Meg takes his hand.

"This is a new beginning! Despite the success in business—I'm now a partner in a money management firm—I just felt I had never quite begun without finishing college. So Meg and I are both at a possible new starting point—the *same* starting point, actually—for very different reasons, having followed quite different paths.

"One interest of mine is worth underscoring at this point: our involvement in the Episcopal Church. I was the founding father, more or less, of a large shelter for the homeless here in San Francisco, and am now president of its Board. So why not the ministry now, if I'm seeking alternatives to the financial world? Well, quite frankly, I've seen through the evolution of the shelter that the lawyer has the power when it comes to instituting 'good.' "

It's Meg's turn now.

"We'll be *different* from many lawyers in the public eye now. The up side of the law is compassion, putting common sense into play for the good of all, becoming astute listeners, sharpening reasoning skills to find the honest way out of a dilemma."

Michael broadens his warm smile. "Meg would not be a good litigator; we both know that. Her superb analytical skills will find a less adversarial niche. I'd like to be a public defender, however, and talk, talk, talk to help some of the same types of individuals as those who are coming to our shelter.

"I know we sound romantic and sloppy. But we're mature people now. We know what the world's all about, we have our priorities in order, we know our own strengths and weaknesses. Forget the bad image of the law. The Bartons are going to be different out there."

■　■　■

*"I'm already dressed for success and I don't mean just clothes.
But will color be a barrier? . . ."*

ROCKWELL PEARCE

Rockwell Pearce, thirty-eight, a tall black with a forceful voice and restrained manner, left his wife and seven-year-old daughter at home in Salinas (ninety miles south) to take up residence in an inexpensive San Francisco hotel to "finalize the goal of law school" for the three-week introductory course. The experiment is not without sacrifice: Rockwell is using his two-week vacation from work plus a one-week "earned administrative absence."

"My confidence is higher now," he reports toward the end of the course, "although the huge reading load they all talk about in law school—and my age—still leave an unsettled feeling. But I've decided to go for it." He straightens up with a warm smile. "I may even try to crack Stanford. Do you think someone my age could get in a place like that?"

The youngest of thirteen children born to a bark stripper and domestic in rural Georgia near Macon, Rockwell moved in with an older brother when both parents died during his early childhood.

"I learned at the start from my brother, a high school principal, that there were two—only two—thoroughly respectable, nearly unobtainable, professions as viewed by blacks: medicine and law. Since I never had much interest in science, 'lawyer' stuck in my mind from an early age. After doing well at a below-par all-black high school, I followed two sisters and one brother to Fort Valley State College (all the other brothers and sisters, except one, finished high school). I wouldn't have dreamed of going anywhere else—the college had grown to know my family and to respect us; the president even knew my mom and dad by first name. I took political science and was active in my national fraternity, Alpha Phi Alpha—in fact, I still am."

Rockwell's eye contact never wavers, even in this busy hotel lounge.

"The draft grabbed me right after college, and that wasn't all bad. I was sent to Tokyo where there was a positive curiosity about American blacks. This was in the early seventies, when international headlines were full of racial troubles in the United States. The Japanese, so homogeneous, were rooting for *my* national assimilation. They made me feel good and self-confident (although I'm not certain they would have accommodated a black woman as warmly). Next came Korea, a half century behind America in so many ways, where I ran an army post office. My environment was almost totally military. Isolated. I found a black American woman there with her family and we married. She's still my wife, a good mother, and does public relations work for a gallery in Carmel, near Salinas. And thank God, she supports my current experiment.

"The next chapter of my life is curious, as I look back. After six years in the military, I realized, a black man needed a little extra credentialing to get ahead. So I was determined to get a master's degree. We liked the greater San Francisco area, so I walked into Golden Gate University, an urban complex with a practical edge to education. I really didn't know or care *which* graduate program they put me into. My hunch is that they needed to fill a quota in public administration, and that's where I landed."

Rockwell sips slowly on a Lite beer. His controlled movement hints at cautious analysis of every step in his current decision-making.

"There wasn't a small city manager job for me when I finished the master's degree, but I got a pretty good assignment with a mega-diet-scheme organization, along with 49,000 others. I even survived two weeks of three hundred calories per day to prove to myself that the damn stuff worked and that I wasn't just a used car salesman. Eventually my wife worked there too, but three years for us was enough—we got out just before Chapter Eleven hit."

Rockwell leans toward me earnestly.

"The black-child-in-Georgia concept of 'lawyer-is-respectable' kept surfacing. I thought of returning to take a crack at Emory's law school in Atlanta, but settled for part-time enrollment next door to us at Monterey Peninsula Law School. Meanwhile,

∎

I was hired by a computer corporation there, am now a manager of personnel and customer services at a good salary, and probably could be a vice president in a couple of years with damn good money.

"But it's now or never for law school." There is a long silence.

"How will I pay for it? Maybe one of the schools will help out, and we have some savings, but I've decided I'll even hustle luggage at the airport two days a week, wearing a little brimmed cap, if I have to. The price of this thing will take a toll on my small family in every way, but we're gambling that it's worth the risk.

"*Risk,* actually, is a big word for me at the moment. Not just my personal risk in starting full-time law school at thirty-eight— but I mean the risk that practicing lawyers take, day after day. I've played around with reading cases enough to know that ambiguity rules. There is *risk* in interpreting ambiguity, in taking the plunge and representing your interpretation earnestly. That takes smarts, an analytical bent, and most of all, the need for something that is driven by *self,* by *me.* I want that."

Rockwell is animated now. The peanuts and beer are overlooked.

"Will color be a barrier? That's a risk too—I think it all depends on what the next few presidents are like. If someone like Sam Nunn from my home state were to be president our cause would prosper. Nonetheless, I'm already dressed for success [Rockwell rubs his blazer's brass buttons], and I don't mean just clothes. All I need is a fresh atmosphere to welcome me in."

∎ ∎ ∎

"Respect, security, and responding to a crisis"

RONALD B. STARCK

"Let's face it: AIDS is becoming a plague, although everyone is afraid to use the word. Monumental social problems related to the disease are emerging. *Some* of us are going to have to stop everything and give ourselves to this cause."

There is a lingering silence. "I've inquired around and am led to believe that lawyering is the most-needed contribution. Legal problems abound, and PWAs [People with AIDS] suffer endlessly, beyond health, as a result."

The speaker is a tall automatic teller machine installer-coordinator for a major San Francisco bank. Ron has been with the bank for five years and is now ready to move on, despite what he considers the decent salary of $36,000 (enough to allow him to put a deposit on a small condo).

He is tall, a marathoner, with salt-and-pepper short hair. Also, he is gay, although the man on the street would probably not guess it. His parents, well out in the suburbs, guessed it early on and that has presented problems.

"They never really supported me beyond adolescence, emotionally or financially. They just didn't understand. . . ."

Ron's father, a telephone-equipment installer, did not go to college, nor did his wife. One of Ron's brothers now works for the state of Delaware, having graduated from college in public administration. Another brother is a policeman.

Ron always had to work for every penny, creating modest new goals along the way. Early on he was something of an entrepreneur, starting with a huge paper route, moving along to a profitable coffee/pop/candy stand during the elementary school years. To support himself in college, he worked at a local department store every day after school and through much of the weekend. He thought he might like landscaping and enrolled in a two-year program at a nearby college in horticulture. He worked a couple of summers at the local arboretum, but found that both the job and the loneliness accompanying it were unfulfilling. He then set his eye on the nearby big city, but continued to live at home as he completed his education at a state university campus, with an emphasis on economics and business.

"There was incredible tension at home. Now and then I would just disappear—take a train to the city and hang out in gay bars. I really didn't know how to handle my sexual inclinations, and I knew that home was no place to sort it out. But then, one awful day, a 'spurned lover' of mine telephoned my mother and told her the whole story. I've never known if my father knows the full chapter and verse but I rather suspect he does. They've probably both known it for a long time. I guess they just decided to live

■

with it, but there were few smiles and absolutely no effort to hear me out. I knew I had to get out of there."

Ron has never been an outstanding student, and that compounded his parents' ambivalence about the way he was spending his teenage time and money. He was a B–C student at the community college in horticulture, and his grades remained at about the same level at the university. But he did very well in a senior year "Money and Banking" course, and that was the deciding factor in immediately pursuing jobs with banks. He stayed with his first employer for five years, working up to assistant manager.

"The first bank was good to me, but my current bank offered more money when all the banks rushed to install automatic cash machines several years ago. I had grown proficient in coordinating the vendors and the banking units related to these installations, and had a good many job opportunities as a result. Nonetheless, I just don't feel of service to society in this professional line. And that's an important consideration, I've decided.

"There's another big element in my life that has to be recorded at this point. My first real lover, Michael—we just split up—was a graduate of Princeton and had a master's from Wharton. He has a good job with a major bank. Although I think he's too caught up in climbing the banking ladder, I'm nonetheless envious of the fact that his environment as a child and young adult encouraged professional achievement. I just didn't happen to have that kind of family. Michael and I had our problems, but I learned from him that I *too* can achieve, even though I don't wear his prestigious school and family labels."

Ron has now applied to six law schools. "Why law? Well, it represents a path of achievement for me and, more important, I think, it represents a need related to the AIDS crisis.

"I don't just talk AIDS—I mean it. But let's face it: Going to law school provides much more for me than the potential of contributing to a good cause. Lawyers have always had prestige, and I need a good dose of that. Lawyers represent authority, and the fact that they *survive* law school means that they are bright and disciplined. Granted, they're people—they come in great varieties—but society respects them, they have security, and they seem to me to be an extraordinarily committed group, even the ambulance chasers. If I can have all that *and* commit to public interest causes, it would be the ideal life."

I ask Ron what level of salary he would need to live at a minimal comfort level in San Francisco. He responds, "Forty thousand dollars." I wonder if he could make that much money devoting himself to public-interest law. He doesn't know, and says he is not eager to find out quickly because the goal might be shattered.

"I've just never felt fulfilled personally—with my family, or professionally, with the banks. All that is about to change. Law is the answer. Check me out several years from now—you'll see."

■ ■ ■

*"Back again to achieve the 'respect of the law'
. . . and maybe Fawn Hall too."*

JOHN WU

"It was, of course, extremely humiliating to flunk out of law school. But that experience has increased, in time, my respect for the integrity of the training. I was there—University of San Francisco Law School—for all the wrong reasons. I didn't really go for a tough legal education. I enrolled because it fit into my 'life plan.'

"Clearly, I entered with a chip on my shoulder. Out of my twenty-five law school applications, only nine resulted in letters of admission. (Now I realize that was pretty good—but at the time it punctured the ego.) USF was closer to home than Syracuse and Lewis and Clark and the others—I decided that if I couldn't enroll at the top of the prestige ladder, I might as well stay home and save some money. That too was probably a bad decision. Anyway, I started with a bad attitude. And it didn't take long for that to show up in my performance. Now, three years later, I must admit I've never gotten over the failure. And I know I missed something important. This Golden Gate introductory course is my bridge back to self-confidence. I really want to try law school again."

John Wu, thirty-one, is the grandson of Chinese immigrants who came to California in the 1890s. His mother died two years ago; his sixty-three-year-old father, a Fuller brush salesman, lives in San Francisco.

John looks Brooks Brothers from head to toe, but confesses he must shop for tweedy lookalikes at Burdine's. Being an ethnic minority simply doesn't faze him although he quotes a recent article listing fewer than one percent Asians among San Francisco lawyers. He expresses extraordinary loyalty to his family, particularly his father, but his points of reference are rarely Asian.

"As a kid, I read all the Norse mythology I could put my hands on. Then I fell in love with Liv Ullmann. Although my parents could not possibly afford it, we worked out my dream: a year at the University of Stockholm (after one year of junior college in San Mateo). Now I have this hopeless crush on Fawn Hall [Colonel Oliver North's famous shredding secretary]. Does this Nordic bent affect my other views and plans? Probably.

"The law lured me early. When I was a fifth-grader, Dad listed the professions and described them. I liked what he said about lawyers. In the seventh grade, a lawyer spoke to our class, and I vowed right then to be like him: he was a smooth talker, smooth dresser, and I was totally impressed. Later, two of my cousins entered law, although one has dropped out to be a chef. And because I'm a media junkie, 'The Paper Chase' put the final touches on my wanting law."

The spoken autobiography flows freely; there is no effort to make it "sound right." John is building effortlessly.

"Law means authority. And lawyers command respect. So getting that degree is my goal. Maybe I won't end up in the profession, but I need to know I *could* have ended up there."

John's current goal is better grounded than the earlier "law school as part of life plan" calculation. He is now a paralegal with a small firm of three lawyers, one clerk, and four secretaries. He has been with the firm for three years (something of a record for John, who jumped from one college to another—finally graduating from San Jose State with a major in print journalism—and one job to another, including newspaper reporter, disc jockey, ski salesman, IBM field engineer, "hippie gardener," personnel manager of a hospital, and Magic Pan host).

With experience under his belt as a paralegal at a law firm, what is his impression of "the working law"? "It's an adversarial system. The good lawyer must be a master negotiator. He must be competitive, indifferent, and detached, combative, supremely analytical, and willing to assume the 'hired gun' role. Is money, or let's say 'reward,' that important? Sure, and rightly so. I think lawyers *deserve* a high reward for their long training, the abuse they take, and their struggle to win."

He speaks compellingly. And it's all on the tip of the tongue.

"I have learned that good lawyers didn't go to law school to learn the law, but to learn the *process*."

John turns on the subtle, mature grin which matches his words of resolve.

"Six years from now I'll be an attorney, somehow involved with torts—I like the concept of insurance defense. I'll have a girlfriend or a wife who looks like Fawn Hall. I'll be making a difference—partly by giving away a good many hours to the disadvantaged who need legal assistance. I'll still be near Dad—I love the man, and he needs me. And I'll have respect. *Lawyers* have respect."

THREE

·

WATCHING:

A View of Lawyers from the Outside

■   ■   ■

Impressions from a few who have *observed* those
lured to law school and on into the profession. . . .

The observers are not generous in their appraisals.
Whether viewed by spouse or ex-spouse, consultant or
placement officer, doctor or politician, the verdict
from the outsiders is clear: entering the law can be
done with clear-headed magnanimity and the
determination to "make a difference," but often the
eventual result is disillusionment due to the necessity
of giving the most time to what one enjoys least and
submitting to a routine that narrows and dulls and
drives one to be anxious and greedy, intense and
manipulative, lonely, and, too often, a compromised
individual.

■

■ ■ ■

Two husbands, two lawyers, two "changed" men.

NANCY HART

Nancy looks like a Marin County woman is supposed to look: deeply tanned, thin, wearing a black wraparound dress with huge Indian silver belt and earrings, exuding a happy glow and a full-energy manner.

"So you think I look Marin County? I *live* there, it is true. And the look may come with the territory, but it's only a façade because, believe me, the youngster from Kansas has always remained close to the surface. I identify with Dorothy all the way—that is, if I understand the girl correctly. Swept away to sometimes glamorous, sometimes scary places, I too have yearned for the familiar and a return to the basic values. But my two husbands yearned even more than I along the way, largely because they were lawyers."

Nancy really is from Kansas—Orange, Kansas. She went to public high school and did well enough to gain admission to Northwestern. But her father gambled away the tuition for private college, and she was forced to return to the University of Kansas. Later she did graduate work at the University of Colorado, where she met her first lawyer husband.

"I'm no authority on the law. And I'm not a lawyer. But I have *lived* with two lawyers, and believe me, that probably equips me with better observations on the law than had I been inside the profession."

There is an intensity to Nancy, but considerable charm. She is clearly her own woman. (At fifty-one, Nancy runs a successful independent counseling firm for young people aspiring to selective colleges. She started the firm nine years ago; it has been copied around the nation.)

"My first husband was a moral, extremely ethical man. The only way he felt he could remain in law was to enter the academy and teach it—he became dean of a large western law school. He

47

tried practicing in a firm after graduating from law school—in and around a stint in the military—and wanted out quickly. He found the firm practice—at least for the associates—to be all paper, a routine devoid of any consideration of values, among a society of learned people who seemed to think that dotting the *i*'s and crossing the *t*'s correctly and with style was the top priority.

"In law school, he had been led to believe that he somehow would make a difference in people's lives. Not finding that possible in the established routine of a firm practice, he retreated to academe. Also, it might be said that the school provided him more security than the firm—but God, don't we all need security?

"I was tagging along, comforting a man in misery until he started teaching. And then I became the observer of law students in and out of our home. They were being readied for an adversarial system that concentrates on 'Win at any cost!' To be successful, they knew they had to pick up on that credo. And as my husband so often said: 'When you set aside your principles, you *forget* them.'"

In California, people seem to be more willing to discuss a succession of spouses than, say, in Indiana. Nancy moved right along to her second husband without shifting gears.

"He's a litigator. In a way, I'm reliving with him the same story, at least as related to the law. So a lot of what he thinks and I feel, through him, has already been said. But to sum up, he is beginning to feel that lawyers have contributed significantly to the disintegration of our country. Need I say more?"

Nancy twists uncomfortably.

"Well, let's have some dessert. And discuss happier topics. We can leave my view of the law by saying, quite simply, that the profession changes people. The change is significant and rarely positive. Now, doesn't that sound like Dorothy?"

■ ■ ■

■

*"Problems related to insurance and litigation are the biggest
bad kids on the block in the medical profession, and the attorneys
are reaping the benefits."*

DR. KARL MACLAREN and DR. DONALD LOREN

An abundance of pizza and beer has seduced two doctors into
candid talk about how the law and lawyers affect their own careers
in medicine.

"When I came to the Los Angeles area from Canada in 1978
to be a general surgeon in a fine, suburban hospital of 350 beds,
lawyers were always in the back of my mind. I *arrived* here fretting
about the law. But the rumors I had heard paled in the face of
reality."

Dr. Karl Maclaren was educated in Manitoba, and following
medical school there, served a five-year residency at SUNY–
Albany. After a number of years back in Canada, he became chief
of surgery at McGill University Hospital of Montreal and held the
post for fourteen years. At the time of the Quebecois movement,
there were enormous financial cutbacks on hospitals in the prov-
ince of Quebec, particularly those of English tradition. Finally, due
largely to language problems his children were encountering in
school, not to mention the new cultural sensitivities inside his
hospital, Dr. Maclaren looked for an opening in the United States
and settled on a Los Angeles offer, much to the delight of his wife
and four kids.

"For years, I didn't even think of lawyers as I went about my
business of surgery. I'd pay about $250 insurance, and that was
the end of it. Now this is an area of increasing anxiety. My own
medical liability insurance bill is something between $25,000 and
$32,000 annually. That covers me for $1 million per incident, $3
million aggregate."

The doctor wants more beer. He is getting heated in his own
restrained way.

"This is an outrage! . . . On the other hand, I've been lucky
thus far. I was named peripherally in one suit that didn't amount
to much. But don't think from my word *lucky* that I'm implying
I should have been sued more. To the contrary, so many suits that
lawyers coax clients to launch are totally groundless—that is, if

■

you consider the unpredictable outcome of most serious surgery. Many of my surgeon friends will agree to a quick minimal settlement in a suit just to get the damn nuisance out of their hair so they can proceed with their practice."

The second doctor, a radiologist, is content to listen. But there is no space for butting in . . .

"How does this mess affect our dealing with patients? Well, it does them a *great* disservice. We require many more tests than are probably necessary, just to convince everyone in sight that there is a problem deserving surgery. We, the doctors and surgeons, are willing to take fewer risks—and often 'taking the risk' results in a cure for the patient (sometimes, of course, it does not). We're very careful not to be too aggressive in suggesting health care, and we never let anyone believe in the possibility of a miracle. We keep endless records, and worst of all, I regret to say, we sometimes are forced to think twice before taking on the bad-risk medical case."

The radiologist, Dr. Donald Loren, takes over. It is quickly apparent he too is extraordinarily serious about medicine and also the legal "threat" to the well-being of his profession.

Dr. Loren has a B.A. from USC, an M.D. from George Washington University. He served with the military as a doctor in Southeast Asia for several years, then practiced at L.A. City General Hospital (affiliated with USC) for four years. "General" has five thousand beds. Now he is a radiologist in a suburban hospital of 650 beds. He is a chubby, happy man. But this subject restrains the spirit.

"The situation has grown so bad that I just can't recommend medicine as a career to my son. But I sure wouldn't want him to be a lawyer instead. The attorneys have done nothing to slow down the factorylike atmosphere of the hospital, which results from the anxiety of litigation. There are too many lawyers circling around the patients, and the majority of them seem awfully hungry."

Dr. Maclaren is smiling. He enjoys Dr. Loren's tackling the topic head-on.

"In radiology, we're not as 'exposed' to malpractice as the surgeons and some others. Still, there is plenty of risk. My insurance bill is at least $35,000 annually. But don't get the impression

■

that this is the only new issue we traditional medical practitioners face. Discounting services is of nearly equal concern—you know, Kaiser and the HMOs. But problems related to insurance and litigation are the biggest bad kids on the block in the medical profession, and the attorneys are reaping the benefits."

Karl Maclaren thinks the two are harping on one side of the issue too strongly. He jumps in.

"You must realize that Donald and I are making what might be called 'generic' accusations. We're not impressed by the law and lawyers in general; but we *are* impressed by our own individual lawyers. Right, Don?"

"Oh, God, I hate to say anything good about lawyers, but yes, that's right. When we're in trouble, they can give exceptional service. What bothers me, though, is when our lawyer says, 'Hmm, I'll look into it.' Does that mean I'm about to pay a goddamn fortune for his education or for his service?"

Both laugh.

"Remember," says Dr. Loren, "that our hospital counsel makes more money than our highest-paid doctor-partner. And that is just to do legal housekeeping for us as a group—that doesn't include his big malpractice deals. He's good, very good, but he sure covers his bases well."

The pizza is gone and so is the beer. But the anxiety about what Dr. Maclaren calls "that one big case that could break you" obviously lingers.

■ ■ ■

LISA TESSLER

The associate director of the placement office at NYU Law is thirty-ish, has a purple fetish (dress, prominent fan on the wall, address book cover)—the NYU school color is purple—and a deep commitment to public service in what she has done and wants to do, and what her law student counselees should at least consider in terms of career or pro bono involvement.

Lisa Tessler is from an affluent suburb of New York. In college in Maine she structured an independent major in social theory and behavior, and has been involved in the application ever since. She has worked for the Oxfam-America Fast for World Harvest, taught in Boston's Chinatown, worked with Indo-Chinese refugee children, and was a professional counselor at Adelphi University before coming to the NYU law school job in 1982.

Ms. Tessler says law students have been lured to the field because of its prestige, security, mobility ("There are good options in law wherever one might want to settle"), the intellectual challenge, and the "acceptable channeling of assertive behavior," but particularly because the starting pay is difficult to top in any other professional field.

What dismays Lisa Tessler is the growing disparity between private-practice and public-interest starting salaries.

"Just a few years ago," states this natural-looking woman with precision, "public-interest jobs paid half as much as jobs in the private firms. Now they pay one-third as much, and there is every indication that the disparity will expand further. Interest in the public sector—not just in agencies like the Legal Aid Society, but also in government jobs—has always been there. But now, who can afford to enter the field at $28,000? How can one live in this city, for example, at that salary, particularly if you leave graduate school with significant debts? Because most of our students opt for the private sector, given the financial realities, they become really interested in which firms encourage public-interest involvement."

She pauses, shaking her head with a soft smile.

"I would describe practicing lawyers as assertive, rational, organized, conservative, detail-oriented—and finally, driven. When you magnify the latter into a firm full of partners who oversee associates, the bottom line is profit, which means hard work and exhaustive billable hours. Too often, then, the firms' and the lawyers' (young and old) good intentions regarding pro bono law are just lost in the rush. Everyone wants to do good— but too often, there just isn't time."

Ms. Tessler comments on NYU's strong commitment to encouraging public-interest law (she also mentions the reputations of Yale and Stanford and Queens College of New York in this regard). Every effort is made, through extensive forums and clinical work, to encourage the young lawyers' commitment to those who cannot afford legal services. For example, NYU sponsors a summer

■

public-interest internship program, giving eighty students stipends to work in the public-interest agency of their choice. And the law students themselves created a fellowship fund to support recent graduates for one year following graduation in a public-interest organization. But still, 76 percent of NYU Law's 1988 graduates headed for private firms, 5 percent went to public-interest jobs, 4 percent to government, 14 percent to judicial clerkships (one- or two-year commitments usually followed by private practice), and less than 1 percent to either business or academe.

This committed counselor likes her "calling" to advise lawyers about careers, but particularly about career conscience. Service to others is her criterion for professional success.

■ ■ ■

"The lawyer's product is murky even when a case is supposedly decided. And they seem to like the murkiness as long as they win."

JEFF LEVY

"My impression of lawyers after consulting with hundreds of them in large New York City firms? That's easy. They are ponderous, overachieving, pathologically allergic to change (really—a dumbfounding fear of change!), barely Pleistocene in recognizing how they should behave in the world of commerce, incapable of evaluating each other (irony: they survive on their clients' ability to evaluate lawyers daily, or at least job-by-job), dull, not as broad as human beings as I would have guessed or hoped, and poor second-guessers (they would have no idea of what to do or how to do it if they were to leave the law). The only group I have found interesting, time after time, is the litigators, but they usually are incredibly abrasive."

Jeff Levy is with a large firm in Manhattan which tags itself "consultants in human resource management and communications." He is forty, short, intense, preppy, has horn-rimmed glasses, a touch of the Woody Allen look, and finds turning a good phrase easy.

"Every day we help clients—usually Fortune 500 types—do a better job in managing people, in resolving key people issues.

About forty-five percent of my own time is spent with major law firms."

We're sitting in the cramped library of his midtown firm, where walls are lined with months and months of *Business Week, Harvard Business Review, Forbes,* and *Personnell* [actual spelling on the box label!] *Administrator* copies. The door is left open and amiable executives pop in now and then to chat (one to suggest that the author could pick up a finder's fee for directing law firms to the agency's services).

"Back at Brown [class of '71], I knew little about lawyers. All I knew was that 'Perry Mason' was boring—and I guess I thought his show was a fair indication of what law was all about. I couldn't help but notice, however, who wanted to head to law school from my class at Brown. Aside from the hopeful draft-dodgers, there were two groups: the high-talent/high-intellectual types, and the very strong overachiever types. I saw no jocks and no 'fungibles' with law aspirations. My hunch, now that I've mixed professionally with a lot of lawyers, is that group two is the more successful set.

"What do we do in a law firm? Well, we help define strategy and style for more effective recruitment of lawyers from law schools and from other firms. For one huge firm, we did 325 phone calls to inquire why third-year law students who had been asked to join them turned the offer down. One of my favorite exercises is in-house training for partners on how to talk more effectively with associates regarding performance appraisal. We split the partners up into two groups—one group elects a representative to play 'partner'; the other group elects a representative to play 'associate.' Then the mock performance-appraisal interview begins. Can you imagine the nervous giggles and twisting in the seats when the partner says tersely, 'Well, Jane, we have to get to the reasons why you're charting only two-thirds the billable hours that the firm would expect,' while staring straight at the floor? This role-playing is a powerful tool, far better than seeing dozens of film clips. The lawyers get involved and better understand their own importance as role models—the bottom line is at least a little eye contact!

"On the whole, lawyers look at marketing as voodoo. They simply don't comprehend law as business. Add to this the fact that they are lousy administrators—although they would be the last to

■

know or to admit that—and you have a pretty good reason or two for them to call in the consultants. Most law firms, in my view, are self-perpetuating aristocracies. Many of the forty-five-and-older lawyers entered law without a doubt in mind. They had a precise hold on the future, as did many of their fathers in the same or at least similar career paths. Law firms were law firms, and areas such as marketing and finance were foreign to them. These are the guys who lead the firms today! They're myopic and frustrated when it comes to combatting the competition, a new phenomenon.

"The new crowd of lawyers is a bit more savvy to the ways of the world. Often the younger lawyers took time off between college and law school, they have more precise expectations of career and lifestyle, and know their way around a bit better than the oldsters (who *think* they know so much more)."

It is clear that this fellow has a lot to say about lawyers. We shift gears somewhat . . .

"Are they interesting? Well, yes and no. I'm always surprised when a firm tells me how diverse their lawyers are—you know, one partner takes a ballet lesson once a month, one writes jazz reviews, one tutors others on computers, and so forth. Firm representatives absolutely light up when describing lawyers' *other* interests. One has the distinct impression that they consider what they do in the office fairly drab and boring so it is the extracurricular involvement that makes people interesting. That's rather sad, isn't it?

"I must say the lawyers I've met who really seem to have broad interests are very limited in number. I'm surprised to find so many, for example, who don't know what I'm talking about when I ask what they thought of *Presumed Innocent*. Can you imagine that they wouldn't know about a national best-seller by one of their own? Some of them just don't have the time—or take the time—to do anything but commute to and from the firm and do the expected while there.

"Another thing I've noticed is that lawyers are very good at 'making work.' The widgetry factor is high. They get accustomed to humdrum research and will create more when the current assignment runs dry. Who wouldn't 'dull out'?"

Levy doesn't "dull out" in talking about lawyers, but he is

willing to share a bit of his own background: New Rochelle High School; Brown for a major in modern Anglo-Irish literature, with a stay at Trinity College, Dublin; a Watson Fellowship to study, in Europe, cross-cultural approaches to the terminally ill ("I was intrigued by the subject, as the English department at Brown had had five deaths in one year—and that sapped the imagination and the energy of us all"). Following his studies, he worked for the Brown undergraduate admissions office for three years, became the director of admissions of Boston-based A Better Chance, a program that lifts disadvantaged minority children to greater academic heights by placing them in college-conscious schools and in colleges, and then spent a number of years at the Wharton School of the University of Pennsylvania as director of admissions, plus other assignments. His new wife lured him to New York City in 1985, where Wharton contacts led to his current job.

"How would I rate the professions in terms of overall respectability, commitment to service, honesty, etc.? Well, I'd put the educators first; then the doctors, then the lawyers, then the businessmen, and finally, the religionists."

He stands to say, "Part of my bias in doing this is analyzing whether we can find a tangible result of their work or not. Doctors cure disease—it's there. A student knows if he or she has had a good education. But the lawyer's product is murky, even when a case is supposedly decided. And they seem to like the murkiness, as long as they win. That promotes detached passion. There is clearly more passion elsewhere.

"My passion now is for lunch."

FOUR

·

IN STEP:

A View of Lawyers by Lawyers

■　　　■　　　■

Here they are: practicing lawyers . . .

One senses the differences, the very personal
differences, these attorneys bring to their profession—
from the fervor of "I'm a hunter, a combatant in the
courtroom," to the plaintive moans of "How did I get
here? Am I caught in the net yet? Are there options
for me?"—The ecstasy of a few to the disillusionment
of the many.

Are lawyers decent? sensitive? happy? fulfilled?
anxious? ambivalent about their quality of life,
personal and professional?

One Los Angeles litigator included in these pages
outspokenly provides a standard we can put to use as
we attempt to learn what lawyers are all about,
beyond the negotiating table: "I'm still in my thirties,
so I haven't met them all, but my general impression
of attorneys is stabilizing: they're serious, pompous,
self-absorbed, intense, insulated from almost
everything but their area of the law, self-indulgent,
and really not very interesting people. On the other
hand, it seems to me that they are, on the whole,
ethical, basically decent people, and surprisingly good
family men, given the little time available
beyond work."

■

■ ■ ■

*"We've produced a system of ending disputes rather than
digging up truths."*

THOMAS H. ALLEN

The all-American boy lives. He is forty-three now. And he's a
lawyer, but not certain that will satisfy forever . . .

Picture this: Tom leaves high school (reputedly the best in
the state of Maine) ranking first in his class, president of his class,
captain of varsity football, captain of both outdoor and indoor
track, president of the Key Club (every public high school's good-
guy organization—the farm club for Kiwanians), eager to
emulate his city councilman father's superb human qualities, and
vowing to marry his high school sweetheart when the time is right,
as soon as possible.

And picture this: Tom leaves one of America's most selective
small colleges (Bowdoin, having turned down runner-up Harvard)
Phi Beta Kappa and ranking in the top three of his class, is president
of his class, captain of varsity football, captain of both outdoor
and indoor track, president of his fraternity (which he convinced
to secede from the national organization because they were reluctant to accept minority members), wins a Rhodes scholarship for
a three-year stay at Oxford University in England, is a bit uncertain
which career path will allow him to emulate the superb human
qualities of his lawyer father and his college teacher uncle, and
prepares to marry his childhood sweetheart.

Now law partner Tom Allen sits only yards from the Portland
harbor in an old warehouse converted to law firm (several blocks
from his father's law firm) with huge exposed beams, atmospheric
lighting, thick Oriental rugs, and a slightly disheveled desktop. An
unfortunate hot dog sign outside his window (THE TASTE OF THE
CENTURY) is the sole element jarring perfection (although hot dogs
are all-American too . . .).

"I've only made one big mistake that I'm aware of," he says,
uncharacteristically throwing his pencil toward an open book in

what seems to be downright disgust with himself. "That was going to Harvard Law School. Or maybe the mistake was in not leaving Harvard and transferring to Yale—but I wasn't certain they'd take me, you see."

Allen looks not a day over twenty-eight. He is runner-thin, "character lines" have evaded him, and he has a lot of brown hair with longish sideburns more Portland than Madison Avenue. His suit is gray-brown, his shirt and tie are nondescript. Understatement is obviously the key. He talks carefully, thoughtfully and rather slowly. He embodies the sincerity of a good counselor. And he has the ability to listen. He has a big smile with a little too much space between the teeth—Huck Finn all the way.

"The stay at Oxford spoiled me, I guess. I took the bachelor of philosophy program and did my big paper on the role of tribal chiefs in the political process of Sierra Leone. At Oxford we strenuously pondered 'What is social good?' or questions like 'What is Quality?' We wrote a lot, and I enjoyed that, even though I knew my progress would be determined by the examination at the end.

"Any good educational system must look at different motivating factors. Law school—at least the Harvard variety—was a crashing bore because it didn't do that, although I hear they've improved. First of all, my class was huge—about 550 as I recall, or 140 in each section. The faculty were too busy trying to be great men rather than great professors. Our sections met all together, day after day, class after class. The combination of the case study method and the Socratic method was perfect for students who were afraid to fail—if you put in your time with all the rote detail required, you'd survive. But there was next to no creative intellectual stimulation. Harvard should have *varied* teaching procedures—Socratic and case-study classes peppered with more clinical experience, big classes and small classes, more writing, more free-for-all discussion. As it was, once our fright wore off, a lot of us tuned out because we felt we didn't need this! It was the antithesis of what they said it was, time and time again: 'We're going to teach you to think.'

"In short, Harvard Law was the only segment of my education that just didn't work. I decided to work hard enough to stay at the middle of the class, and that's exactly where I ended up. It's odd, you know: I've always thought I was clever enough to leave my options open—don't know why I didn't try to get out of Harvard and move over to Yale. Harvard had the reputation of getting students ready for private practice and for the big firms; Yale had (and still has) the reputation of more of an intellectual approach to law and an emphasis on public service. Anyway, Harvard, for me, was a big mistake."

Allen sits stolidly in one place and, aside from a few "Sorry, I'm busy" responses to his secretary's inquiries, concentrates on what he is saying with a small gesture here, a small gesture there.

"I forgot to say that between Oxford and Harvard, my wife and I—we married right after college—spent a great year in Washington. It started by my assisting Senator Ed Muskie plan for an upcoming campaign. The job was issues-oriented and stimulating. Diana had trained in Montessori teaching, and she enjoyed her job too. But we noticed that people in Washington more or less assumed the personality and the style of their elected bosses. You became a stand-in for your boss at parties and meetings. That didn't appeal to us, so the little part of me that had craved big-time politics was put to rest fairly quickly. Diana and I decided it was time to settle down and start something for ourselves . . . all the more reason that a rocky law school experience, as I got ready for the 'long term,' was a little unsettling."

Allen starts playing with the venetian-blind cord. But the story keeps on, methodically building.

"In retrospect I guess I decided to go to law school because I didn't *have* a career—maybe politics, maybe teaching—I just didn't know. And law school seemed the kind of education that allowed one to keep open options. In short, my big question was 'What makes society work?'—I remember asking myself questions like that over and over again at Bowdoin. How do buildings get built? How do corporations get formed and what do people in corporations do? How do we know, for all society, what is right and what is wrong—and how does it get conveyed? Well, law seemed the broadest umbrella for looking at those big questions. I had chosen the most challenging major at Bowdoin—English— only because the English professors seemed to be asking those questions. I had considered being a political science major, but the profs weren't asking the big questions there, or so it seemed in my introductory courses.

"Ultimately, choosing a law firm became a key exercise, because so many of the questions Diana and I were asking ourselves about quality of life were wrapped up in that decision. I didn't want another collegelike fraternity that compromised diversity and intellectualism. We tried the big Boston firm at first, but couldn't picture ourselves commuting into the city from the suburbs, living among people who were just like us. So a return to Maine started looking better and better, although we wondered if Portland, with only 65,000 people, might be too much out of the mainstream. As it has worked out, the answer to that is probably a qualified yes—and for all the good reasons, at least in our view."

The venetian-blind pull is returned to its place and Allen starts twisting his pencil in his hands. Each new paragraph is started as though he is allowing someone the time to hit the "return" key.

"I chose this firm because it seemed so democratic. It's not very old, and one of the founding partners wanted to make certain his new firm was not of the traditional mode like the firm he was leaving. That means that every new associate here is welcome to review the books—that's astounding! Everyone is expected to have an open door. The founders wanted to convey to the younger lawyers that the practice of law was not life itself—there would be time for family and community service, also. And that's what we're trying to keep in place here, although the world is changing and the young people coming out of law school seem much more materialistic. We're a big firm now, by Portland's standards, and all big firms are forced to become more of a business—too much so. We care more about 'billable hours' than we used to (seventeen hundred per year are expected here for those who anticipate partnership—many put in a lot more), but we're sure trying our best to keep the human element in the workplace."

Allen goes on to explain that his own work is in civil litigation. He is in court regularly with corporate and commercial securities disputes. His interest in litigation evolved after sampling a number of specialties.

He returns to the venetian-blind cord.

"Litigation allows freedom. How one handles the case relates directly to outcome. Choices regarding how far to go with discovery, etc., don't pop up in all specialties of law. There is choice here, and I couldn't live without it.

"It's fashionable for lawyers to say to you writers that law is grand—we wouldn't trade it for the world. But that is such an overstatement, and rather dishonest. Most of us, I think, initially go through a four-year learning curve after we leave law school and get into practice. Then there is an exciting accelerating curve of four to ten years where we keep learning, but the practice begins to show results. We're all extremely encouraged by that. Then, somehow, routine sets in—we don't learn as much, we know how to approach most every case from our little bag of tricks learned over the years, and we quietly grow nervous that life in law after forty-five might not be so satisfying.

"I'm tackling that dilemma right now. It seems to me that the 'good life' has three strong ingredients: commitment to a good profession, commitment to mate and family, and commitment to community. My scorecard at this point, I guess, looks okay. My wife says I work too hard and don't spend enough time with the family, but I'm home every night for dinner at a reasonable hour, even though I might work back here at the office at least two nights a week. I drive to work with my father every morning—we live two blocks apart—so that important contact is kept alive. My marriage feels very strong and good, I'm with the kids each weekend, and we take great summer vacations like backpacking and climbing in the wilds of Wyoming last year.

"But at this point I feel myself pulling away from law a little to give more time to community. We all just have to spend time with people who need help. And in my case, I need to recharge batteries with a variety of activities as well. Portland is a great place to do it—every helping hand is important, and the place is small enough that every situation provides a pretty good mix of people. We're not large enough to form into monotype organizations.

"One of my great joys at the moment is the Portland Stage Company, our repertory acting group. I'm president of the board now. It's a nonprofit organization, and the funding challenges are large. But the best part of that involvement is having learned that theater is real! *Long Day's Journey* or *Painting Churches* become serious counseling sessions for those touched by chemical addiction or aging parents.

"I still give a lot of time to Bowdoin—I'm an Overseer, chair

■

of the tough Physical Plant Committee, and am inevitably involved in a few more activities there. I love it. Also, I'm helping to select Rhodes Scholar candidates from Maine colleges. I was on the commission to rewrite the Portland city charter recently, have worked with child welfare, children's theater, United Way, and a bunch of other things. And I fly-fish and spend all the time I can muster planting and nurturing apple trees, usually on my parents' farm at Sebago. There is nothing I enjoy more than watching apple trees grow."

Unlike almost all others interviewed for this book, Allen never once looks at his watch. But this quiet discussion is eating the morning away . . .

"Who knows, I'll probably run for city council soon. And there might be other goals beyond that. We'll see. But I'm beginning to realize that the trouble with law is that you spend most of your time solving private disputes that don't make a bit of difference to furthering the common good. And the disputes themselves are often such a crock!—like a bankruptcy case I'm on now where discovery is taking almost two years, and we all seriously wonder if there is really a case. It's a crock! This kind of thing doesn't utilize my full skills—surely a lot of lawyers feel the same way when the learning cycle calms and the tedious where-are-we-going-with-this? case consumes so much time.

"Litigation is out of control. Much of the activity now is to cover lawyers' rear ends. We've evolved a system of ending disputes rather than digging up truths. Ultimately, someone wins—the case comes to a close. But the final result always remains murky. So many findings are taken from inference."

He stands.

"Nonetheless, I've learned a lot about how people put buildings up and how corporations get formed. Is that enough? I'm not certain."

What more is there to the American Dream? Stay tuned, and watch Allen. . . .

■　■　■

■

"The atmosphere in the government sector insulates me as a woman."

LESLEY MARTIN

"Should I be happy or sad that almost everyone I meet says, 'A *lawyer?* . . . You don't *seem* like a lawyer—you're not aggressive, you're not manipulative, and you're not a bowl-them-over kind of egoist'?"

Lesley Martin is in her mid-thirties, articulate but soft-spoken, gracious, and—yes, one has to say it—feminine. But you might recognize her on the street as a lawyer: quick-paced, in plain dark blue suit with matching shoes, plain white blouse enlivened by a simple gold chain, and toting a well-stuffed polished leather brief-case. Her black hair with strands of gray somehow confirms the impression of a woman with considerable purpose.

"I was never bred to be a career woman, even though my father was a successful lawyer and—if the truth be known—a real social climber. Although he had the stamina and the intelligence to move up the ranks from CCNY to Cornell Law School to a successful entertainment law practice, similar goals were just not thought appropriate for his two daughters. That was my first problem.

"My second problem was, in a way, related to the first. I carried such emotional baggage as a woman—in this case, a dis-traught daughter—to law school that I didn't do particularly well, and that was quite out of character for me. But the second problem goes well beyond me and my own personal circumstances. It is this: What does one *do* if you don't happen to end up in the top half of your law school class?"

The first "problem" first . . .

When she was halfway through high school in Fairfield, Con-necticut, Lesley's father decided to take another wife—not a pop-ular choice with others in the family—soon after her mother died of cancer. As the household broke up with considerable hard feel-ing, Lesley and her sister were "sent away" to a prestigious private school not far from home.

"Actually, although my sister and I were heartbroken at the turn of events—partly because we loved our public high school—Dad seemed rather pleased that there was a good reason for having his children in a school whose name everyone recognized. I plugged away in my new school and just kept working hard at my studies because I knew the college admissions hurdle was not far ahead. My friends would probably have described me as too studious, smart and serious, but friendly too. When the big moment of getting into college arrived, I remember asking myself where my parents' most impressive friends had gone. As a result, most of my applications ended up being sent to women's colleges. I finally decided to attend Mount Holyoke because its campus was so gorgeous and because I just didn't think I was Radcliffe or Wellesley material.

"There was enormous pressure from my father for us girls to perform well academically—which seems odd now as I look back, because we were just being groomed to be class housewives (which my sister is, by the way). All this pressure became deeply internalized. Mount Holyoke was a good choice, actually—you know, very respectable academically, and back then, a haven for the good-citizen types.

"I did really well, and soon discovered that I loved French and was a natural in foreign languages. (You know, I've met so many lawyers who majored in French. Just coincidental? I'm not sure.) I was in sports, a bit of student government, did some student teaching, and was elected to Blue Key, the honors students who show high school kids and parents around the campus. In short, I was the model of what my father wanted me to be, even though inside I was being all chewed up by his new marriage and living *his* goals for me rather than my own."

This woman could be a newscaster. She speaks directly, convincingly, and in complete paragraphs. And with considerable charm.

"Then I did something extraordinary—well, for me, given my protected background. I took off for California—not just for the summer, as my father suspected, but instead for three years. And there I was in Berkeley, proud to be rather completely out of character. It was the big era for rebellion, of course, and I lived out a very conservative version of that. At the time it was emancipating—and I put in enough hours at a public health agency to pay rent—but now, in looking back, it was a waste of time. I may have gained some semblance of independence, but I lost three important years of continuity.

"I wanted to be in New York, so that's where I headed next. I landed a decent job using my French as assistant to an African undersecretary at the U.N. But I quickly learned that significant advancement at the U.N. was closed to Western women—Third World women, okay, but not Western women.

"I knew I'd have to go to graduate school to get ahead. But I was baffled: What does a woman study to *be* when French and art history are the primary interests and areas of expertise? The teaching profession seemed full at the time. So suddenly law school just loomed forward. I couldn't imagine being a lawyer, but law school was a good extension of the liberal arts, everyone said, and I knew the law degree would give me credibility. My father was really my only exposure to law—and let's face it, I really liked the way his mind worked."

Every time *father* comes up in this conversation there are searching pauses.

"The top schools in New York were tough to crack, I knew, but Fordham decided to take a flier on me. *Fordham?* I know, a Jesuit law school with a rather homogeneous student body for this bred-for-polished-Jewish-wifedom didn't quite fit the grand plan, but I decided to go ahead. And because I'm so tenacious, I decided to go full-time and finish without interruption. I did all of the above, and totally on my own resources. Proud as I was to get through, I knew I was not giving a Mount Holyoke kind of performance there, partly because the education itself was so dry, so disciplined, and so totally lacking in any form of personal creativity. But also, I was emotionally confused by it all—still, I must admit, torn up about the disruption of my 'normal' home life and more important, confused about the role of women outside the boundaries drawn by parents and one's own social culture.

"The great part of being at a Catholic law school was the faculty/administrative habit of looking out for the person who wasn't doing all that well. And, let's face it, that was me. The dean himself was incredible in guiding me through some hard times. Besides encouraging counsel, he picked a group of us to do background research and writing for his *New York Law Journal* articles. That, plus the attention of a labor law professor, provided the little personal push I needed to make it through."

The story does not seem easy for this woman to tell, but she pushes on. And now, "problem" two.

"It is expected that the top students in the law school class, regardless of what they represent as human beings, will take the lucrative big-city private-practice jobs with possibly a clerkship or two along the way. Although people say they won't be lured into that tradition, there just aren't many exceptions to the rule! The rest of us had to struggle with deciding on what was left—government jobs, which pay dreadfully and are known to be often so b-o-r-i-n-g, the possibility of getting one of the few desirable public-interest jobs (that wasn't for me since I had heard that the huge caseload and physical circumstances resulted in endless frustration and not getting the job done—not to mention the dreary pay), or boldly striking out on one's own, which is rare for the lawyer trained in New York City.

"Anyway, I was lucky. That wonderfully helpful labor law professor had heard that a few dutiful lawyers were needed in one of the key agencies of the New York City bureaucratic complex. I took one of their jobs, and eight and a half years later, here I am at the same place."

A pause, a toss of the hair, and a sip of cold coffee.

"There is more than one irony as I analyze my current situation—or plight, maybe?—compared to those who graduated well ahead of me in class rank. On one hand, the top group of my class at Fordham are at the approximate $140,000 level at this time in the big firms, big cities—well, a little less in cities outside New York. And what are we of the same class, further down in final rank, making? I'm actually doing well in the government sector, and with a recent promotion, I'm pushing $60,000 a year. But on the basis of salary, I'm obviously the loser.

"In another couple of areas, I may be a winner—even though that may be known only to me. I crave independence now, as a lawyer and as a woman. In my government agency, we have independence—as an office, and as respected individuals within that agency. My friends at the big firms, with few exceptions, lament being tiny cogs in huge wheels and getting stuck researching minutiae for the big case, always dependent on top partners for direction and rare appraisal of performance. I certainly have to work cooperatively with others at my job, but there is great latitude for meaningful movement. I like my environment and I like my job.

"Also, my atmosphere in the government sector insulates me as a woman. I have the feeling, based on so many experiences of friends, that the big firms do everything within reason to *attract* good young women to their workplace, but then, perhaps unintentionally, create considerable obstacles for women truly to succeed. Maybe the clients rather than the partners are the culprits, but something happens to women between getting the job and making partnership. I'm protected—I think that's the only word—from that, due to government understanding and checks on gender discrimination.

"Aside from the money I make compared to others, I'm relatively happy. But in retrospect, I wish I had had the *choice* of what kind of law practice I wanted to be a part of. My class rank, due largely to circumstances well beyond my abilities related to the law, pushed me into the job market with a considerable deficit. What causes me to lose a little sleep is that I'm not certain that it can ever be overcome! Legal headhunters won't give me the time of day in searching for a private firm, due to my law school record and the fact that I work for the government, even though my job is extremely responsible and I have wonderful recommendations at this point. How sad that one steps onto a treadmill at the end of law school with little hope of moving up—moving over, yes, but moving up, no, except within one's own sector.

"I'll continue to do well in my own area, probably getting promotion after promotion with limited horizons in remuneration. And again, what I'm doing is interesting: Was someone discharged, for example, from a New York City job for incompetence or because of subtle union-related protection of a competing worker? This is fascinating and important stuff. But I'm not happy with the tradition in legal hiring that has decided my stratosphere for me."

A pause, then a big smile, one of the rare ones . . .

"And what ever happened to the 'wife and kids' concept? I'd love to be married and hope it will happen. But I'm fully into my career now. There probably will be no kids as a result. The tide has turned. I'm one of many women out there with readjusted priorities. But it has not been easy getting to this point. I haven't marched in any parades, but my path toward a redefined role has been full of quiet bumps. The effect is with me still."

■ ■ ■

*"I'm dealing daily with rape and murder and kidnapping,
just making sure everyone gets a fair hearing."*

ROBERT C. JOHNSON, JR.

This law office doesn't have the big plants and the mauve carpets. It is on the tenth floor of a nondescript building in a historic, atmospheric, crowded section of downtown Boston. There are tired murals of the Boston Tea Party on the waiting room walls and the chairs are stark and stiff. The receptionist/secretary, an attractive black woman, is wearing a trendy man's undershirt. She informs me that Mr. Johnson is still in court in Roxbury and will be a bit late for our appointment. I return from coffee in half an hour to find him in, but a little rushed. ". . . I'm spending the weekend in the country. Can't wait . . ." He is gracious and accommodating, nonetheless, and gets right to his story.

As we begin, I notice African prints on the wall of his small office, papers piled in cardboard boxes on the floor with labels such as "Personal Injury," and pictures of Robert Johnson with famous politicos: Johnson with Governor Dukakis, Johnson with Senator Ted Kennedy, Johnson with Shirley Chisholm.

"The early days are, in many ways, the most vivid. I was born in what could be called 'Black Appalachia,' a poor rural area outside Chattanooga, Tennessee. Dad died when I was four, so Mom moved to Boston, leaving my two sisters and me with my grandparents until I was twelve. My grandparents made a tremendous impact on me. Granddad was a preacher and a carpenter, a role model to everyone in the area. And Grandma lived what he preached. I remember this bum showing up almost regularly on our front porch. He would just sit there patiently until Grandma spotted him and quietly came out of the house, whispered a few words of assurance, then fetched him a little food. He would leave as quietly as he came, only to reappear the next day."

Johnson looks rather formal in a dark suit with purple tie.

But it took no time at all for his shoes to come off. His stocking feet are on top of the desk now as he talks at a fast pace, recounting early days with ease. His eyes are wonderfully expressive, as are his gestures.

"Mom remarried in Boston, and we kids were called up north. But her new husband died, and we inherited a stepsister. I'll never forget the Dwight School, near where we lived on the fifth floor in the South End. There was no discipline problem there, to speak of, because the principal and teachers ran such a tight ship. We had to *square corners* as we walked in the hallways. If we didn't, we got two strokes on the palms with the teacher's batten—about one yard of solid oak, and *nasty* if soaked in vinegar. My biggest honor was to wash the blackboard—I'd sit up front, and the teacher always rewarded the most alert students by letting them wash the board. I washed the board a *lot . . .*"

Johnson has a great smile. It registers often as he talks on, looking out the window at Boston. Now his feet are on his chair, and he is squatting there (a difficult feat, it would seem).

"By junior high school, I guess they all knew I was a little different—I was interested in school. They'd pick on me, and I was always in fights. In the sixth grade, I was stomped by one big guy, the height of shame. After it happened once, it never happened again. I learned to say with some authority (God knows where I picked it up), 'Come on, come on—I'll kick your ass.' I was holding my own and they laid off.

"At Boston English, my high school, sixty to seventy percent of the teachers taught and the rest didn't do a damn thing. My French teacher would always go next door during class and drink with one of the gym teachers. When he left the room, all the bullies would take over—it was pathetic. Then the guy wouldn't give any tests at all, but would automatically dish out A's to the Chinese students, B's to the whites, and C's or D's to the blacks (about half the kids in the school were black). I didn't learn a word of French until college. Then the biology teacher would tell us all the questions he was going to ask on his tests—our good grades made it look as though he was really teaching us something. Christ!

"Going to college, by the way, just never entered my mind. No one in my family had ever gone to college and it was a foregone conclusion, I guess, that I wouldn't either. And Boston English wasn't exactly college prep. But by the second year of high school I caught on to taking the good teachers. I was in the top five percent of my class, and started going with a lot of the other smart kids to the South End House, a community center, where I got to know Mel King, one of the most respected black politicians in the city. One day he just said, 'How'd you like to go to college?' And my nod and smile in return changed my life, I guess."

Johnson wheels around on his chair and lets out a big breath of relief as though the story has been on edge to this point. He continues, high speed.

"Mel King told me about A Better Chance, a program to get bright disadvantaged and minority kids to private schools to prep them earnestly for college. Before I knew it, I was heading over to the Commonwealth School in Boston, a progressive day school full of Waspy and Jewish kids from professional families who wouldn't have dreamed of *not* going to college, and wanted highly selective ones at that. The headmaster there, who had founded the school (he's from a wealthy, prominent family), was a taskmaster and one of the really great men I've met. In short, I worked my butt off. Still, though, I was at the bottom of the class early on.

"A couple of formative things were happening just about then. Mom moved us into a pretty rough housing project called Orchard Park. All I remember from the first days there was a huge guy grabbing me by the collar and saying, 'Hey, man, are you messing with my Phyllis? I'll crack your ass with my bare hands.' It scared the hell out of me. The project was like a prison—everyone was vulnerable. But it prompted sort of a bond with some of my Commonwealth School friends—I'd bring them to visit the project, and they started taking me home to see how they lived. Interesting . . .

"Then too, I got involved with a teenage action group that encouraged playwrighting. I seemed to have a natural knack at this and my first play, *Coffee and Sour Cream,* was produced to really decent reviews in *The Boston Globe* and the *Christian Science Monitor.* Hey, man—at this point I was off and running!

"How would my secondary school friends have described me? Well, probably as responsible and militant. I wasn't as militant as the Black Panthers, but almost. Outside of school, I helped Mel

King run for this and that public office. I was walking a fine line between my old community and my new school. But I was hanging in there academically. What started as C's became B's at graduation. Princeton rejected me but Bowdoin admitted me and I was off to—of all places—*Maine* for college."

At this point, I gaze about the room, stretching a bit. As I spot a color photo on the windowsill of two handsome teenagers, Bob Johnson says: "You're looking at the best part of my first year of college. That big guy on the right was conceived in my freshman dorm at Bowdoin."

A huge, proud smile.

"I exchanged a year to Tufts in Boston to be with my girlfriend when she had the baby. Then back to Bowdoin. All kinds of new horizons opened up. I tried astronomy—I had always used the stars as a kid to get away. I'd look at the stars and find some kind of peace, stability. The stars always seemed to be constant in a universe that wasn't. Well, I tried astronomy during a summer at MIT. I had always liked math and science, you see, but my headmaster at Commonwealth quietly told me that he thought I'd do well in the humanities—history and English. He proved to be right. I tried biology at Bowdoin but I was really more taken by a history course about Africa and some of the other humanities.

"But suddenly I found myself a race leader at Bowdoin. Actually, there were quite a few blacks in my class but I pushed right into leadership. We had a Mahalia Jackson concert to get an Afro-Am House off the ground. During all this, I must say, I was very aware of a Bowdoin black upperclassman, Virgil Logan, who always seemed to provide a bridge between the black students and the white. I noticed how effective his style was, and found myself trying to copy him. I learned a lot from the guy. . . .

"Anyway, I knew all along that this education was going to be put to work for social change. Anything that got in the way I scoffed at impatiently or abandoned. I was in a fraternity my first year, for example, and then bailed out—it just didn't feel right. But I became sort of a team player, although still pretty radical. I played soccer, was on the judicial board, student council, and some of the other mainstream stuff. I was involved and creative—helped to start the Brotherhood Internship Program, for example, through which Bowdoin students went to Boston for a semester to help in the community centers, to teach math and English and lead all kinds of social projects."

Then Johnson turns toward me and puffs out a little.

"Two big things happened that meant a lot to me. At the end of my junior year, Bowdoin gave me the Franklin Delano Roosevelt Cup for '. . . that student whose humanity, vision and courage contributed most to making Bowdoin a better college.' And then, at graduation, I won one of those fabulous Thomas Watson Fellowships that allowed me to travel anywhere for one year—I went to East Africa and Kenya to study black migration from our continent to theirs.

"All the way along, of course, I wondered what I would eventually do for a living. Going to divinity or law school had appeal, although at some point I thought I would return to Africa for a period. But after I got caught up in things at graduate school, that just never happened. But not everyone knows, you see, that a lot of black Americans return to Africa, the homeland, just like Jews return to Israel. That story really has to get out more."

There is a quiet moment—there aren't many in this conversation—as though Johnson is reminding himself of this old goal and making a new resolve.

"Anyway, law seemed a powerful tool. It struck me—in the little I had seen—that a lawyer could do anything. Also, I knew I was best when I was in a combative situation—*that* fit law. And I was deeply concerned about protecting people's rights. It just seemed to me that law might be the closest training to fit the bill for what I thought I could do and wanted to do, although I wasn't certain. I decided to try for the best, and put in applications at Yale (rejected), Harvard (wait-listed), and Cornell (admitted). Once again, I was off to some remote place for more education.

"But Cornell didn't prove to be remote at all, at least for social activity. I got involved in bringing in lecturers to address the Attica defense trials issues, and started a prison project twenty miles away at Auburn where, coincidentally, H. Rap Brown was incarcerated. Although Cornell Law itself was very conservative, there were around fifteen blacks in my class of 125. I did a lot of stuff with the Black Law School Association. Maybe too much! My first year was really rough academically, and I, of course, was questioning the relevance of the law school training for what I wanted my future to be. I decided to study concurrently for a masters of professional studies at Cornell in Afro-American Studies. That brought some meaning and totality to the law pursuits. The whole package made sense, although it was tough to manage. But by the third year of law school, I was really in the swing of things academically—even pulled a few surprises like an A in my trusts and estates course! With my J.D. and M.P.S. in hand, I was ready to take on the world—but *how*?

"I had no interest in the private world of corporate law firms, unlike most of the others in my class. Since summers had been spent teaching Upward Bound kids at Brandeis and Boston College, I thought public agency work might be interesting. And that's what happened: I got a job as director of affirmative action for the Massachusetts Board of Regional Community Colleges—fifteen of them, in total. And right away I knew that my law training was a big bonus—it had given me the power to analyze, to write clearly, to act in an authoritarian manner, and to read statistics and legal gibberish with understanding. We hired two new female presidents, two new black presidents, and I felt good about the social progress that could be made at this level of authority.

"I moved up to director of affirmative action at the University of Massachusetts–Boston, and taught intro courses in law around greater Boston in different colleges. At this point, I had become convinced that involvement in law could indeed bring about significant social change. At U Mass–Boston, for example, we achieved the distinction of having more black faculty than any other college in America. But that wasn't enough—I started challenging the chancellor on affirmative action issues, and ultimately sued U Mass over a tenure dispute."

Bob Johnson is rolling now, and moving up and down slowly as though in aerobics class, crouched above feet *on* the desk chair.

"I decided to run for office, for state representative. I picked up about one-third the votes, and some fair coverage from the *Globe*. But along the way, I really was saying to myself, 'This fucking system ain't worth shit.' And just about this time, my wife, who has held good jobs in the academic community of Boston, is saying that the once sensitive and caring man she originally knew during college days had changed, beginning with law school, to

■

someone cold and calculating. We split after having two children. But everyone is on good terms now, and I'm seeing the separated daughter of my old headmaster—life takes odd turns, eh?"

The head nods to and fro, up and down.

"And here I am trying to start up a private firm with one other black lawyer. I'm doing criminal work, discrimination law, and my clients are usually, but not always, black. I'm dealing with little businesses that get into trouble. [Johnson gave me a newspaper article featuring one of his clients, a woman who ran a snack shack at a bus terminal in a desperately poor area and couldn't pay her rent to the bus agency because her stand was robbed so frequently.] Am I making as much of a mark on society as I did in government-related law? I don't know, but I do know that I have to make a living.

"I also know that I'm a damn good lawyer. I can make a witness fall apart on the stand. In fact, much of the law school training proved relevant to what I'm doing. On the other hand, law school didn't do enough to make us look at the whole of society in preparation for applying our trade. We weren't trained well in negotiating, for example—and in the big world, that's the way problems should be settled and often are settled. Instead, most lawyers just have the win instinct, want to achieve that at any cost, and take it personally if it doesn't happen. The client too often gets overlooked in the rush to victory.

"What will I look like ten years from now? God, I don't know, but I want to write more and spend time in the country— I like to walk through the woods like anybody else, but haven't spent much time in doing it. I have no hope of being a big legal giant—in fact, my living comes largely from my commercial real estate investments. I support the good guys—give money to Dukakis and Kennedy campaigns, and serve on boards of places I believe in, like my old day school. And Dukakis appointed me to one of the state college boards of trustees. If he should end up being president some day, I might get a minor post in Justice or Education, and I'd like that.

"But, for the moment, criminal law keeps me in touch with all the people—I'm dealing daily with rape and murder and kidnapping, just making sure everyone gets a fair hearing. The drug dealers I represent are the only ones that put me in a real moral dilemma—do they *deserve* their 'rights'?"

There is a new pensive posture, feet on the floor.

"You know, I do have to say that I don't have a very high regard for lawyers. I can't think of a one I've met who I thought I could really trust. And yet I'm glad I'm in law—as an advocate of people's rights. Sure, there are problems with the system—it takes so long for some resolutions. Although there are some great judges, some others are a fucking joke. At times this really does seem like a 'white man's system'—but, on the whole, I can't imagine a better system and I just go in there and do my best, take it less personally than I used to, and think that even though I lose a case, hopefully there is better law in place because my case was well designed and well fought. I guess Grandpa's preaching and being stomped by a bully in sixth grade all remain with me. I'm still trying to put it all together in law, and that's the right place to be. For me."

■ ■ ■

"Law has had me at war for thirty-five years. Every case I've had left me shell-shocked, fatigued, full of fight. One could say I've played all my life, because I like what I do so, but no, I've been sent to innumerable fronts of war. It hasn't taken genius to win.
It has taken energy. Energy."

GERRY SPENCE

Well out lonely John Dodge Road, several miles from trendy-for-the-outdoorsy-set Jackson Hole, Wyoming, a huge sign intrudes on a white birch grove: STOP . . . DO NOT PROCEED BEYOND THIS POINT . . . THESE PREMISES PROTECTED ELECTRONICALLY. With permission, one proceeds cautiously. At the end of the meandering driveway looms a towering, ruggedly stylish home and a towering, rugged lawyer. If Bill Blass wanted to decorate in the woods, this would be the spot; if Paul Bunyan had gone to law school, this would be him.

It isn't long before we are settled in his lush office, and Gerry Spence is peppering forth colorful phrases.

"Ever see an Arabian stud standing coolly in his stall? Beautiful eyes, calm demeanor. But let him out, the docile beast becomes himself—with nostrils flared, he roars. It's not acting, for Christ's sake. It's the roar of natural energy, of passion.

"I don't know what happens to me in front of a jury. But whatever is beautiful and natural inside me roars forward—all the energy, all the passion is let loose. And *passion* is the key word. Most lawyers just don't have it—they became lawyers because someone expected it of them—the family, the college, the friends, the society."

As the ringing phone distracts this Buffalo Bill, I have time to gaze about the office: a chandelier of antlers, fine prints of Indians, horses, and sheep, old guns, an antique cart posing as a cocktail table on heavy plush burnt orange carpeting, and generous windows inviting the nearby towering Grand Tetons indoors. The rangy sixtyish lawyer with long hair, baggy black pants not quite covering his full backside, green casual designer shirt, and dark, tired sneakers, raises his voice on the telephone. "Well, how would you like to take a case that lasts for at least four months? It would be good for you, would force all your energies into one arena for an intense period. Think about it. You need it. We'll talk later." He hangs up, kicks aside a roll of paper gathering on the floor from his computer printer, and slumps again in a huge leather chair.

"How was I lured to the law? Because I could speak and write, was precocious, and loved to stand up in front of an audience and show off—an anomaly, I guess, since I'm shy."

The famous trial lawyer throws his head back and grows softly reminiscent.

"My dad was a chemist at a cement company. He and my mother both went to college, but not much money ever came in. In fact, they were rather simple, poor, hardworking people. I knew that they expected me to get out of the nest as quickly as possible and take care of myself, to 'earn my space on this earth,' as Dad used to say. But I didn't know what I'd do. I knew I didn't want to be a chemist or a teacher, the only two professions I had really seen in action. But I read a lot. And one day I stumbled upon a book that changed my young life: *The Great Mouthpiece*. I had never ever met a lawyer, but suddenly I was determined to be one.

Funny: No longer did I feel restricted by money or poor social position or the conservative Methodist Church. Instead, I looked forward to using law as a rapier—it sounded so goddamn romantic! I was at Laramie High School at the time. At fifteen I ran over to see if the dean of the University of Wyoming Law School would talk to me about law. He did, and that was it. I had finished college and law school by the age of twenty-three, eager to start."

Spence snaps out of his reverie, and pulls on the big smile.

"You know, it's odd. If my wife didn't force me out of here now and then [Spence works dawn to dark in this home office, taking brief walks and going to his office in downtown Jackson Hole as infrequently as possible], I'd be a goddamn hermit. But then there is that other side of me that surges in front of the jury and always wants more. It's unexplainable."

Enough of the personal story. Spence has too much to say about what lawyers *are* versus what lawyers could and should be.

"My sons both have said they want to be lawyers. I tell them to go where they'll be taught the least. Law school professors, in my view, are the drones and morticians of the profession. After a year or two with law professors, students have lost their idealism. Ever see second-year students line up for big-firm interviews at the law school placement offices? They look like pink-eyed rats, dressed alike and trying very hard to act alike. Unfortunately, they're cerebrally overweight. The passion, if it was ever there, has been suppressed by the constant diet of word games in law school.

"The American Bar Association is largely to blame. The ABA is ultimately responsible for the whole system by credentialing the schools, credentialing the entrants by those dreary exams, and credentialing the profession itself. I'd *remove* the ABA! There can't *be* uniformity in law—Chicago doesn't need the same kind of lawyer that Wyoming needs. And no uniformly prescribed exam can test the heart of the matter of what makes a good lawyer: passion and intuition.

"How would I select a law school class? First, I'd just do away with the LSAT. I'd give a passing glance to the college transcript, but I'd interview the hell out of every candidate. Does he or she write poetry? Play music? Do photography? I'd take the one who wrestles over the one who plays tennis, the one from Peace Corps over the one from Kappa Sig. I'd ask the candidates:

'What's the worst thing you ever did?' The first one who retorted, 'None of your damn business!' would be the first admitted. I'd take protestors and doers, and the angry ones over the pacified. I'd take more minorities and the offbeat. Nothing is more expensive in this profession than encouraging and/or hiring the wrong people, I don't care how goddamn smart they are!"

A handout from Spence's office indicates that the Wyoming native became the state's youngest prosecuting attorney at twenty-three.

After eight years of trial work on the State's side (where he never lost a criminal prosecution), he entered into a general trial practice. Among insurance companies, he could win any case in a pinch. At forty, representing corporate America against the little person became repugnant to him, and in a typically compulsive clean sweep, he discharged forty insurance companies, and from that day forward devoted his life to cases for the "little person," refusing any longer to work for the banks and the insurance companies and for the "non-breathers," as he calls the corporations. Since then, he has tried and won many prominent cases including a 10.5 million dollar verdict for Karen Silkwood against Kerr-McGee. He has never failed to acquit a client charged with murder.

Spence continues. "It's true. I don't give a shit about corporations anymore. If you want to represent people, you grow passionate for justice—now I represent just people.

"My father was a hunter. He loved it. I've spent much of my life revolting against my parents, but now I know I'm imitating them, time and time again. Like Dad's hunting—*I'm* now a hunter, a combatant in the courtroom. It's just like the forest: I walk through quietly but resolutely, ready to make a purposeful kill. You must have great *love* to kill, to combat, to *advocate*.

"The guy with the best case doesn't always win—too many trial lawyers lose by attorney-judge kiss-ass tactics. You have to realize that neither side represents black or white—to win, you must make the most of shades of gray. No one's fully guilty; and no one's fully innocent. The lawyer's job in court is to find the client's redeeming qualities and convince the jury. And yes, I play 'hardball'—an ABA descriptive term—to convince them."

Spence is rolling now. I have the feeling the "I'm in front of the jury" button has been switched to on. He is the Arabian stud let loose.

"Law has had me at war for thirty-five years. Every case I've had left me shell-shocked, fatigued, full of fight. One could say I've played all my life, because I like what I do so, but no, I've been sent to innumerable fronts of *war*. It hasn't taken genius to win. It has taken energy. *Energy*."

The big man has been slouching in the leather chair, shouting at the wall, hands cupped. He is ready to switch gears and grows quiet, awaiting a new question.

"Aside from some of the traditions of the profession itself, what are the greatest obstacles? What can ruin lawyers? Easy: booze and politics, and I've been sidelined with both. I ran for Congress in Wyoming and was whipped by a very plain but prominently named man. And drinking sidelined me too. But my wife and I gave up drinking totally when we married, and that's eighteen years now."

Gerry Spence has allowed me an hour, and the time is up. But there is a postscript.

"I rise every morning at five and average a fourteen-hour day. I'm consumed by all this, so time counts. By the way, you didn't ask me when I'll retire. Don't bother. I'll die in court."

A big smile. A tough handshake.

The solemn white birch grove lining the long ribboned driveway doesn't calm me immediately. This interview was a tidbit in Spence's day, but I am exhausted.

■　■　■

"I wanted a credential to use later, when and if I wanted a profession. But I didn't necessarily want the responsibility that came with it. Law seemed just right."

BARBARA E. SMITHE

"Can you imagine spending your vacation reading law? Some here in the firm do just that—they eat it and breathe it. Not me. A frozen daiquiri on a sandy beach sounds considerably more alluring. And, believe me, it gets structured into our family schedule every year, big cases or not. Balance in life is essential; time for one's self is essential; law too easily consumes, and too many lawyers just sit back and let it."

The speaker is a thirty-eight-year-old woman who specializes in litigation and was made partner last year at a major, prestigious Manhattan law firm. She is married to a lawyer, a partner at another firm, and they have two children, three and one.

"Yes, I made partner but it wasn't easy. I chewed my fingers to the bone during the final months before the firm made the big decision, and I put on lots of weight. You should have seen me—not too pleasant, but the pressure got to me. To top it all, I was pregnant for the second time around. Once I was a partner, the work didn't change that much outside of the fact that I delegated a lot more, but I *felt* so different! When the baby was due, I was working on a big case and was here until four hours before delivery."

Ms. Smithe is sitting at a huge desk in a corner office with a view of the Empire State Building. Someone else has obviously just moved out—picture hooks hang empty, books are in boxes rather than on shelves, and the furniture is a little worn.

"Excuse the mess. I've just been here a short while since maternity leave. During the time I was out, there was great shuffling of offices due to the fact that my firm merged with another. It will be a while before we're all settled—but it's great, because the merger made litigation the largest department in the firm."

Ms. Smithe lived in a middle-class suburb during her childhood and competed to get into Hunter College High School, a selective public high school on the Upper East Side of Manhattan. Both of her parents went to college.

"At Hunter I was able to graduate a year early. I don't mean to sound conceited, but studying and school just came easily to me. I was diligent, but not obsessed with top grades. They came naturally. I was something of a loner—in fact many of the girls there were, because we commuted to school from all over. The school was able to create loyalty among us, but traditional high school activities like rooting for a nearby boys' school football team? Forget it. We all lived in different places and lived private lives. It forced many of us to become adult rather early. That was the rouser political protest era, of course—I graduated from Hunter in 1970—and yes, I looked like a hippie and protested a bit, but my heart wasn't in it. I'd much rather have spent time shopping at Bloomingdale's, and did, a lot. And I'd travel in the summers, sometimes alone, which I liked.

"When I got out of Hunter early I tried for the big name colleges. Harvard and Yale and Wesleyan turned me down, but Vassar took me and I went. In fact, I *adored* the place—everything about it. I thought I wanted a co-ed college but a women's college still makes a lot of sense to me—men tend to take over, you know. Vassar was just becoming co-ed and there was a lot of tension and, quite frankly, some weird men. One famous guy who wore drag now and then around campus was elected president of the student body. I guess my contribution to campus politics was loaning him jewelry."

There is great enthusiasm whenever Vassar is mentioned.

"It really was a wonderful place for me, and a wonderful time of life. Yes, there were a lot of drugs—and on the other side of the coin, I met Muffy, Fluffy, and Buffy for the first time—but I moved while there from trendy academics to becoming something of an intellectual. I majored in philosophy, concentrated on Plato, and took a lot of art history, a demanding and superb major at Vassar. Again, academic success came easy, but this time I was really interested. Now and then I'd have a 4.0 semester, even though I grew erratic in actually being on campus. I fell in love with this guy at Princeton and arranged all my classes at Vassar so they met on Tuesdays and Thursdays—from Friday through Monday I was at Princeton. As time moved on, though, my friend—who became my husband—really tuned in to Vassar. We ended up spending as much time on my campus as his, which is so unusual. Most guys just won't do that, but I found the right fellow."

There is a kind of automation in the way this woman speaks. After being asked a question, she just sits there and delivers with a little smile and a little animation. Her manner is extremely matter-of-fact—"lawyerlike," one might say. But she doesn't look like most lady lawyers look—she is dressed in pastels with huge shoulder pads, a very long dress, tiny pearl earrings, and has close-

■

cropped hair. And she is rather svelte. There is no hint that soon after making partner she found it necessary to embark on a liquid diet for months to ". . . get back to normal."

"Why I went to law school is still something of a mystery—there was no cogent reason for it. In fact, my mother recently found my old college essays in the attic and relived the day when I told her I was going to write on the prospective joys of motherhood, much to her chagrin. On leaving college, not much had changed. However, I did want some kind of credential. I didn't necessarily want the responsibility that went with it, but I wanted the credential to use later when and if I wanted a profession. Law school just seemed right. Having been a philosophy major, I loved analysis—there was plenty of it at law school.

"Since my husband-to-be was at Boston University Law, I wanted to be in or near the same city—but Harvard rejected me, and so did Yale in New Haven. Columbia said to come ahead, and I did, but I hated the place. The professors and classes were good but there was absolutely no cohesive spirit among students, as there had been in college. It was a factory. There was no soul to the place whatsoever. For example, my father had grown very ill and I spent hours in the hospital with him in midtown. Since I lived down in the Village, it was difficult to use the Columbia Law Library, way uptown, at night. So I asked one of the deans if they might arrange to let me study nights at the New York University Law Library, which was so much closer to the hospital and to my apartment. The quick response was 'Absolutely not!—the NYU students might think it a precedent and ask to use *our* library.'

"As the years passed, I thought I might be judging the place too harshly—that is, until recently. A representative of Columbia Law called to congratulate me on doing so well at my firm. Then she asked if I would be willing to tithe—can you imagine it, ten percent of salary!—to the law school. I told her that my experience there hadn't been totally satisfactory, but I'd be happy to send her one hundred dollars immediately. She coldly responded that that level of donation was not worth the paperwork, and I need not bother. Then I discovered Columbia had hired an outside agency to make these calls on their behalf. It's *still* a factory!"

Ms. Smithe, when she is finished with a topic, abruptly stops talking and waits for the next question.

■

"How difficult is it to manage a full family *and* a full partner's load here? Well, it is working out okay, thanks largely to a wonderfully cooperative husband who is every bit as busy at his firm as I am here. We get up at 7:30 and have breakfast with the kids, then walk the older one to school en route to our subways. We employ foreign girls to live in and look after the kids during the day—we had one from Ireland for several years who was wonderful, and now we have a new one from North Dakota who is not quite as trustworthy. But it works out. Obviously the big case can keep me at the office well into the night, and the same for my husband. But the big cases seem to come at different times in our lives, so one of us always seems to be around to relate to the children. Normally, we're both back at the town house by nine at night. I must say, though, that there is a real lack of flexibility in our lives now—you know, a two-career family with children. We have a little house on Martha's Vineyard and spend a lot of weekends there—but it's far away. We may sell it and find something closer to home, like the Berkshires."

A silence. And no new questions.

"But I'm really content. The litigation department here is like a small firm, we're so cohesive and tight-knit. There's not a severe hierarchy among us and we don't work just to put in hours—we work until the job is done. As for me, ninety percent of my time for the last two years has been spent on one case—a complicated liquidation of a bankrupt Caribbean insurance company. It will take four to six years, all told. But it's a very interesting case, and I feel close to the clients now. I'm working with British solicitors and barristers and get to the islands a lot, too."

Silence.

That was it. A matter-of-fact lady talking about her matter-of-fact life in the law.

■ ■ ■

"You put in a little more than you take out."

PETER WEBSTER

"On the whole, I love it. If one of my favorite professors at college had not said, 'Peter, you will go to law school'—even though I didn't know exactly what that meant—I'd be in the family business selling veterinary supplies or teaching school, either of which I might have enjoyed. But law is just right for me. I don't do anything here I consider drudgery.

"Sure, there are the dogshit cases that we wish we'd never agreed to take. It is natural, I guess, to put that set of papers on the bottom of the pile, day after day. And then the phone rings and you learn it is that goddamn Mrs. Jones inquiring about her little boundary dispute. You bring the papers up, but the next day they sink to the bottom again. After a few more calls from Mrs. Jones you can't postpone the matter any longer, and you do the job and it isn't so bad after all and you wonder why you didn't get right to it in the first place. So that little stuff is all that I have to complain about—not very serious, huh?"

Peter Webster, forty-seven, is a jaunty, jolly fellow. His spacious office with two huge floor-to-ceiling plants is in Portland, Maine's newest and showiest postmodern building with lots of marble and mauve carpeting, of course. Webster sits many floors up in a glassy corner showcase and has so much room to spare that without the giant trees it would be embarrassing. His desk is tidy and on a very hot summer afternoon he looks fresh as can be: tan poplin suit, striped shirt, and festive Liberty of London tie (he told me the brand name, adding that his wife is responsible for *all* his ties).

Webster is a success in his field. One book named him "one of the best lawyers in America" in 1983; *Who's Who in American Law* included him in 1986; he heads the grievance commission of the Maine Board of Bar Overseers, the agency that oversees and disciplines the entire lawyer body of the state; his alma mater, Bowdoin College, uses him as head counsel (a considerable tribute, since there are hundreds of Bowdoin alumni lawyers); and he is one of the three partners on the administrative committee of his large firm in Portland.

"Gawd, I don't know how it happens. College, for me, was all fun and games—president of the frat house, gregarious, fun-loving, and I played poker half the nights I was there. Yes, I got to work now and then—ended up a dean's list major in government. I guess my story may be typical of a lot of people who end up in law. You know: high school president of the class, ambitious, involved, editor of the yearbook, and 'most likely to succeed.' Then you go on to college and become international good guy and someone says you have the generalist talent to make a good lawyer, and zap, that's what you do and it works once you set your mind to it."

One expects Webster to deal the cards at any moment. There is a remnant of the frat house air to this happy-go-lucky fellow.

"In college, I looked for a few minutes at chemistry and math, and one memorable professor—a really good shit!—tried to convince me I'd be a good teacher. (You know, he may have been right.) Anyway, my political science adviser said law school was what I ought to do, and I did it.

"It was obviously time to get serious. My parents set standards that were to be followed, period. Dad, in Wakefield, Massachusetts, didn't even finish high school, but he became extraordinarly successful in his veterinary supply business. He was truly a self-made man, and put us all through college and graduate school. My brother, a Boston University graduate, runs the family business now, and my sister, a Radcliffe alumna, is a vice president of Citibank in New York. So I knew before I started that my poker-playing days were numbered.

"But law school was something else, good intentions or not. First of all, the bleak weather around Cornell didn't help one bit. But the worst part was all the little assholes in my first-year class who raised their hands at the beginning of the class and just kept them in the air until class was over. I hated it! At Bowdoin, you see, all the professors patted me on the head every time I turned around. In law school I was only getting kicked in the rear. And I still didn't know what it *meant* to be a lawyer. So I wanted to get the hell out of there. Dad came over to visit and told me I had to stick it out for at least a full year—that I couldn't just quit. As almost always, he was right—by the end of the first year I had a sense of place and was doing okay in the classroom, even up against all those little twerps. By the end of it all, I graduated in the top quarter of the class. Considering the meager beginnings, that was a miracle.

"It was the summer work that got me all excited about the law. Once I worked for a congressman who put me on a project in the Bureau of Indian Affairs. It was really interesting research.

The issue was whether some fairly obscure Indian tribal rights, long ago signed over by the U.S. government, superseded Oregon's and Washington's strong state regulations regarding the catch from the Columbia River. Another summer I did research in the bowels of Langdell Hall at Harvard for a Georgetown Law School professor who was visiting Cornell. That ordeal contributed greatly to my being a patient man and a careful researcher, which, after all, is the heart of law. And soon I was on my way to the 'big firm,' Portland style. At that point—in 1965—this firm had only nine lawyers—now we have about fifty-five. I sampled real estate law but moved slowly toward a corporate and commercial practice.

"The great thing I have now is a real mix. Maybe fifteen percent of the time I'm working on projects for Bowdoin. Actually, working with a college is just like working with a small corporation. There are employee relationship problems, pension plans, contracts related to architecture and construction, the rare discrimination case, alleged violations of teaching contracts, etc. But working with a college is a great balance to the real corporations— there is a strong element of collegiality, and perhaps best of all, almost always a squash game at the end of the day."

(Who wouldn't want this guy as a lawyer? There is serious undercurrent, but always a happy manner and a generous worldview.)

"The heart of all this is going beyond the letter of the law with your clients. Yes, you talk over purchase and sale agreements, but there is no restriction against offering a little good advice on how to run a small business, having seen a bunch of others make the same mistakes, time and time again. Law lets me get to the people. Sure, the details can become burdensome. And now and then it's difficult to keep so many balls in the air at one time. At times, without ill intent, we overburden ourselves. The lousiest part of my day is coming back from lunch and finding fourteen pink call-back slips. But I try to get to every one, every day before I leave.

"Lawyers have to watch themselves carefully. Overextension is easy to fall into. And that, I've learned through my grievance committee work, can result in client neglect. But the checks and balances in a place like Maine probably quietly force us to balance

■

our lives a bit more successfully than in some other places. I feel I *have* to be a United Way leader, a trustee of the school, and a bunch of other things—also, I like it a lot. People just have to work together to make society go."

We head down to the building take-out for a pasta-seafood salad, seltzer water, and the biggest cookie northern New England has seen. Peter Webster just keeps "shooting the breeze," intelligently. And he says hello to everyone on the elevator, and most everyone in the casual little restaurant.

Following one big bite: "It seems to me you should put in a little more than you take out."

There is a long gaze toward the tall pine trees in the courtyard.

"*You put in a little more than you take out.* That's all there is to it."

■ ■ ■

"Law is just the organization of chaos."

GREGORY S. FEHRIBACH

Attorney Gregory Fehribach is an associate with a reputable firm in downtown Indianapolis. The dark-paneled walls in the waiting room are standard, as is the harried receptionist, attempting to answer phone calls while lawyers lean out of office doors to shout friendly but insistent orders.

But on entering Fehribach's private quarters at the firm, the traditional atmosphere—well, the scale—changes abruptly. The desk is a typical lawyer desk but in miniature, and the coat rack is knee-high. The lawyer himself is three feet, eleven inches tall, and in a wheelchair.

"The law has lured me since high school when my German Catholic parents started harping early on, 'Get a good job, like all the rest of the kids.' I was always a good student and a real achiever—you know, Eagle Scout and all that goes with it. I picked Ball State in Muncie for college because it was so accessible for me in a wheelchair—*flat*. They elected me student body president there. Next was Ohio Northern Law School, also selected principally for accessibility for the disabled."

This smallest of lawyers speaks directly, quickly. Now and then he whirls in his wheelchair without missing a phrase.

"Why law? I'm not certain why it was so obvious to me as early as high school. Perhaps it was basic gratitude—lawyers have always helped me out. That was during a period when disability seemed a potential problem, personally and professionally. I no longer view it that way at all.

"It pains me that the current image of law and lawyers is negative—and there is no doubt but that is the case. It seems to have started about a decade ago with such an intensive pleading process. Law 'of the people, by the people, and for the people' has been lost now, partly because one needs to be a lawyer to understand all our unnecessary jargon and legalese. There is simply no justification for making law so complicated for the public. That's one reason I just want to stay in general law, to have a family practice."

The wheelchair takes a turn or two while the young attorney collects his thoughts.

"Sure, there is vanity in this profession and there is bound to be. But the greed and the amorality are not as rampant as the public seems to think. I'm determined to play some part in dispelling the rumors—there are plenty of us who are basically good, honest, hardworking attorneys who are genuinely *concerned* when someone is run over, when someone's car is bashed, when there is an owner-tenant dispute."

But Fehribach isn't all sugar coatings.

"Law school isn't one bit relevant to what we're doing. I hated it. That training was the catalyst bringing together many of the negative elements of the law as practiced today. You know, law is just the organization of chaos. In sorting it out, we too often forget that the process begins and ends with people. . . .

"Which brings us to what may have attracted your attention to me in the first place [a newspaper article] . . .

"Disabled people are supposed to be able to eat out, to get to and from a job with relative ease, to get into public events, to have access to education. I find I'm spending more and more time boosting the cause. These are pro bono hours, by the way. It irks me that the Five-Hundred-Mile-Race grandstands are basically inaccessible—a group of us are working diligently to correct that.

■

On the other hand, Indianapolis, in becoming the 'amateur sports capital of America,' has done a good job in making the natatorium, the Hoosier Dome, and some other major facilities accessible. The city hosted the Pan American games—*most* of the facilities were disabled-accessible. I was chairman of the Disabled Support Services Committee and we were really upset not only about some issues facing the hearing-impaired, but particularly, the inaccessibility of the Speedway for the grand super-duper opening. The '500' is the symbol of it all in this town, and we're determined to see that corrections are made there."

Fehribach suffers from hereditary osteogenesis imperfecta, a brittle bone disease making him prone to easy breaks. But that didn't restrain him from flinging himself down a too-steep "handicapped ramp" with a near-disastrous finish to prove to the director of the city Department of Transportation that the slope of the ramps around town was not quite right. This engaging fellow wins points one way or another.

"I'm going to be a good lawyer," says Fehribach at twenty-nine. "Also, I'm in a position now to make life somewhat more comfortable for others who have problems like mine. Law speaks, and I'm glad to be here."

■　■　■

"Life is a moving target. Things look wonderful from afar,
but as you get closer, flaws appear."

JOHN ELLISON

From the bottom of that tower of stainless steel on Park Avenue in Manhattan it is a long ride to the forty-fifth floor. The law firm receptionist's room is as large as many hotel lobbies, with a wall of glass featuring reach-out-and-touch-them skyscraper tops and the Hudson River, angling straight out to the lady with the torch.

After the appropriate phone call, I am asked to walk down an oak spiral staircase one floor. Smaller lobby, to be certain, and a new receptionist poring over ads for discount trips to Mexico. As I am seated near her, personal whisperings between telephone answerings become audible. "I'm not certain I can take this place much longer," reaches well above the murmur level. She then looks at me shyly and smiles as though she has shared a secret.

Four lawyers whisk through this small outer room, one at a time, always rushing, never speaking. All are coatless, all wear dark blue pants, all sport red ties. The fifth to come along is my interviewee, a college classmate. He also wears the club's red cravat.

As John and I walk to his glass box in the sky, I experience a few flashbacks from the past. Perhaps his wedding in the big church next to the Waldorf-Astoria is the most memorable.

Among the ring of graduate schools around the nation, the rumor passed among old friends and classmates that John Ellison was about to marry the daughter of a major bank's vice president in a big ceremony at St. Bartholomew's on Park Avenue. We all made every effort to attend, and the show was worth it. Society weddings may be commonplace for some, but not for the assemblage sitting on the groom's side. We felt home again, however, when we saw John's father stroll up the aisle carrying a huge antique family Bible.

There was unintended humor at this wedding. Someone had the grand idea of placing gardenia trees at the end of each pew at center aisle. One gardenia casts a pleasant scent, but hundreds of gardenias can, for some, prompt a touch of nausea. And more than a few of these people were attending the wedding. Quick departures from the massive sanctuary were the rule of the afternoon, and others who stuck it out needed recovery time before proceeding to the reception.

At Duke, John was a big man on campus with an academic tilt. Everyone knew he was near the top of the class, but he didn't rub it in. Y activities, Student Union, and fraternity involvement rescued him from the books long enough for us all to know that he was a most pleasant fellow, a bit direct and argumentative for a Southern boy, but pleasant nevertheless.

By coincidence, John and I ended up at Yale, post-Duke, but on opposite sides of the well-ivied campus. I was taught early on that we at divinity school collectively liked all students in town except those at law school. Somehow, they remained different and seemed rather pleased by that.

John and I had lunch a couple of times during that three-year period, but there was strain. He was combative, preferred elegant excesses of language, and had developed a strong, up-front sense of self. I found him a chore to be with.

But now, as we walk toward his panoramic-view law office, appropriate for the fifty-three-year-old partner of a big-city firm, I know in a moment I am talking once again with my friend of undergraduate days. The John of law school had been a passing phase.

I am, however, lucky to be an interviewer rather than a paying client. John is not capable of saying just yes or no. Every topic has an array of gray shades, all to be explored. What was to have been a two-hour interview has to abruptly end after four hours due to other commitments.

John is the product of a tiny town in North Carolina. His father, a teacher of math and science, became a school superintendent and then a hospital administrator. He had graduated from Duke in the mid-twenties. John's mother had not gone to college and worked in a department store and a beauty parlor prior to marrying. His sister is now a schoolteacher in Virginia.

"Looking back on college, academic involvements, including debating, linger most in my mind. I got to do good things like research at Harvard. Through a social science grant I did a paper on seditious libel in England. It was on that trip to Harvard that I stopped off to look at law schools, including Yale.

"Graduating close to the top of my class at Duke provided a choice of the best law schools. Harvard had the reputation of being the big school with a rigid curriculum. As I visited Harvard and Yale, everyone seemed to enjoy Yale more—too many were eager to get out of Harvard. The atmosphere of the two places seemed strikingly different and I thought Yale the winner. But a professor there cautioned, 'Well, I think you'd like it here; but first we must ask if you can get in.' That comment threw me for a loop, and into momentary rage. I couldn't *imagine* that my Duke record could leave me standing outside the gates of any goal."

John talks and talks and talks in a most cordial way about the early days. As the bold winter afternoon sun begins to sink beyond the Hudson, he pops up and down to alter the slant of the miniblinds, one huge panel at a time.

"Law school was okay. In fact, I wouldn't change the way

the better law schools teach today. We learned law by mastering a framework for further understanding of the legal process. Without the framework on which to fit all aspects of the practice, I would be lost."

John describes himself as the "class rounder" in public high school. It was a small graduating class, but he was Mr. Top Everything: president of the student government, a high-ranking student, head of debate, and on the varsity football team. There was no thought of attending college anywhere but the University of North Carolina at Chapel Hill or Duke. The family college won out with little effort. John entered Duke as one of the few Angier Duke Scholars, the most prestigious honorary award given incoming students.

"I knew I wanted to be a lawyer all the way along, given my quick mastery of Robert's Rules of Order and my natural inclination to preside. It seemed I could argue and defend handily, and I always loved debating. Everyone said—and I listened—that law was a natural for me. Having devoured crime books as a little kid, I thought law sounded like fun and a professional area that might fit my talents. In short, the decision came early. As I recall, there was no consideration of options."

John looks remarkably like he did in college: blondish short hair, with the well-chiseled face of a disciplined athlete and a touch of an "aw-shucks" demeanor.

"My interest in debating reached a high peak at Duke. I won the southern region and moved on to the nationals. Debating was not work but fun. My partner and I had a class act and knew we were in the *most* civilized extracurricular endeavor.

"Perhaps a high point of my legal education came in the summer following my second year, when I was a summer associate at a really prestigious firm in New York City and spent a good bit of time on a project for a former Secretary of State. That experience gave me confidence that I could handle the big time. As so often happens, I ended up at the firm where I worked during that crucial summer after 2L, and it proved to be a good choice. The firm did a lot of litigation, which interested me from debating days on. Actually, I had offers on leaving law school from the most prominent New York firms. The one I picked seemed a little more interesting and appropriate for me than most—but looking back, one wonders how you reach that conclusion at a young age, viewing the firms largely through the rumors within academe.

"Dorothy and I made a couple of big choices as I entered the firm. Since she had gone to Chapin and Smith, the big-city environment and all its appropriate extensions were routine. We were both convinced that it would be silly for me to waste time commuting to the suburbs. We could put the children in private elementary schools in the city and send them off to boarding schools later. We both liked the fact that we could get in a cab and *be* somewhere in minutes—all those amenities the city has that one travels so far to find elsewhere. Also, it seemed to us that big-city parents were subjected to fewer Americana pressures—Little League ball and all that, for which Dorothy and I have little use or time."

The sun is setting now as John continues, often staring at the skyscrapers, slouched in his chair. One has the feeling he has rarely been asked to talk about himself.

"The crossroads at the big firm proved unfortunate for me, as I was not made a partner at the end of my eight-year probation. In a 'class' of seven, only two made it—one, predictably, a woman. This didn't come as a great shock because I knew my orientation at a highly regarded firm would give me great inroads elsewhere. Nonetheless, not making partner clearly was a setback, perhaps my first big one ever. In retrospect, I probably had been too critical of other associates and partners along the way, and had not been appropriately involved in the in-house political game. I guess I was honest in exercising my priorities, but am not sure now those were the priorities of the firm. So be it, I'm not angry at the system.

"I wanted to remain in litigation and in New York City, although some in my class at the firm left to do other things. I considered leaving with the others—to do independent lawyering—but still had the gut feeling that I was most effective and most satisfied in a large-firm setting. Being general counsel to a number of large corporations had its appeal, but my wife and I decided that I should continue to look for a big-firm alternative to my initial one.

"Actually, that was easier said than done. Big firms tend to hire young people straight out of law school rather than 'senior laterals,' which is what I was. Given my eight years out of law school, it was obvious that I had not made partnership at my first firm. I carried that small burden into the job-seeking environment.

"But all's well that ends well," says John, with a circling gesture that includes the grand appointments of his office and the spectacular view. "I like it here, although I must confess I bridle now and then under the firm's leadership in my area—leadership that was in place before I moved in."

For the first time, I sense resignation in John's tone and manner.

"I bill out at $250 per hour and work very, very hard, usually putting in over two thousand billable hours per year. A handful of our top lawyers bill out at $350 per hour here, so I'm mid-to-high scale. In moving here, I fared okay economically, but was set back a bit in status due to the fact that this firm has its headquarters in another city. I do spend most of my time on fascinating cases, though: I'm involved now in New York City asbestos litigation related to schools, shipyards, etc. I really enjoy the magnitude and importance of it all.

"I guess, in total, I'm eighty percent happy professionally. Dorothy and I love the city, although our children have quite honestly had some problems. Law has been satisfying and Dorothy has a fun job as director of admissions of a good little private elementary school."

As early February darkness comes upon the city, John and I decide to move to the Yale Club for a drink. The same John continues speaking, but walking out of the firm's building somehow releases his philosophical edge; he is suddenly less an on-line professional.

"We all want to be happy in what we're doing. I love litigation and enjoy most of my time, most days.

"But do I have regrets? Absolutely. I probably could have bcome more publicly visible, and should have. Lawyers who get press somehow gain more confidence of clients, even among those who are the most sedate, withdrawn, and sophisticated. I've never understood how the press can find good lawyers ahead of good lawyers finding good lawyers, but it happens. Alas, the press has never found me. Have I been too busy to be bothered? I probably should have *sought* visibility."

John sips a glass of white wine methodically. He nibbles at unsalted peanuts even more sparingly.

"If the truth be known, I'm a bit disenchanted these days by the direction of the 'large firm.' The business side of the firm seems to be threatening the practice side of the firm. Managing the practice is such a huge affair that it interferes with practicing law. I've never been bored with practicing law, but I'm painfully bored by all the internal sniping related to the management of the firm. Would I be saying this if I had a stronger role in the leadership? I don't know. But I do know I cannot dare show disenchantment inside the firm. Meanwhile, I'm plugging along with a consistent low-profile style. I don't get to share cases with the table-pounders, and don't really want to, but realize that maybe I *should* want to."

John starts popping peanuts faster.

"Civil and commercial litigation allows me to help a client stand up for his rights. I can't be shy and I can't be unscrupulous or dishonest because I'm constantly in front of judges who are too wise. I have learned over the years that you're not considered less tough by being less full of crap—sheer bluster gets ignored in serious lawyering, despite what television asks the public to think. Sure, I have to have an ego to be a litigator—I even went up against Louis Nizer once!—but there are limits to the rewards of pushing it.

"What's my life beyond law? I'm on the board of our Park Avenue church, and another church in the Village. I'm on the board of a mission in Chinatown also. These volunteer involvements make me sound more religious than I am. Also, I'm part of a spelunking group at the Museum of Natural History—we'll be traveling to South Dakota to investigate caves in June. I guess that's my most bizarre involvement. The rest of what Dorothy and I do is utterly predictable for a professional couple in New York City.

"God, it's taken me a long time to tell you all this, hasn't it? Let's finish by saying that I think life is a moving target. Things look wonderful from afar, but as you get closer, flaws appear. It's taken most of my life to get *close* to law and my life in New York City. And you know what? I think I could move to a little town in North Carolina tomorrow and be a very happy lawyer."

We shake hands and he heads off to dinner with Dorothy before a Carnegie Hall concert.

■ ■ ■

"My generation . . . looked at law as a profession. Too many of the younger ones look at law as a business."

PAMELA ANN RYMER

The blond lady of forty-seven looks like the manager of one of the better departments at Nordstrom's. She is classy and understated even though her black dress has huge white polka dots and pouffy Barbie sleeves. She is tall, thin, and could appear on the cover of *Vogue*.

But Pamela Rymer is a federal district judge in Los Angeles,* appointed by Ronald Reagan in 1983. Her name keeps appearing in substantial newspapers and journals on "hot lists" for this or that nomination—in *The New York Times* on the prospective (Republican) attorney general list, in *The National Law Journal* as a possible Supreme Court nominee under a Republican administration.

She accepts the attention gracefully, but is tight-lipped about all the second-guessing. Why is she such a strong candidate for a top nomination on the bench? Those around her say she is extraordinarily hardworking, conservative, tough at sentencing, and fair. In hearing that description, Ms. Rymer says, "Well, what more could one ask for, if it's true?"

Pam Rymer went to San Mateo High School, near San Francisco, where she was distinguished in class offices and sports as well as in the classroom. Her father was a wholesale distributor, and her mother taught junior high school to help put together the money to send her to Vassar. "I wanted to go East to college, and Mom thought Vassar had the best reputation of the women's colleges out there, so off I went."

According to Rymer, she wasn't particularly scholarly at Vassar, but full of zest when it came to helping out with the Rockefeller

*In May 1989, Ms. Rymer was nominated to the Ninth Circuit Court of Appeals.

for governor or speculative Goldwater for president campaigns. A favorite professor in political science, her major, suggested that she go either for the Ph.D. in poli sci or to law school. The latter sounded like the better choice, although she didn't know a single lawyer and didn't know anyone else at Vassar even considering that route.

"But Vassar taught me that I could do whatever I wanted to do without making a big deal out of it. So I quietly pursued law school."

Yale turned her down, but Columbia and Stanford admitted her. The decision was easy, she says: Stanford was close to home.

"What a reverse from Vassar! I was one of six women in a class of 140—four of us graduated. But Stanford taught me how to think and talk like a lawyer. Would that we had had a bit more clinical experience, but that *is* part of their program today. Otherwise, I thrived there. Also, I accelerated so I could leave early to help the Goldwater campaign. They hired me as director of political research and analysis. After the campaign, I joined a firm in Los Angeles and was an associate for six years. I loved it—did First Amendment law and some antitrust cases. But in 1975, another lawyer at the firm and I thought it was an ideal time to split away and open our own firm. We did it, specializing in business litigation and antitrust."

Judge Rymer only speaks when spoken to. Her answers are short and extremely cautious. But she has a lot to say regarding the practice of law yesterday versus today.

"Lawyers always have been and probably always will be very hardworking. And they're broad-gauged: they can deal with a wide variety of problems. I'd like to think the public service component is high too, but one does wonder at times. What *has* changed, most definitely, is the fact that my generation and those older than I looked at law as a profession. Too many of the younger ones look at law as a business. Money is a great thing—I believe in it, even for judges—but when the money starts breaking apart firm loyalty and collegiality, we're all in trouble. And that has clearly happened.

"These changes have had a profound effect on the practice of law. Collegiality—that common core of values and shared assumptions of how one practices law—has always been an important concept. It is being replaced by an individually oriented practice of law. The group is gone, and that is both sad and bad.

"There is another important change. Because firms just can't say no to new clients, it seems, conflict-of-interest problems pop up frequently. More and more, we have motions in the courtroom to disqualify."

Ms. Rymer isn't exactly certain how her nomination to the district court bench happened. But she says she'd be happy sitting there the rest of her days—if, of course, a nomination to a higher bench doesn't materialize.

"My court handles any squabble that raises federal questions—regarding tax, labor, antitrust, health plans, or fights between citizens of two states if the disputed amount is over ten thousand dollars. Also, we take on federal criminal cases—drugs-related or major white-collar criminal cases, for example. I spend a lot of time in trial, and a lot of time with pretrial motions. Also—and this was a surprise to me—the time spent on management is great: you know, in speeding a case along, in deciding how much involvement all parties should have, in just deciding how a case can be simplified. And the caseload is heavy. We might have 220 cases in inventory at a time. . . .

"My greatest frustration on the bench is the lack of support of the government for the judiciary. Lawyers in the firms have high-tech computerization—but we're still in the horse-and-buggy age because we're not provided the money to make essential changes that would speed everything along. Computerization should not stop at the courthouse steps. On the other hand, there are many joys to this job—the greatest is simply in providing an environment that is fair and reasoned for resolving disputes."

Judge Rymer is talking more now. But she is reserved and deliberate.

"I can't tell you how important good clerks are to what goes on in my courtroom. What do I look for in applicants? A severe commitment of time and talent. That means that I interview all my finalists to discern attitude—I'm not satisfied, as some judges are, with just looking at the students' résumés. I have two clerks at a time, each spending one year with me. They do legal research, memos, they're a superb sounding board for me, and they create bridges between the judge and the lawyers in the case. Basically, they assure me that the case is ready to proceed. Although their attitude and commitment are important, they also have to be making the most of law school. . . .

"Which brings us back to law school. I think legal education is the most rigorous of educations, and that is a value unto itself. The rigor of the education is as it should be, since the lawyers in our country are on the cutting edge of almost anything that counts. But law schools should make professionalism and ethics underlying themes of the entire curriculum. That might result in lawyers giving more time to public service. My involvement in the California Post-Secondary Education Commission (I served for ten years, but probably gave, cumulatively, two full years of time) added tremendous balance to my life and perspective."

Pam Rymer must go. It is mid-evening, and she rises every morning at 4:45 a.m. to walk one and a half miles around a golf course before doing some last-minute studying to prepare for the daily trial period, which runs from eight a.m. to one p.m. She normally gets home about seven p.m. There are breaks, however. Tennis is her favorite getaway activity, and she squeezes it in two to three times a week.

"Would there ever be time for a family? Sure. It may happen someday. Meanwhile, I love my life. And so will a lot of young people entering the law. If they're honest with themselves, have the ability to say no, resolve not to serve themselves more than their clients, and commit themselves to the oath of the court, we'll all be the better for it."

■   ■   ■

"If I can't clone myself in an associate, I'll do the work myself."

PETER S. BRITELL

It was a quiet dinner party in a small, rather stylized Manhattan apartment. Although there were only six of us, that meant one or two too many for the table in the dining alcove, so we were all in overstuffed living room chairs with lots of candles scattered about, precariously balancing food on trays.

Everyone seemed to be paired off in conversation in different corners of the room. In one corner, a musician was talking with

an architect. "As a property owner and sometimes builder or ren-
ovator, I've never been able to figure out where the responsibility
of the architect ends and the contractor begins, particularly when
they don't seem to speak exactly the same language," said the
musician rather earnestly.

The young architect acknowledged that it was a tough question, that he faced it on site often. He was about to give his view
when an unexpected answer shot across the room from one of the
other pairs. The "answer" came not with a smile or as a hypothesis
or even as a starting point for discussion. It was just delivered as
the answer.

This verbal cannonball came from Peter Britell, a forty-seven-
year-old partner with a major New York law firm with offices
high up in the Pan Am Building. Britell—surely one of the few
major firm partners in Manhattan with a scraggly beard, but one
of the many with a blue-striped shirt topped by a stiff white collar—
always seems to have the answer. But his answers usually make
sense and tantalize by being rather academic.

Peter Britell loves the law and feels there could be no other
professional place for him, even though he "just fell into it." Britell
was not born with a silver professional key in his mouth, but his
hardworking parents did create a rather comfortable path toward
career placement and success.

It started in remote Amsterdam, New York, where his Italian
Catholic father, who had dropped out of school in the sixth grade,
married a Jewish woman who had gone to college and had strong
professional aspirations for the men around her. Britell's father,
who converted to Judaism in marriage, moved from truck driver
to setting up an insurance and brokerage house that sold farms at
auction—the largest business of its type in New York—and a
textile business that sold goods mostly to the U.S. Army. In time,
he did very, very well.

The high schools in the area weren't good, so Peter's mother
and father decided that he and his brother should go away to prep
school, which they could now afford. The Taft School, a conservative boys' boarding school in Connecticut, was the choice for
both boys (Britell's brother is now a doctor in Seattle).

"I really pumped it out at Taft. The others in the class of
'seventy (there were only six of us Jewish kids) voted me most

likely to succeed at graduation. I ended up number one in the class, managing editor of the paper, and started a literary magazine. I can't tell you how unsophisticated I was and *felt* on entering Taft with my non-Ivy background, but obviously everything came out okay. I had been eager to go to one of the service academies since I was a kid, but glasses at eleven years old put me out of the running. So Princeton looked good for college until I met their pretentious admissions rep. Then my college adviser said one day, 'Look, you're number one in the class. Number one's should go to Harvard.' So I did, and that was that.

"At Harvard, my whole life revolved aruond the *Crimson*. I had always been good at writing, even scored an 800 on my English achievement test at the end of Taft. By sophomore year I was city editor of the *Crimson,* a big honor for one so young. But then I fell in love, lived in Boston my senior year, married early, and concentrated only on my studies, particularly my thesis for European history which was about an early proponent of social democracy in Spain. The push on academics paid off: I graduated magna, was Phi Beta Kappa, and the master of Leverett House said my work on Spain was the best undergraduate thesis he had ever read."

It is not difficult for Peter Britell to tell his story. It is matter-of-fact. But he lights up when the subject of law is introduced.

"I guess I wanted to be a novelist—in fact, I wrote a book after Taft but nobody wanted it. But as I was finishing Harvard, law just seemed right for continuing the kind of education I had started—liberal studies, you might say. I got lucky and was admitted to Yale, Columbia, and Harvard law schools. Why did I pick Harvard? Easy: it's the best."

Not even a snicker . . .

"Law school was great. I *knew* how to write, but Harvard Law taught me how to *read* all over again. I needed that, but didn't realize it. A good lawyer needs a strong academic base, and it is largely in skills of reading and writing. Law school gave me that, forcefully. I'll never forget my first class with Professor Clark Byse, the model for Professor Kingsfield in "The Paper Chase." He was exactly like he was depicted on television. In short, he scared me to death. I knew from the moment he entered our classroom that my life was about to be different—the difference evolved in paying greater attention to detail."

Britell can't talk fast enough now. His enthusiasm and love for everything related to law animates him.

"A good lawyer needs a strong academic base, but people skills are just as important. Law school doesn't *touch* the people skills—and I don't think it can. That's why older lawyers are better lawyers—they've had time to develop all the connections between the ideas, the analysis, *and* the people on the other side of the table. That just doesn't come without a good bit of experience."

We switch from Britell's chronology to observations on the law and lawyers in general.

"I'd describe lawyers as professional, craftsmen, and workaholics."

He ponders a moment and then continues.

"Well, I don't know why I first said 'professional'—that is just a built-in response, I guess. But we certainly do our share of professional training, so I guess it should stick.

" 'Craftsman' is more on target. Like a concert pianist, or someone in the martial arts, or a master carpenter, we develop an art form by disciplined study and learning, then by apprenticing, then by constantly stepping back to judge and refine the application. All kinds of academic and personal connections come into this honing of the talent. It's not quite like the doctors' profession where some of the younger practitioners may be better because their training is closer to the new technology. Our expertise builds on old forms. But we constantly renew attempts to master the skill more fully.

"Ask any lawyer's spouse—we're also workaholics. Law is labor-intensive! When the big case is upon you, you work until it is done. I average a workday of eight to eight, but in the fall and winter there are plenty of Saturdays spent here, and the eight to eight crumbles if the pressure is on, regardless of season. The client controls. . . . And then there is another related issue. I find it tough to delegate my work to juniors, to the associates. The client is relying on *me*—and if I can't clone myself in an associate, I'm not satisfied and I'll do the work myself. That's why my practice is 'lean,' despite the fact that I'm in a big firm. And that's why I'm a workaholic—that's why so many of us are workaholics.

"Every aspect of my real estate practice presents sharp edges, you see. I can't afford dull responses. Most of my work is negotiating agreements—on financing property, on contracts to buy or sell or construct, etc. But the tough part comes when two parties *think* they've reached an agreement and I step in to point out all sorts of fuzzy or unaddressed areas. Then there are almost inevitably disputes, as so much is at stake in these huge transactions. We're talking about air rights, massive construction contracts on skyscrapers, tax easements, neighborhood disputes regarding the environmental consequences of the structure, and a host of other problematic areas. There can*not* be dull responses to these sharp issues. So we work until we're satisfied. And very often that means we forgo the fabled January trek to the Caribbean or the August trek to the Hamptons. But I'm lucky—my wife loves my love of the law, and we work together to resolve the time sacrifices, often with the kids in mind. (I have two little sons now through a second marriage—and two college-age daughters through my first, disastrous marriage.)"

The offhand mention of the first marriage somehow stops Britell dead in his tracks. Then he picks up steam again.

"Attitude is the most important element in a lawyer's success. I *know* the other party and I are going to work out a deal when we enter negotiations. It has to happen! If the other party has the same attitude, it does happen. That kind of perspective can apply to firms as well as to individual attorneys. Some firms just can't get off the dime. I was with one that grew into the posture of always fretting about movement. Now I'm happy as could be with this firm which thinks as positively about the law and about movement as I do."

Britell is a watch-watcher. It is time for him to move from this conference room in the sky to a client meeting. His muted smile emerges, as he rises from the table.

"A final thought . . . Both of my second marriages—wife and firm—are just great.

"A second final thought: The more free a society is, the more lawyers it has per capita. That's why we have so many. We should be proud of that."

Boom. No contest. And he is gone.

■ ■ ■

■

Puck under wraps.

RUSS LI

"Here I am at a big, prestigious Manhattan law firm. But I'm not really interested in partnership. No one believes me when I say that, but I'd know if I were fooling myself. I have this nightmare now and then that I wake up at sixty-five years old, look around, and see nothing but a solid wall of binders housing the cases that I blew my mind on through the years. I say, '*This* is what I've done with my life? The big joy is sitting around with a few other retiring attorneys joshing about how we screwed the other guys in the Blatzo case twenty-two years ago? Okay, I've been a pretty good Wall Street partner. But is this fulfilling the good life?' "

Russ Li sits almost motionless behind horn-rimmed glasses. ("Like them? They combine my academic lawyer side with my Puck half.") The surroundings are formal—one of the smaller conference rooms of his "white-shoe" Wall Street firm. The room is all beige with an antique Oriental chest providing the appropriate backdrop.

Li, now thirty-four and a seventh-year associate, was born in Singapore of Korean parents. An early transplant to Tacoma, he attended public high school before moving to Yale for his bachelor's degree and then to Harvard Law. But Li looks like a New York lawyer now. His suit, granted, is a bit different from the norm: it is a deep mauve ("Made in Korea—possibly the only one in the firm?") with a somber plain dark tie hanging several inches below the belt with a subtle Royal Opera House logo.

"Part of this nightmare is that I'll end up like the senior partner I'm working for now. Everyone agrees he is a great lawyer—one of the best in the firm—but, Jesus, what a drone! He's now on a nine-day vacation, his first in years. He's not a young man, and he's in this firm from eight a.m. until ten p.m. Then he takes the train home, sleeps, and comes right back, time after time after time. He *will* wake up someday—soon!—and see only a wall of volumes of his cases. Is that it? Maybe for him, but not for me. I'm just back from vacation too—more than his nine days, and mine was spent a little differently. I slept one night on an open trail in the Rockies before heading overseas to see my family. In winters I like to ski Colorado and don't intend to sacrifice it just to say 'I'm a partner!' "

Li explains that he has often fallen short of what was expected of him—what *others* expected of him, that is. He was magna at Yale, but says he could have graduated summa if he had worked harder. He loved Yale undergraduate days ("I'm one of their rah-rahs now") which started with nine freshmen rooming together collectively speaking seventeen languages.

"I was dismal in social situations—in fact, so dismal that I decided to take ballroom-dancing lessons so I could at least get out there at mixers and attempt to master a technique rather than miserably hide in the corner watching all the others be jolly. I was in this brainy residential college and my friends probably thought I was inscrutable, bright like everyone else there, but not a real tool. To everyone's great surprise—particularly mine—I won the Athlete of the Year award one year for just participating in the intramurals, although I was fairly decent in squash. As a kid I was a figure skater, so all the games with footwork were easy for me."

Li sits absolutely still, his dark, long-on-the-top hair not tempted to shift. But the smile is puckish indeed, and breaks through the formality of the posture often. His words are clipped, although now and then he grows verbose, almost out of control with enthusiasm, as in describing Yale undergraduate days.

"I had no vices. Can you believe a college kid with no vices? But I really couldn't find my niche academically. I went to college wanting cosmology and ended up majoring in history and philosophy after taking summer courses at the University of Oregon to 'find myself.' I must admit, however, that the most memorable part of the University of Oregon summer was wandering into a dance course called 'Elementary Dance I: The Basics of Rhythm.' I thought it would advance me, out of sight of my Yale friends, in my ballroom dancing, but lo, everyone in the room was female, in a leotard, and ready for ballet. I felt it would have been chicken to leave so I learned ballet. And guess what? I've never left it. I still take two lessons a week."

Li explains that his Yale undergraduate career really was

serious, particularly toward the end. He focused on political and social philosophy and was deeply influenced by John Rawls, Robert Nozick, Roberto Unger, and Ronald Dworkin.

"I was so intrigued by this school of thought that I carried the enthusiasm right into Harvard Law, thinking it would provide a continuation of liberal studies. But that didn't quite work. Law school was much narrower than I thought it would be. I did okay, but just okay. Law school was a good combination of the intellectual and the practical, I guess, but I learned a hell of a lot more as an undergraduate. Part of my problem at law school was that I kept doing things to interfere with my studies. Was I just trying to get out of the field since I didn't know exactly why or how I had wandered into it? Probably . . .

"During law school, I sort of majored in dance. I worked with the Boston Repertory Ballet, danced and choreographed with the Harvard/Radcliffe Dance Company, and took a nine-city tour with them just at the time of some big law exams. I even performed at Jacob's Pillow at Tanglewood! A curious law school career? Yes. But among other things, I was at law school with a lot of other people on a sure route to paying off all my educational debts. Not the most honorable of motives.

"Actually, I did some serious things in law school. Professor Arthur Miller needed a lot of research for a television show he was starting on law. I was part of 'Arthur's Army,' getting him ready for prime time. Also, I worked with a firm in Rotterdam one summer, and my second summer was right here."

There is a big smile and a slight, unusual shake of the head.

"And here I am. They've been great to me—after two years as an associate here in New York, they sent me to the Geneva office for two and a half years. And now I'm working under a lawyer who probably couldn't be a better role model for most young lawyers—that is, if you want to commit your entire being to the law and the big, prestige firm."

Silence for a moment.

"I have a little problem with all this. Actually, I *am* a 'running dog of capitalism.' That is said ninety-five percent in jest, but the remaining five percent has to be considered. Let's face it—I'm spending most of my hours in a firm like this *benefiting corporate America* aiding accretion of capital. I'm a tool of management! Is all this affecting the quality of life of society in general? I don't know exactly, but it doesn't fit too well with my worldview. At the same time, I'm not doing anything here that is incongruous with benefiting society. At my tenth reunion at Yale they asked us on a questionnaire if we were busy doing anything we thought, deep in our souls, was unethical. I really had to say no. But, deep in my soul, I can't put the word *ethical* in caps, either.

"I spot a lawyer or two—note I said 'one or two'—in the hallways here who are good attorneys, and then go out and fully lead a different-than-expected life. I trust most of the attorneys here are Republicans. But one of our best tax lawyers really works hard for the Democratic party and finds time for it! He uses his podium in life quite well, it seems to me. So there are lights here and there that give me heart."

We talk about the near future.

"No, I don't expect to be here for long. Yes, I *might* make partner, but I doubt if this atmosphere provides the kind of life I really want to lead. I respect lawyers—I've never met a sleazy one, although I keep hearing they're out there. Lawyers are extraordinarily busy, they learn to successfully juggle a range of skills from scheduling to organizing to telephone effectiveness to writing to research to careful analysis. We all learn to think in a different kind of way—to get to the heart of the matter, to cut through the extraneous and the irrelevant. The problem with that is that we tend to look at *everything* in life that way, always ready to figure out an advocacy position—it's a habit that drives me nuts at times.

"My biggest problem is that I don't take the time to go out and look for the options. Will I get stuck as a result?—I can't allow that to happen, but here I am, seven years down the path of associate and I still don't know the other opportunities out there for me. One reason I went to law school was to have options—but what are they? Where are they? I'm fairly serious about a woman now—she's a staunch Catholic—and everything is going to have to get figured out fairly soon. Friends say I could probably succeed in providing a legal link between the U.S. and Korea, but I don't know . . .

"I have this feeling I'm on a fast track to the wrong place—to the wallful of case studies. Jesus, I'd better look around. But how *can* you look around when you put in 2,600 hours per year

THE LURE OF THE LAW

at the office? My spare time is spent watching the professional dance companies come through New York. And that is one little joy that cannot be lost, fast track or not."

It is time for a meeting with a client. Li stands, straightens his tie, formally shakes my hand, and moves purposefully down the hallway. Puck is buried deep.

■　■　■

Considering the test scores, still overachieving . . .

RICHARD REYES

As a new freshman at Bowdoin College in Maine, Richard Reyes carried a bit of a grudge against standardized testing. Moderate SATs had kept him out of Dartmouth. But he quickly fell in love with Bowdoin. And now, at thirty-nine, he is an Overseer of the College.

"Look, I'm from New Hampshire—and everyone in New Hampshire *knows* when they're seventeen that reaching the summit of life is admission to Dartmouth. As number two in my class, and a New England champion debater, I presupposed Dartmouth would take me. But lo, my dreary SATs kept me outside the gates. Standardized tests have always been my nemesis, including during the initial round of trying to get into law school.

The tests, which had seemed to obstruct his goals, are well behind this New York–style Portland, Maine, law partner now. The overachiever whom the tests could not adequately define is still overachieving. Not only is he a key partner with one of the leading firms of Maine and a youthful trustee of his prestigious college; he also is the just-retired president of the Greater Portland Landmarks Association, is current president of the Maine Historical Society, the Bowdoin trustees' representative to the public television station WCBB, serves on the Judicial Records Committee of the Maine Supreme Court, and has somehow found the time to revise totally his little town's (Durham, Maine) subdivision ordinance and land use ordinance. (The Reyes home, a twenty-five-minute commute from big-city Portland, is a National Historic Landmark: the only three-story, hip-roofed, center chimney house in the state.)

"When I grew up in the mill town of Dover, New Hampshire, Dad was the local judge. [In fact, he ultimately became New Hampshire's chief justice, is now retired, and lectures around the law school circuit.] I guess he was the role model regarding a future in law. But for a long time I wanted to be a college professor of American history. Volunteer efforts related to Americana still consume most of my spare time."

As one listens to Reyes, a clean-cut, fair-haired fellow with a supertidy office of antique desks, maps, and Maine memorabilia, there is a backdrop of constant distraction through the huge window behind him—ships and sailboats buzzing in and out of the Portland harbor. Reyes's firm has just moved into this postmodern mega office building, high above Maine's waters.

"It was a little tough being an arts-oriented student in that small blue-collar New Hampshire town. How would my classmates have described me then? Well, as supersmart (it just seemed so in that context), an overachiever, a hard worker—no, make that very hard worker—and Mr. Clean. I was editor of the newspaper and loved debating. My archrival, who was valedictorian after our neck-and-neck race for the top, taught me a lot of lessons. Although I was something of a minor athlete, he had zero skills in that category. So he sort of needed my protection for his enthusiastic involvement in his own areas of interest—the drama club, for example. He wouldn't join the drama club unless I did too—to keep from being the only boy. I proposed a deal: I'd join the drama club if he'd consent to be my debating partner. He agreed, and ultimately we swept the whole state and regional championships. Great guy!—he's a successful professor now. You know, people like that are helping you jump life's hurdles when you least suspect it."

Reyes speaks like he looks. Everything is in place. There are not excessive words or phrases. The point is there, always put forward with considerable warmth and seriousness. There is immense credibility to this man.

"Anyway, it wasn't really too long a journey from that high school to the law. My view of lawyers, now that I've met so many over the years, fits my self-description almost perfectly. We're an analytical crowd—'problem-solvers' says it best, I think. We're rational. We handle pressure well or we drop out along the way and move quietly to another profession—I've watched some great minds drop out of law abruptly because their shoulders just weren't broad enough to handle the pressure. Most important, I guess, is the fact that we're almost inevitably conservative. I mean that as applying to a number of areas: politically, socially, personally. For example, our profession could have spawned some of the great captains of industry, but it wouldn't happen because lawyers find it very difficult to risk their money. We're conservative at every turn. We're also loyal, and incredibly hardworking. It's the right place for me!"

Reyes tells the story, now with a smirk, of constant batterings by admissions officers because of the standardized tests. Toward the end of his Bowdoin career, distinguished in the classroom and out, he learned of his 560 on the Law Boards, utterly out of keeping with his college grades but utterly in keeping with his SAT level. (There are critics of the Educational Testing Service who say that one's 'level of testing' will not change, despite high or low performance in the classroom.)

After getting an early rejection letter from Harvard Law during his college senior year, Reyes learned he had won a Keasby Fellowship (second in prestige only to the Rhodes) for two years of study at Cambridge University in England. At Cambridge, one option for his major was law, an undergraduate discipline in England. He studied torts and contracts and all the subjects he would have taken to start his law career in America, and he loved every bit of it. He knew then that law was his field—the interest in American history would have to be avocational.

Toward the end of his Cambridge period of study, Reyes again applied to prestige American law schools. This time, the Keasby honor and his successful performance at Cambridge seemed to have put the moderate Law Board scores in backseat position. Yale and Cornell said "Yes," but Boston University was the only top law school that would give him a year's credit for his two years of concentration on law at Cambridge. He was off to Boston.

"Law school was great. Although I hated anything related to tax law, the field of litigation called on my old debating skills, and I thought I had found my niche. Then summer jobs introduced me to new areas like municipal law, where one could deal with school

∎

boards, zoning committees, and the volunteers that make society tick. So here I am in a firm that represents many small towns in municipal law.

"Actually, I have rather large corporate clients—one of the largest paper companies in this well-forested state, for example—whom I represent in small power production interfacings with utilities: hydroelectric questions, waste disposal, landfill, where to bury sludge, etc.

"My relationship to the paper company is intriguing. I did some small assignments with them related to the Department of Environmental Planning. I guess their counsel liked what I did and asked if I knew anything about federal law that permits private companies to sell electricity to utilities. I said, 'I don't know anything about it today, but I'll be an expert by the end of tomorrow.' Well, I was—and they give me more business than I can handle now on a variety of matters.

"Does the corporate lawyer in Maine wish that he were in New York, where all successful corporate lawyers are supposed to be? Absolutely not. I know I *could* be there, because I've won several cases against Wall Street's best. But two kids, an outdoorsy wife, an allegiance to family and community and profession all wrapped into one probably wouldn't fly in New York."

A knowing grin, and a swivel toward the harbor view . . .

"But I have some New York kinds of problems. Our family leaves tonight for a one-week vacation. There is no way in the world I could leave my clients for more than a week—several of them during the past few days have been less than kind when I've told them I'm escaping to an island off the Maine coast for a few days and will provide an able associate for them to consult with, should the need arise. They're upset. 'When *my* case is on the fire, lawyers don't vacation!' That scenario happens around the calendar, so I just have to pick the least hurtful week.

"My wife is upset, really upset, that we have the means, the happy family, and the adventurous spirit to get away a bit, but can't because of the law. I mean, this is a real problem . . . So it's no different in Maine than in New York. The island we're going to has no phones. 'Great!' one might say, but I know I'll row across the harbor each day to make a key call or two at the pay phone."

On cue, the phone rings.

"John, I know it's crucial to meet with your group next week, but as I told you, I'm taking a one-week vacation then and I just can't join you."

A lengthy silence while the other party profusely carries on. Then . . .

"Okay, okay. On Wednesday, I'll row across to the harbor and call your office on the pay phone. Have the four parties set up for a conference call at ten a.m. We'll take care of it."

A sad smile and a shaking of the head toward the interviewer.

"No, it's okay, John. Talk to you Wednesday."

It is time for the young partner to head off to the island, just a row away from the telephone.

■ ■ ■

*"I'm still not making over $35,000, but my work is
extremely meaningful."*

ELIZABETH STERNBERG

Beth Sternberg is committed to good deeds. Forget the affluent urban background, the Seven Sisters college, her brief stay at a prestigious Wall Street law firm, and even a recently acquired imposing sapphire-with-diamonds wedding band ensemble: Beth is content to sacrifice the material up side of the law and, with her professor husband, serve the public interest at dreary pay to make life a bit more comfortable and safe for the disenfranchised.

Beth is a staff attorney for New York Lawyers for the Public Interest, an organization packed into tight quarters on the upper floor of a brownstone (now red) at Third Avenue and Fifteenth Street in Manhattan. Her apricot corduroy skirt and sweater are simple and worn. Old silver heels have been abandoned under a work table in favor of scruffy penny loafers. And she talks in a manner consistent with her appearance.

It all seems, somehow, rather down.

This is ironic—Beth obviously loves what she is doing, and she is practicing her kind of law at considerable sacrifice. But there is little joy to be found in her discussion of vocation, not to mention the surroundings she has created. Nonetheless, her commitment seems real and her agency is downright essential in today's profit-oriented social and legal context.

New York Lawyers for the Public Interest was founded over a decade ago to "provide a mechanism for bringing New York City's large private law firms together with public interest clients." NYLPI coordinates pro bono work by major law firms on NYLPI–sponsored projects and also solicits the firms' financial support for NYLPI's lawyers' direct involvement in the rights of the mentally and physically disabled, neighborhood preservation, and a host of other public-interest areas requiring legal resolution. Through both the pro bono involvement and direct financial assistance, the organization's forty-one member law firms "provide a concrete expression of private bar commitment to public interest law." In 1988, NYLPI's participating firms provided legal assistance to eighty-three projects, approximately half of which required litigation, the remainder involving tax or real estate or corporate matters for small neighborhood organizations such as day-care centers or substance abuse or job training programs.

As most observers of the law today lament the paucity of pro bono effort in attorneys' weekly routines, a sampling of the NYLPI roster of projects provides hope:

Age Discrimination in SRO Housing (Wachtell, Lipton, Rosen & Katz). The firm is serving as counsel with the East Side SRO Project of MFY Legal Services in a lawsuit instituted to prevent the eviction of 22 working women who are long-term residents at St. Mary's Home for Working Girls. These women, who are 45 and older and have lived at St. Mary's for periods ranging from 5 to 16 years, have been given notice that they must move from the residence because of a four-year residency limitation which had never previously been enforced. Plaintiffs have commenced an action seeking declaratory and injunctive relief and damages based on violations of the Human Rights law, breach of contract, waiver and estoppel.

Tax Assistance for Animal Rescue Organization (Donovan Leisure Newton & Irvine). Pet Rescue is a volunteer organization that cares for and finds homes for abandoned dogs and cats.

This firm is assisting the organization in resolving problems related to its tax exemption.

Counsel to Develop Shelter for the Homeless (Shearman & Sterling). This firm is assisting the Harlem Heights Community Housing and Development Corporation in the development of a housing project to provide 30 units of both transitional and permanent shelter for homeless families.

Discrimination Against Women Printers (Weil, Gotshal & Manges). This firm is representing current and former female employees in the printing industry in New York City in litigation challenging sex discrimination in the terms and conditions of employment. Since the turn of the century, the printing industry has been notoriously sex-segregated. Male and female employees were represented by separate union locals until 1977. Women continue to be denied fringe benefits and wages equivalent to those received by men. On behalf of the women, the firm is seeking back pay; an equalization of the benefits they are to receive in the future; and injunctive relief ordering a reclassification of jobs within the industry.

Negotiation of Long-Term Lease with City on Behalf of Consortium of Chinatown Groups (LeBoeuf, Lamb, Leiby and MacRae). This firm is representing five not-for-profit organizations serving the Chinatown community to establish a consortium which could then enter into negotiation with the City to lease, on a long-term basis, the City-owned building in which all are currently located. Negotiations with the City to keep rents at a rate manageable for small non-profits are currently underway.

The staff attorneys of New York Lawyers for the Public Interest, in addition to coordinating major law firms' pro bono involvement, work daily on their own caseloads—a sampling:

Benjamin B. v. Cuomo
NYLPI filed suit in the Eastern District of New York on behalf of six mentally retarded persons who had been housed in a psychiatric hospital on a ward with mentally ill patients for

several years. The plaintiffs did not receive any treatment or training appropriate for mentally retarded persons.

Heard v. Cuomo

This case has been brought by the Coalition for the Homeless on behalf of all homeless mentally ill persons who have been discharged or conditionally released from New York State psychiatric centers or hospitals administered by the New York City Health and Hospitals Corporation without a "written service plan" providing specific recommendation as to the type of residence in which the patient is to live and a listing of services essential to the patient in such residence.

Hill v. Board of Elections

This action was filed in Supreme Court, Kings County, by NYLPI to assure access to polling places for mobility-impaired persons in New York City.

School Transportation Cases

The Education for All Handicapped Children Act requires states to provide transportation to school for handicapped children. The three plaintiffs are wheelchair bound adolescents who live in non-accessible buildings. No family member capable of carrying the student up and down the stairs is available at the time the child leaves or returns from school. The New York State Commissioner of Education ruled that the obligation to provide transportation was only from curb-to-curb, thus the Board of Education did not have to provide an attendant to carry the child from his apartment or front door to and from the bus.

Andrew B. v. Sobol

This case involves the unusual issue of whether a child with a very high IQ can be classified as learning disabled when the child achieves only at grade level rather than at his expected potential. Plaintiff is a bright twelve-year-old who has been able to achieve only at grade level or slightly below and has increasing behavioral problems in school.

Beth Sternberg is participating in what is, for her, a natural forum. She has always been surrounded by the city. And she has always been surrounded by lawyers.

Beth's father was a lawyer for the Internal Revenue Service, where a promotion always meant a move: during her childhood, from Long Island to Maryland to Miami to Philadelphia, and back to New York. She grew accustomed to being a transient in public schools, always leaving behind friends just made, and decided to quietly concentrate on her studies plus a little involvement in student government.

"My interest in law was always in the background. I may have been the only kid in my class who could not only name all the Supreme Court justices, but could also name which presidents appointed them. That was never on a test—I just made it my business to know it."

Beth's mother, a well-educated mother of four, and her uncle, a lawyer, mentioned from the early years that Beth would surely be a lawyer—her interest in social justice issues surfaced even when she was a child.

"Also, my uncle always said that I *talked* like a lawyer, whatever that means. So I just naturally looked toward law, largely because of family influence. But I knew that being a tax lawyer, like my uncle and father, was not for me . . . Bor-r-ring!"

Having skipped from one high school to another, in Miami and Philadelphia and New York, Beth followed her mother to Barnard College in Manhattan where her friends, she says, probably considered her "smart, studious, hardworking, with an insatiable passion for theater. They called me 'White Way Sternberg.'"

While at Barnard, Beth was quite involved in the Jewish Student Union and other Jewish-oriented organizations, student government, the student newspaper, and a variety of volunteer social justice projects.

She did no more than cross the street to attend law school at Columbia which, in retrospect, she liked because "They made it their business to worm a curl of *something* out of you. On the other hand, I found law school boring and not nearly as much fun as college. I found that I had to leave law school to make the experience 'real.' I did projects for the NAACP Legal Defense Fund, for example. But Columbia now has a good human rights pro-gram—I'm so glad that has finally happened. Columbia *was* good in allowing us to take courses beyond law in related fields, so I was able to avoid a lot of commercial courses and load on more from great professors in the social sciences."

This interview is slow. Beth always pauses to think and looks at her desk or the floor before speaking. She rarely smiles but, nonetheless, transmits a certain passion regarding what she be-lieves and what she is doing.

"During law school I had the customary yearning to sample what a big firm would really be like. After my second year of law school, I was a summer associate at one of the Wall Street firms here in New York and really liked the experience. So I decided to join that firm following graduation and stayed three years. I rather liked litigation, and they had me doing a lot of work on one of their huge corporate cases. It was good to earn some real money— actually the three years there allowed me to put away a tidy nest egg."

There is a slight, sheepish smirk. "Although the firm was generous in allowing me to give considerable time to pro bono cases—for example, another associate and I spent over three hundred hours preparing an amicus brief for the first sexual har-assment case to go in front of the Supreme Court—the fact remains that I knew early on that I wasn't, in the big-firm context, making the type of contribution in law that I wanted to make."

The phone rings and Beth calmly discusses procedures re-garding the case of a disabled student's constant harassment on a public school playground. The pause gives me time to glance around the high-ceilinged office with baby blue woodwork and filthy windows. There are Classic Coke cans everywhere—some empty, some full. A cellophane-wrapped, unopened perfume box is on one table, surrounded by uneven stacks of papers. There is a photograph of a cemetery on one wall, and on another, a Wall Street–oriented cartoon—which, quite frankly, I don't under-stand—from *Harper's* magazine.

The phone conversation ends . . .

"Through old friends and contacts, I landed a job as deputy director of the Equal Employment and Public Accommodations Division of the New York City Commission on Human Rights. It seemed, on the surface, a context in which I could make my own special contribution and a wonderful balance to the big firm. But I quickly learned that there were so many problems related to the massive bureaucracy that I would have to move along to more directly serve the public good.

"This particular city commission was rampant with tension: for example, the issue, among lawyers, of *quantity* versus *quality* of work, which clearly resulted from the six-month-to-one-year backlog of cases. There were unfortunate quota systems, there were severe time constraints, and there were great tensions among the mostly minority, full-time civil service workers there. On the whole, it was just a depressing situation. And many of the cases that came to us were frivolous at best: so many people would come forward saying they had been treated unfairly because of race, color, or creed when, in actuality, many had been fired from jobs, for example, for excessive absenteeism. Too many cases were submitted for no rhyme or reason.

"There were some cases, nevertheless, of clear discrimination: age discrimination in the police department, for example. And we had an interesting case of a blind person who was not allowed to take his guide dog into the Bronx Zoo—no one had ever raised this issue before. At first, the zoo authorities said that the dog would frighten the animals. But in a short time we were able to convince them through a few tests that guide dogs would not be a threat, and now the dogs are allowed.

"Now and then we did find cases of blatant discrimination—taxicabs repeatedly passing by black men, for instance—but it was frustrating trying to nail down the individual case that would provide a symbol for the larger issue."

Silence, and a long glance at the floor. "In my view, the city commission did not use its power effectively to combat discrimination. The whole thing was just too complicated in organization, and the commission did not focus on cases that symbolized *patterns* of discrimination. My disenchantment there, however, was limited to that particular commission. I could see that other commissions of the city worked quite smoothly and effectively. The new AIDS unit, for example, is doing great straightforward work."

Beth seems to be warming to the conversation somewhat now, but the positive comments are strained.

"I found *this* job in my Columbia Law placement newsletter. We have four staff attorneys at NYLPI and we really dig into our cases, quickly and directly. We try to move on 'impact cases' that will affect large numbers of people. Part of our funding comes from the state, part from federal coffers, but much of our funding comes, of course, from our member law firms. I'm still not making over $35,000, but my work is extremely meaningful and the hours are sane—I work from about ten to about seven.

"My husband is a professor at a law school on Long Island. He is not well paid either, and consequently we are in a small, one-bedroom apartment in a Hispanic neighborhood on the Upper West Side. We're really quite happy there, and happy with our lives."

Beth has a meeting.

I descend the narrow, creaky staircase and notice another public-service-law–oriented program on the lower floors. Out on crowded Third Avenue, the people with obvious problems look a bit different to me now. If they could only find their way to Beth's congested, unheralded office, a small band of lawyers is willing to assist them in asserting their rights as citizens and to help them maintain the bottom line of human dignity. But I know also that the service provided is at considerable cost to the lawyers themselves, quite beyond salary.

■ ■ ■

"Lawyers: serious, pompous, self-absorbed, intense, insulated, and self-indulgent."

NORM SHERMAN

The telephone message at my hotel from a friend, the director of admissions at a southern California college, invited me to meet her and her lawyer husband at a little restaurant in Venice, a beach town not too far from central L.A.

Not knowing the territory, I arrive early. And, my, what a scene unfolds. . . . Gold's Gym has an open-air spot where the Stallone-type female and male hopefuls pump a lot of iron; bikini-clad women swirl on roller skates through the milling multitude on the boardwalk; and tacky, tacky shops abound, thronged with an army of those who purchase billed caps with animal ears or little mirrors decorated with shells and beads. There is atmosphere indeed. The ocean rolls in, but the crowd doesn't seem to notice.

Californians are casual in dress, even at the opera or in the finest restaurants. But "California casual" would be labeled formality in Venice. Lo, into the restaurant walks the young lawyer looking like he has just taken the Number 4 train from Wall Street to the Upper East Side. He has on the universal big-law-firm uniform: very dark suit, white buttondown shirt, red tie with a hint of paisley design.

Nice guy! After a chat with his wife about college admissions and California football rivalries, Norm Sherman and I settle in to talk law.

"I know we attorneys all look alike, whoever we are, and wherever we go. But it's not our fault—it's yours. People *expect* lawyers to look this way. The clients who pay a lot of money expect it and even the judges expect it of attorneys performing in front of them. But give us a break: English professors tend to look and dress alike, and so do plumbers. I'd just as soon get out of this uniform now and then, however."

One reason I am eager to talk to Sherman is that he heads up the lawyer hiring program for his large downtown-L.A. firm (fortieth floor, Wilshire Boulevard). Most firms name one young partner the "hiring partner" as a rite of initiation to the partnership. The hiring partner is usually affable, organized, and pretty good at "sales." One could add the usual outspokenness of lawyers and have an apt description of Norm.

"Our firm nurtures the killer instinct. And that's largely because we specialize somewhat in litigation—of just over one hundred partners, there are always fifty-five to sixty litigators. We certainly are active in other fields of law, but, as you know, many big firms tend to be known for a speciality in something."

After being fairly fussy in ordering wine, Norm continues. His usually verbose wife is content to listen.

"How would I describe lawyers in general? Well, remember I'm still in my thirties, so I haven't met them all, but my general impression of attorneys is stabilizing: they're serious, pompous, self-absorbed, intense, insulated from almost everything but their area of the law, self-indulgent, and really not very interesting people. On the other hand, it seems to me that they are, on the whole, ethical, basically decent people, and surprisingly good family men, given the little time available beyond work."

Dinner is served, but Norm is enjoying this discussion, and just keeps talking.

"We only visit the best eleven or twelve law schools to look for new talent. Top firms, in my view, can't afford to go beyond that. The young people we're seeing these days are interested in the big bucks, no doubt about it. They are intrigued by the huge financial mergers, the huge settlements in a variety of legal areas that they've read about. On the other hand, there is a curious swing toward a revived interest in doing pro bono work at the Legal Aid Society, for example, or sexier stuff like dealing with undocumented aliens. I don't know if they're interested in this free lawyering because of guilt over the big salary chase, or if there is reviving common concern for the common good. But my firm will support any cause a person feels passionate about. So if the young associate wants to put in nineteen hundred or more billable hours *and* undertake a lot of pro bono work, great."

The restaurant is now jammed (and the vegetables under-cooked).

"My travels to law schools are fascinating. Good law schools teach you to think like lawyers—that's not a difficult assignment, it seems to me. But the top law schools teach young people to *think,* just to think. And *that* makes a potentially great lawyer."

Norm's wife reminds him that his (expensive) food is getting cold. She takes the opportunity to agree with everything he has said . . . (until, that is, what he says next).

"One thing that gets to me in law—but maybe this relates to all the professions—is how *superb* some of the less well recognized are, and how shoddy some of the 'greats' are. For example, I think a lot of the judges are really mediocre—they're less interesting and certainly less well motivated than many other lawyers. I really don't know what to make of that. On the other hand, I wouldn't turn down being a judge."

Ms. Sherman talks more about the college scene. Curiously, the lawyer tunes out.

"Insulated"? "Self-absorbed"? "Not very interesting"? Well,

maybe just tired. But soon after we end his subject, the lawyer is ready to go.

And does.

■ ■ ■

"Unfortunately, I'm not good at being obnoxious, and I'm a terrible actor. The two combined almost disallow my 'success' in law."

MARK SAUNDERS

Mark Saunders said he could fit me in on a Saturday, when he was to attend an all-day seminar for lawyers on "search and seize" at the San Francisco Hyatt. We decided lunch would provide the best opportunity.

Granted, it is Saturday *and* San Francisco, but I didn't expect a lawyer—any lawyer—to show up in Reeboks, wash pants, and an open, trendily oversized white shirt. His gentle, wry smile helps set the stage. "This one is different," I think to myself . . .

"How can one point to a single factor that was the lure to the law?" says he. "Impossible . . . but if I had to find one, it would be my grandmother. She was Mexican and had the notion that she was quite aristocratic. She wanted to be European, not Hispanic. . . .

"She and my grandfather emigrated to California in 1917. After roaming from one little town to another in search of work, they settled up north in a small town of about 25,000 people."

Having downed a grapefruit juice that the earringed bartender was visibly disappointed in serving at this upscale financial-district eatery, the lawyer inspects his huge hamburger and sends it back for a longer stay on the grill. He accomplishes this with warm smiles, soft comments.

"Granddad ended up working for years at the lumber mill. But Grandma knew there were better ways for the rest of us to make a go of it in America. She thought *lawyers* represented ultimate respectability—they all made millions, rode in nice cars, and spoke fluently. As a matter of fact, she was probably close to the true picture of the lawyer in rural America in the twenties through the fifties (given, of course, a little salary inflation).

"I was not the only one influenced by her. My mother ended

up marrying a lawyer—a real mistake. He bolted when I was two and never bothered to keep up with his two kids—I have an older sister—at all. Yes, he paid a little alimony, but there was no interest in the family he spawned living on the other side of a small town. I didn't even know who he was—if we had passed him at the drugstore or on the street, my sister and I would not have realized it. Then, one day when I was thirteen, this man came over to us on a plane and introduced himself as our father. We talked for a while—interesting, in retrospect, how lacking we were in emotion at the time—and all I could remember thereafter was his eloquence, his strong persona, and how smart he seemed to be. Clearly, he became another heavy influence—subconscious though it was—to my ultimately entering law."

Mark speaks quietly, picking his way carefully. He pauses now and then to imply the start of a new paragraph.

"I lived with my grandparents, mother, and sister. We kids were sent to parochial school—kids without a father were thought to need discipline, you know. I guess it was clear to all that I was bright and an achiever. Funny how I researched imaginatively about colleges—I settled on Columbia in New York, as I wanted to get as far away as possible. Meanwhile, I got to know my father a bit better and discovered, among other things, that he was a very heavy drinker, a rugged individualist with a very high self-image, and had a law degree from Berkeley (which only confirmed my notion to get out of California for higher education). To his credit, he did help Mom and my grandparents put me through Columbia. Still, I qualified for a hefty scholarship.

"At college and in New York I became more myself. The intellectual experience of Columbia was marvelous, and I took full advantage of it—majored in political science, pulled a 3.4 average, and graduated in 'seventy-one. Beyond studying, I just took in as many concerts as I possibly could. During summers, I returned to California to work at the lumber mill to make more good money for college."

After a bite or two on the big burger, a long pause leads to a quiet shake of the head.

"But those were hard times for young people. There were campus protests—heavy protests—all about me. I avoided that scene. But I did fall for the cynicism of my turbulent college genera-

■

tion. Although I was working fairly hard at getting an education, I was quietly wondering, 'Why knowledge?' The 'futility of knowledge' became something of a motto for me as I plowed ahead.

"At graduation, I didn't know what to do. I had developed into a cynical snob. I wouldn't have dreamed of going into business—in fact, I didn't know *what* I'd go into. So, back to California and the lumber mill became the only safe answer. I lasted about a year, buoyed by the 'futility of knowledge' theme. Then, all of a sudden, the futility of getting stuck at the lumber mill, like Granddad, hit me. At *least* I had an education to use—could I teach English or sociology? I convinced myself I didn't have to believe in teaching as a career—it could be viewed simply as my trade, not unlike working at the mill."

The wry smile again . . .

"But some force irrationally led me to the University of San Diego Law School. There was an almost equally strong force telling me to jump off a bridge somewhere—the futility theme was obviously still strong.

"First-year law students in our system are taught to compete against themselves and each other. It is a devastating introduction to a trade. I was discouraged at the end of that year, but decided to continue in a different, less threatening atmosphere—Golden Gate Law School here in San Francisco, which is known for a calmer approach and training for public service. At the time I thought it might be good to go into criminal law—it seemed more socially useful than serving the rich in other specializations. Golden Gate's sensitive approach to law served me well."

The hamburger is gone and more grapefruit juice has arrived. The casual lawyer is telling his story somberly, seemingly unaware of any of the hubbub around us. He is a man of deep concentration.

"Now qualified to be an 'artisan,' I became a public defender for three and a half years, averaging eighteen thousand dollars a year. Long, long hours were spent in drunk driving court, with those accused of minor theft, etc. Quite frankly, many of the people I was assigned to just hadn't been dealt a full deck in the first place. They were more often obnoxious than not, impatient with me because my services had been essentially imposed upon them. In total, I represented hundreds of people and ended up in twenty-five or so court trials, most of which I won."

Another long pause.

"It was a bewildering experience, and my constitution just couldn't stand up to it. I was often assigned four or five clients at once, and there was no way I could do justice to their cases or situations. And on top of that, of course, was the ugly fact that this was a very lonely existence—these clients were not exactly the type who would send flowers or a Christmas card later if they felt well served. I just couldn't take it anymore and quit.

"Not long after, in 1979, I opened a tiny office near the Tenderloin—too near the Tenderloin—with another ex–public defender, a Chinese fellow who was just too nice and mellow to be efficient in law. The upshot was sheer incompetence—malpractice just waiting to happen. I had to abandon the partnership with him, and moved to upscale Union Square where I'm dealing mostly with divorce cases and varieties of breach of contract. But now there is a new chapter of disillusionment.

"I'm not with a firm, really, but a complex of ten cooperating lawyers in one building drawn by a magnet, a very visible constitutional lawyer I had read a lot about and greatly admired. (I've since learned that even prominent constitutional lawyers must spend more time dealing with society's real losers than winners.) But there I remain, plugging away in my own little practice, working only about eight hours a day and pulling in a salary just into the six-figure range. (You may be surprised to hear me talk of the latter, but if one wants a little house with a garden and two bedrooms in the Bay area these days, salary concerns legitimize.)"

It is time for ice cream. And that means time for summation. He remains ponderous, careful, thoughtful.

"No, I'm not certain it was wise to fall to law. But here I am. Law today needs people who love gamesmanship, who enjoy scheming. I just don't. One always hopes there might be something more. But, dammit, there hardly is. I just enjoy advocating the rights of people who in some way have been exploited. If I can help a little, I'm content. Usually the case does not come in blacks and whites, only shades of gray. But if I can keep someone from bankruptcy, say, through negotiation, then good purpose has been served.

"On the whole, law is no longer an instrument for social change—it is a tool to be used in a class struggle. And that requires practitioners who value aggression, salty talk, an obnoxious de-

∎

meanor, and rude behavior. Lawyers almost have to be very ego-centric to survive in the race today—somehow, staring out of their fortieth-floor windows nurtures their worst instincts to keep hold of the power at any price.

"If I was really motivated to charge toward *my* definition of legal success, I would get more involved in free-speech cases, censorship law, perhaps be an ACLU lawyer. But I'm not sure I want to fight the fight again, and I really want to avoid large organizational approaches to law.

"Quietly, I still look at law as public service. I bring to it diligence, and I'm painstaking with the facts. My current situation allows that. Unfortunately, I'm not good at being obnoxious, and I'm a terrible actor. The two combined almost disallow my 'success' in law."

Another long pause. And the final bit of vanilla.

"Maybe that's why I'd rather be an opera singer or pianist. But my grandmother and father didn't point in that direction. I and too many other lawyers just fell into law without much thought. And here we are, blandly practicing a trade."

■ ■ ■

"I'm lucky to be working for something larger than myself.
Would that everyone in law could do that."

SIMON SIDAMON-ERISTOFF

"I'm *really* pleased about my new job with the Trust for Public Land. Sure, I took a huge cut in pay switching from the law firm. But at a private firm you serve the client, not necessarily one you *want* to serve or a cause you believe in. There were endless minutiae—I knew there would be for a young associate, and I was lucky to have a great mentor—but it got to me after a while. Now I'm combining law with my love for the environment. I feel like I'm really doing something, even though I'm paid less. And yes, the fact that I can afford it helps."

A big pause. And a big smile.

"I'm just a lucky guy, just a really lucky guy."

It is so . . .

Simon Sidamon-Eristoff is recently back from a family re-

■

union in Russia. Several generations ago, Simon's family ruled the largest dukedom of Georgia. In 1921 some of the family emigrated to America to escape political upheaval. But now the American cousins of the Georgians are treated like royalty on their returns to the homeland.

There is, however, more than international romance to this family story. Simon's great-grandfather was a partner of Andrew Carnegie. The family did well when the business was sold to U.S. Steel.

Simon Eristoff (he tends to shorten the last name—"*Eristoff* means 'prince' in Russia, by the way") appears to have used his advantages well. And quietly. At thirty-two, he is understated, calm, and handsome, with a chiseled face. He dresses conservatively—black shoes and all—the only hint at aristocracy being a tiny monogram on the shirt pocket.

Eristoff was sent to St. Bernard's School in Manhattan for grammar school and then off to the countryside for boarding school—the Milbrook School, not far from the family weekend home in Highland Falls, New York.

"I thrived at Milbrook—you know, editor of the paper, prefect, a decent student as a result of being fairly conscientious and energetic, and I had the good fortune of scoring well on the SATs."

Princeton, Simon's father's school, was next. (Williams rejected him but Middlebury and Princeton said 'Come ahead.')

"I really worked hard at Princeton and the place was totally invigorating. Also, it was there that I spotted the difference, early on, between the premeds, the pre–Wall Streeters, and the prelaw students. Maybe it was just my perception, but it seemed to me that the prelaws were the brightest group—hardworking, systematic, ambitious, and usually likable."

Eristoff converses directly, always with a suppressed smile, bright eyes, and a careful ear. He is very mannerly, but his alertness and enthusiasm are never lost.

"I've always picked up on the best opportunity afforded me— the best college, the best law firm, the best mentor. The best law school I was admitted to was Columbia, but I didn't enroll until after a dazzling one-year trip abroad—first with my aunt in Nepal, then skiing in Europe.

"By the time I got back to New York for law school, I was

accustomed to playing around—a year of travel abroad will do that, you know—so Columbia was a rude awakening. But the education there was really good for my needs. As a law student, I could also take courses in other parts of the university: urban planning, architecture, and the business school, for example. It was a broad approach to the law, and I liked that. Early on, real estate looked good to me as a specialization because it was practical—a contract or tax action is somewhat esoteric, but a building can be kicked."

A wide grin . . .

"I wasn't great as a student there initially, but I kept moving up and had a decent record by the time I graduated. After my first year, I married Nancy—see? lucky again—and that made all my pursuits more serious.

"On the whole, I'm an even-keel kind of guy. My story really isn't very dramatic, I guess—the right prep schools, falling into the right college and the right law school, and then the right law firm."

In the summers during law school, Eristoff secured a paralegal job through his aunt, who worked at one of the city's leading, moderate-size law firms, interned for a judge whose wife was a partner for that firm, and returned to the firm as a full-blown summer associate after his second year at Columbia.

"In joining the firm full-time after law school, I remember saying to myself that life would be just fine. And it was.

"The big firms pump out a letter-perfect product. The client gets the job done quickly, if that's at all possible, and done well. Every base is covered—if one lawyer can't speak to an area, he'll find a specialist down the hall who can. There were tremendous resources at my firm, and I had great respect for the work.

"But the best part was the partner I spent most of my time with in the small real estate department. He was the consummate technician—I never really got to know him well, but he taught me almost every practical thing I know. He insisted on perfection, and I certainly tried to deliver it. In the process, I learned a hell of a lot, sometimes the hard way.

"When he left the firm after some internal misunderstandings, I went with him to another big Manhattan firm where the quality and seriousness were just as good. But then an irresistible opportunity came to apply my training in law to the environment. I had to grab it—and my partner mentor sincerely wished me well. We remain good friends."

Eristoff is one of two lawyers with the New York office of the Trust for Public Land, which is based in San Francisco. It is a national nonprofit conservation organization, a fifteen-year-old spin-off of the Nature Conservancy, which provides strategy and monies to add to the nation's parklands and preserved open spaces, often near urban areas. One of the projects in Simon's region, for example, is to acquire land on the New Jersey side of the Hudson River to create the Hudson Waterfront Walkway, an eighteen-mile linear park stretching from George Washington Bridge to Bayonne, providing great views of Manhattan and the Jersey waterfront.

"There is enormous variety to this public-interest assignment. We acquire the land most often from wealthy individuals or corporations, resulting in an endless variety of contracts to be drawn up, tax questions and boundary disputes to be resolved, etc. The trust is an innovative project, and requires my application of the law to be the same.

"I think the happiest people are those who are externally oriented and who are helping others. That's why many big-firm lawyers get bored, get dry, because they're doing corporate matters that become exraordinarily impersonal. Happiness comes with seeing a result, a result that benefits others. I'm thrilled to be in a place now where I can dream about—and actually touch—the forest and not get hopelessly lost in the trees.

"Well, I've said it before but I must say it again. I'm lucky. I'm lucky to be working for something larger than myself. Would that everyone in law could do that . . ."

■　■　■

"Most lawyers, it seems to me, simply can't balance their energies: the goal of success and more money chips away at them until they have succumbed to a dangerous kind of myopia."

H. JAMES THOMAS

News of law and lawyers tends to concentrate on the exceptional, right from the starting line: Only the exceptional students from the exceptional colleges have a good chance, it is said, for a good law school, and only the exceptional students from the exceptional law schools have a good chance to land the best-paying big-firm jobs, the jobs almost everyone dreamed of when considering law as vocation in the first place. So what happens to the unexceptional student who wants law and who enters the vocation with a relatively undistinguished academic background, both at college and law school?

H. James Thomas made it through George Washington University Law School by the skin of his teeth. The most prestigious law schools had turned him down, as had the Ivyish colleges four years before. To add to his set of "disadvantages," he entered law school with mononucleosis, missed the first six weeks of classes, and started cautiously with catch-up a top priority. He rarely surpassed C's, but graduated nonetheless.

"The big firms in Philadelphia didn't give me the time of day," says Thomas, a happy-faced twenty-six-year-old, slightly plump with a tailored beard. "So what was I to do? Well, there was nothing to do but kick ass for a while and hit the yellow pages to hunt for a job around Princeton, New Jersey, where I had settled on living, partly because of a new relationship that I wanted to work. I started under "Lawyers" in the A's, and didn't have to move very far, to the G's, before a one-man-shop attorney by the name of Goldman (who sounded quite respectable over the phone) said he needed a paralegal who might progress to become an associate. I grabbed the opportunity!" says this up-front young lawyer who has succeeded in passing the Pennsylvania bar, and has just taken the New Jersey bar exam.

Jim wonders if the fact that he is an adopted child somehow led to the "security of law." He thinks there is probably a link.

His adoptive parents are bright and professional. The mother, with a master's from Columbia in speech pathology, is now a recovering alcoholic (her grandfather and father were alcoholics also) but remains engaged in her specialty of oral myology. Jim reports that his fifty-five-year-old father is "type A and overweight and all that goes with it. He had us jumping for years. Most of the time, he has worked for American Can, although he is now on his own, manufacturing tops of cans called 'ends,' which he sells to beer companies. After he finished his master's in business in Arizona, we moved from Puerto Rico, and then to Connecticut, and on to Colorado. I'd have to question my stepparents on a lot of points in terms of my own development, but they certainly provided me with good schooling: a challenging start in a wealthy commuting suburb of New York City, and a fine private day school outside Denver for the high school years. My adopted sister, a star field hockey player, is still in college.

"Scoring myself, I'd have to say the record all the way along was adequate but not exciting. In secondary school I ran a little track and led Human Growth Seminars, which was sort of a teenage est. I was a nice kid. But despite a good grade-point average, my standardized test scores were quite average—so average that Stanford, Columbia, Bowdoin, and Yale told me to look elsewhere for college. I settled on Colorado College, near home, and took a junior exchange year at the University of California, Santa Barbara.

"What was my 'lure of the law'? Well, what *else* could I do with a history and humanities interest outside of teach or go to law school? The latter won out, but without serious commitment. I was doing a senior thesis in college on cable television economic law and all the regulations related thereto. It was interesting, so my political science side won out as vocational planning began. In fact, the communications field looked interesting to me from the start, and it still does."

Jim's smile and casual demeanor remain constant throughout the interview. The lack of big-firm, big-city influence is evident in this congenial fellow.

"Criminal law, once I got into law school, looked rather interesting too. During my third year I spent a lot of time as a public defender. Interested as I was in the real service of this job, it was apparent to me that this was an area of law that probably didn't pay unless I became F. Lee Bailey, and the chances of that were slim. My eyes are still on communications law, an interest furthered by clerking after my first summer of law school for a fairly sophisticated communications firm.

"For the moment, Mr. Goldman has me doing everything: a little real estate, a little trust and estates, a little corporate law, a little contract law. He bills me out at $85 an hour—he bills himself out at $150. We're in a tailored office in an upscale commercial cooperative park with old brick and manicured new lawns outside

Princeton. It's really good for the moment—I even oversee the billing. My hunch is that if I do well here, the larger firms in Philadelphia, or whatever else is within commuting distance of Princeton, will start to smile at me. The relationship with my lover has been cemented now so I want to stay right here.

"That brings up a very important topic: the attorney's personal life. I'll probably never be the big-banner successful lawyer who hits the newspapers. My goal, actually, is *not* to become that. Most lawyers, it seems to me, simply can't balance their energies: the goal of success and more money chips away at them until they have succumbed to a dangerous kind of myopia. I want to keep the liberal arts–type thinking and values *alive* in my vocation of law! Most lawyers, it appears to me, are professional—I certainly want to be professional—are concerned, and genuinely want to relieve whatever tension exists for their clients. But most are too profit-motivated and become provincial to life within the borders of the profession. Also, many older lawyers seem disenchanted to me, probably because they find themselves caught in the net of the ingredients I've just named."

A final big smile, a stroke of the beard.

"My casual choice was right. I like the law, and society obviously needs attorneys. But there is life *beyond* law, and I intend to live it."

■ ■ ■

"Lawyers have a societal obligation. People who don't understand the burden of that should look elsewhere for work."

ROBERT D. RAVEN

The nice, gentle man next door, retirement-age and a lookalike for *Mission Impossible*'s Peter Graves, is the 112th president of the American Bar Association, the American law profession's highest elective office. One California newspaper, the *Sacramento Bee,* said that sixty-five-year-old, white-haired Robert Raven, at six feet two inches in height, Hollywood handsome, an antitrust litigator and senior partner at the huge prestigious San Francisco law firm of Morrison & Foerster, "couldn't look more like an ABA president if he had been sent by central casting."

But appearances so often mislead.

The energetic, very young Robert Raven does look "establishment," a seeming natural match for the conservative, clublike ABA. But the route he took to get where he is and his suggestions for change within the national organization and the practice of law fall well outside traditional boundaries.

For starters, Raven attended a one-room school with thirty kids ("give or take a few, according to the year") and two teachers for eight years in rural Cadillac, Michigan.

"Thanks to that school and the example of my mother—a graduate of a two-year 'normal' college—I learned to enjoy reading. And soon it became a passion. Now and then Mom and Dad would get irritated because they'd send me down to the mailbox to get the mail, but I'd sit on the grass and read the new magazines, only to show up late for my farm chores or a meal. I guess that early fondness for reading was my original 'lure to the law.' Little did I realize it at the time."

The second-oldest of eight children, Raven attributes another basic instinct to the early days. "Dad (who didn't go to college) was an extremely hard worker. We kids couldn't help but be impressed by that—and on a farm, there was no other choice for us all. I don't remember Dad ever settling into an easy chair without falling asleep. It is just natural now for me to work hard, to put in long hours." During the exhausting yearlong campaign for the ABA presidency, Raven *still* billed over two thousand hours at his firm, a time commitment to lawyering expected of the most ambitious associates striving for partnership.

"We eight kids scattered to a variety of jobs—one is a nurse now, one a county agent, one a telephone lineman, one a meat company driver; we're just all over the place in what we decided to do and how we decided to live our lives. As for me: I did well in high school—where I met my wife, by the way—was president of the class and a pretty good athlete. But I milked my last cow when it was time to head off to Detroit in 1941 to build aircraft engines for eighty-five cents an hour. I enlisted in the air force soon after Pearl Harbor and was a gunner-engineer on B-24s in the Pacific.

"What happened after the war changed my course of life. The GI Bill made it possible for me to go to college. A deer-hunting friend of mine had gone to Michigan State for engineering, so I decided to enroll too, but my eye was on forestry. I always liked trees, and couldn't imagine a better life at that stage than concentrating on them.

"At this point, at twenty-three, I married my childhood sweetheart who had just come out of the war too—she was a sergeant in the marines. I really didn't know what I wanted to do—the forestry idea was superficial at best. And I wasn't really a very good student until I married. But one of my economics professors was a lawyer and he recommended that I read up on Clarence Darrow and Arthur Vandenberg. Well, that was it. I was intrigued by what I read about law and lawyers. When my wife said firmly that I should be what I *wanted* to be, I decided to try law school. Because we both liked our brief exposure to California during the war years, I decided with her encouragement to try Cal–Berkeley's Boalt School of Law."

The irony of this uncomplicated, down-home story with straight down-home delivery is that Mr. Raven is being interviewed on the thirty-fourth floor of a brand-new glass-and-gloss building in the heart of San Francisco's financial district in what seems to be a floating conference room among clouds with God's own smashing panoramic view of the bay. The only reminder that a law firm exists around us is the handwritten sign on yellow note paper taped to the refrigerator door in the antiseptic small kitchen where guests are invited to pour a cup of coffee while awaiting lawyers: "Please don't take anyone's lunch but your own—This causes dismay among some of the lawyers."

Robert D. Raven is the salt of the earth. He effortlessly and directly states what he believes without the least hint of imposing a point of view on his listener. He is calm, congenial, and takes his time. His wording would not always please William Safire, probably, but his manner would. In short, he inspires confidence. In this era of lawyer-bashing, he hardly fits the stereotype of the senior partner in a big, big firm.

The one-room-school background and the casual, thoughtful demeanor, however, are but the superficial aspects of this man's "difference" in the large-firm context. And in the American Bar Association context.

"What will be my legacy as president of the ABA? Well,

creating a structure for long-range planning, in the first place. The organization is made up of 346,000 lawyers, you see, and there is bureaucracy on top of bureaucracy. It will be as tough to turn as a battleship. But organization is not the arena that piques my interest most. It is something more important. It is the lack of access of America's poor to the services of law and lawyers."

Raven picks up the pace . . .

"Eighty percent of the legal needs of the poor of our nation, mostly minorities, are not met. If the federal and state and municipal systems won't address the problem adequately, then we in the legal profession have to. And the problem, of course, goes beyond the poor: because they're not eligible for public legal aid, many middle-class people find legal assistance utterly inaccessible. So, the theme of my presidency in the ABA is simply 'access to justice.' "

Creating something of a stir in conservative organizations is not new to Robert Raven. Although he has not been a mover (Raven joined Morrison & Foerster as its seventeenth lawyer in 1952, immediately after completing law school, and has been there ever since, helping to boost the firm's growth to nearly four hundred lawyers today), he has always been a quiet shaker, even within his own firm. When "MoFo" was charting plans for its new offices in the sky, Raven suggested (without success) *no* offices for the lawyers—they could gather in conference rooms and be out on the road with the clients, keeping files and paraphernalia in their secretaries' private offices.

Within the firm and out, Raven has been a force for enhancing social responsibility within the law. Morrison & Foerster is now known for its ambitious pro bono program and its diverse roster of lawyers; for example, thirty-five percent of the firm's attorneys are women, including fifteen percent of the partners (as compared to six percent nationwide). The firm also has an aggressive campaign for minority hiring.

Raven's efforts addressing "the social responsibility of the law" have not gone unnoticed beyond his firm in San Francisco. In 1971, the San Francisco Bar Association's "young turk" lobby, a group of law graduates of the sixties, surprisingly picked Bob Raven as their presidential candidate because everyone (including the Establishment) seemed to like and respect him, he was involved, and his thinking seemed consistent with their eagerness to convert the San Francisco Bar from a social club to a social force. He won. An ambitious bar association volunteer program for assisting the underprivileged quickly followed. Ten years later, Raven became president of the California Bar Association, and once again a well-financed campaign to support legal services for the poor was quickly put in place. About that time, President Reagan proposed to cut funding of the federal Legal Services Corporation. Raven organized a march on Washington—over 150 lawyers including the presidents of forty state bar associations—and the Legal Services network funding was saved. Now, with the new administration, he is working to see the program and its monies greatly increased.

Raven is viewed as more than a social reformer in law circles. MoFo attracts powerful corporate clients, and Raven's own client list is impressive. According to the October 1988 issue of *The American Lawyer,* ". . . Raven is an impeccable strategist with a soothing, efficient style. Over the years, Raven has built a diverse client list, from cement companies to Bay Area Rapid Transportation, the city's futuristic metro system. In a massive ongoing case that may substantially influence the future of the computer industry, Raven is representing Fujitsu in the four-year software copyright case brought against it by IBM."

"It is mentors," says Raven earnestly, "that create good lawyers. I was lucky to have a great one at this firm—a litigator named Herbert Clark. He was committed to the needy, and among other things, helped start the San Francisco Legal Aid Society as well as the strong pro bono program here. He gave me tough assignments from the start—showed confidence in me, which helped me have confidence in myself. He was always there when I needed him for good advice, and I needed that often.

"The law schools, you see, have a tough time sorting out what they can and should do—the 'why' of theory versus the 'how' of practice. Some law schools create good professional bridges—the strong clinical program at Penn is one example that comes to mind. But they really have to concentrate on the theory—so who will pick up the more practical side of training? The bar associations within the profession will have to share some responsibility, not to mention the firms. Graduates of law school hit the ground

■

running, you see, as soon as they enter practice. We must remember that forty-seven percent of the attorneys today are sole practitioners, seventy-five percent of the nation's law firms have fewer than ten lawyers, and around eleven percent of the firms have fewer than fifty lawyers. So who has the time, not to mention the know-how, to teach the new lawyers how to write a deposition once on the job?

"Although the huge firms can have their problems related to 'quality of life,' we also can afford some basic luxuries. So we have just hired a full time 'professor' to work at this firm to help the young and the old with legal writing and a host of other skills. I wanted the firm to put a classroom in our new set of offices, but that was asking a bit too much. The fact remains that one only becomes a good lawyer by *continuing* education beyond law school. Mentors are essential; if they're not available, or unwilling to share their time and practical expertise, the profession must pick up the pieces."

Robert Raven is full of suggestions for change within the traditional law firms—he questions the partner/associate division, for example, and wonders if this system might not be effectively replaced with a stock-sharing concept among new and seasoned lawyers.

But it is in discussing social reform that Raven's true vitality shows.

"You know, a lot of lawyers worry about the image of the profession. They *should* worry because the system just isn't working and the image is painfully close to the truth. Some people in Sacramento, our capital, said to me one day recently: 'The people who sent Willie here [Willie Brown, the black Speaker of the House] don't understand or use your system.' That really upset me.

"*Correcting* the system is not a 'liberal' notion. Access to justice is not a political cause. The preamble of the Constitution says 'to establish justice.' That doesn't mean *pursue* justice, it means *establish* justice. That's what we all should worry about—in our professional associations, in our firms, and in our lives."

A long glance at the clouds and the bay . . .

"Who should go to law school? Well, people who understand that because we have more rights in America, we need more good lawyers in America. And they must be people who *like* other people, who don't mind stress, who don't want or need much leisure, and who are determined to help society. We don't need more people in the law who look at their profession primarily as a business. Lawyers have a societal obligation. People who don't understand the *burden* of that should look elsewhere for work."

The words read tough. But from Robert Raven—"the consensus builder," as a fellow attorney tagged him—they sound mellow and inviting.

One would wish for this ABA president an even more visible platform.

■ ■ ■

Keeping the social conscience afloat . . .

CHANDLER CUMMINS

Did all the social activists of the early seventies who "turned professional" sell out?

Plenty did, it would seem, as one talks to the thirtyish associates in major law firms. It is now difficult to find ideological space between many of them and their role-model partners from earlier eras.

There are, of course, bold exceptions. One is Chandler Cummins, at thirty-seven a new entry to the field of law.

Chandler shuns the label "communist" now, although once he thought it appropriate. But "socialist Marxist" still fits. Determined not to compromise his worldview, he is an associate in a law firm that exclusively serves the International Brotherhood of Electrical Workers. He works "with the workers," as he'd resolved to do during Harvard undergraduate days. The route to this seemingly ideal role for him was colorful, somewhat turbulent, and speaks of the continuation of family values as much as the priorities of his strident college activist colleagues.

Back at Weston High School, in an affluent suburb of Boston, Chandler was, in his words, "a golden boy." He played the lead in *Once Upon a Mattress,* was president of his class, played good soccer, lived with a Belgian family during an exchange year abroad (he spoke mostly French), took more than the usual load of advanced placement courses, and graduated at the top of his class. Harvard was, quite naturally, the next stop.

Chandler had good luck in family beginnings. His father (MIT and Brown) was director of admissions at MIT. His mother (Wellesley) was the always-active volunteer, working with the League of Women Voters, the Unitarians, and other groups. His brothers and sister were all bright and on the path to educational and professional success. But an underlying ethic in this family was, according to Chandler, "community, involvement in community—contribution to the common good. Dad, for example, was quite involved with the NAACP."

As Chandler entered college, the big issues of the day were the draft and the accommodation of blacks in society. It was 1970, and his sister was already at Radcliffe on an activist track. Chandler joined in with high spirits.

"I had always been good at compromise, working effectively in the mainstream. High school leaders learn that type of thing fast. And here I was, all of a sudden, a radical, genuinely moved by the issues of the day and the immobility of the then-perceived Establishment to join us in righting the wrongs of society."

With a rather proud smile, Chandler says, "It didn't take long for me to be arrested, blocking access to Harvard's main administration building, University Hall.

"Actually, I felt betrayed—for the first time, *betrayed*. The freshman dean happened to recognize me in the crowd of unknowns barring entry to the building. Why did he recognize me? Because I had been one of the few who had gone in to talk to him about all of these problems of society that I thought we at Harvard needed to act on. He had never been a very good listener.

"Now, my attempts to communicate had suddenly landed me in some trouble. (Better just to demonstrate and not be 'known' to the administration? It seemed that way.) Meanwhile, our group carefully avoided destroying property or hurting anyone. We were 'admonished' by the administration for blocking entry to their building and soon afterward, we were back at it again. The end of the story, of course, is that the students' concerted efforts around the nation worked. We pulled our country out of Vietnam, a senseless national effort from the beginning.

"I switched then to giving more time to counseling projects

like the Big Brother program, and volunteered to go to Africa during my junior year to teach impoverished black kids carpentry. My political leanings were strengthened during that period—imperialist economic systems seemed so irrelevant to those peoples' needs. In returning to America to finish college, I trekked through Ethiopia and Sudan for five weeks with a buddy who ended up at the University of Wisconsin Law School. Quite frankly, by this time, I was wondering how revolution could be formatted to dramatically change the United States—I guess 'overthrow' is language too strong, but the intent was there. I had always thought that had to happen via organized governmental change. Now I was becoming convinced that an organized working class could accomplish the goal. My thoughts then could be summed up by saying that I knew 'GM was in the business of making money, not cars'—and that applied to corporate government as well."

Chandler starts wolfing down Chinese food with noisy chopsticks.

"I was lucky. Having drawn number 247 in the draft lottery, I could proceed with my education and activism without the threat of disruption for some cause I really didn't believe in. On return to Harvard, I volunteered at the Roxbury Day Camp and jumped into other community social efforts, and took too many courses, probably, that related to my political quest. School suffered a bit as I became 'experience-oriented,' including summers in factory work. Nonetheless, I ended up with a decent record at Harvard. The next steps required more real decision-making, introspection, and questioning of how deeply committed I was to 'the cause.'

"The answer was clearly 'Yes, I'm committed!' and I was off to Baltimore—there was less competition there in organizing factory workers than in other Eastern cities. It was 1975. 'What are the issues, now that the war is over?' was the big question for us activists. But the goals of social and economic justice did not need a war to buoy them.

"I married that year. My wife was also a hard-core activist from the Harvard-Radcliffe stream whose father was a lawyer. She started working in the Baltimore garment factories, helping with newsletters and worker organization. I joined the Teamsters and started driving trucks—was fired four years later for leading a demonstration. Meanwhile, the 'movement' was falling apart. I'd guess that less than one percent of the hard-core activists were still involved in getting to the workers of America for revolutionary change. Everyone was heading back to school. Between 1978 and 1985, the radical troops just evaporated from visibility."

Chandler, a mustached, trim professional in a slightly disheveled suit, had suggested we have lunch in a Chinese restaurant near his firm. He was somewhat self-conscious about the eatery's "being too loud and looking a little grand," but his story unfolds as easily as over picnic in a park.

"Was I part of a cult? Well, you might say so. The fewer we became, the more strongly we had to support each other and draw in. Those few that are still out there are cultist indeed. They have to be to survive.

"Anyway, my wife and I moved to D.C. for a better Teamsters' job. I remained working-class oriented, but that didn't blind me from better opportunity within that context. I like those people—they're honest, on the whole, and that's rare today. But I was growing depressed and burned out. The gnawing question kept returning of whether I was using my education and skills to best advantage, political goals notwithstanding.

"One day Dad came to visit and suggested I look at law schools. If he had suggested this six months earlier, I would have spit at the ground. If he had suggested business school, I probably would have hit him. But at this point law school made some sense. I trucked over to George Washington Law School in my leather jacket and boots and asked a labor law professor if I could talk with him about his field. And that was it—here I am.

"But in looking back, I have to laugh. When I entered law school, I saw most lawyers as sleazy, fork-tongued, dishonest, and building professional gain out of distortion and manipulation. Now that notion has been altered somewhat, but not fully: I do see a lot of sleaze within the profession and manipulation of working-class people. On the other hand, I know so many lawyers who are exceptionally hardworking, honest, ethical, and responsible—and not all of these are in the public service field, to be certain.

"Getting through law school was a chore. I drove oil trucks from six a.m. to four p.m., attended class two hours each evening, studied nights and all weekends. Along the way, I also pounded nails, did some work with the National Labor Relations Board, and clerked for a labor law firm, which convinced me I was on the right path. Meanwhile, my wife was working on a master's in social work. She deserves so much of the credit for our making it through that period—together.

"My politics now? Well, our biggest political involvement at the moment is the PTA. I guess we still call ourselves socialist Marxists, but we know that political philosophy never fully came to grips with the positive side of our democratic traditions, which are important, real, and a responsible vehicle for change. But change *is* still a top priority with us, particularly the economic structure of the country.

"Yes, I wouldn't mind being a partner in this firm. But still, I would make approximately half of what others are making at corporate firms. And that is okay with us. We'll continue to live in a county where there is a mix of cultures and socioeconomic classes, although the question of quality in neighborhood public schools does bother us.

"We're healthy and we're prospering. But *our* kind of prospering remains different."

He puts down his chopsticks and we leave.

I feel I have met integrity, head-on.

■　■　■

"The law is so phallic! . . . It doesn't leave much room for sensitivity, which must be why so many guys are happy in it."

ALYSON SINGER

One hears there are a lot of these young people—those who've become very disenchanted after just a few years practicing law. But most of them don't speak up, somehow fearing that their job will be jeopardized.

Not Alyson Singer. She is dissatisfied and willing to talk. She, in short, finds it ironic that a job so dull brings her so much respect.

"Granted, I've only been out in the world of law for a couple of years, but lawyers seem to me to have an inflated sense of self and are overbearing to mask an underlying insecurity. When I think of lawyers now, I think of legions of dark-suited people marching in a line, not looking to the right or to the left, but straight ahead."

She is a second-year associate at a well-regarded Los Angeles firm, headquartered in Chicago. This is Saturday, and she is lounging on a huge sofa in skin-tight cut-off sweats and high-laced yellow shoes like Granny used to wear, with massive silver chains around her neck and wrists. There are huge silver circles through her ears. If it weren't for the chains you might think she was just back from aerobics class. She speaks right up . . .

"You know, it's really odd. It's symbiotic—I mean, who feeds on whom? Even though the lawyers' name is shit among so many, there is still *such* respect accorded us. 'You're a lawyer? You *must* be smart.' And I think that very phenomenon is why a lot of women head toward the law—just to prove something to themselves. Law is so specific that people think they can come to grips with their lives by being a part of it. Or maybe it's just that women talk so much more honestly about all this.

"The law is so *phallic*! You know, 'Get in there and push!' It doesn't leave much room for sensitivity, which must be why so many guys are so happy in it. Most women I know just don't want to behave this way. And I think there are more effective ways to win cases, anyway—through mediation rather than ramrod litigation. But if you don't do it the ramrod way, you may not be praised by your superiors who are accustomed to only that. Anyway, law school taught us the ramrod way. We all sat there in deadly fear of being called on, watching a few supposed 'stars' in class around us charging forward, day after day. It was like boot camp. So how can we be expected to do it any other way now, particularly as novices with everyone watching and judging?"

Alyson worked and waited to get into law school, once her mind was made up.

She is from well-educated parentage in Freeport, New York, on Long Island. Her parents are public school guidance counselors and her one sister is a young Yale alumna currently ski-bumming and waitressing in Colorado. ("Can you believe it? Now *she* wants to go to law school, only because there's nothing else to do.")

■

Alyson had "different" tastes in high school—in clothes, etc. She thinks she probably seemed industrious and destined for success to her small group, which was outside the main cliques: "the JAPS, the druggies, and the nerds."

"Anyway, I did all right. I ended up at the bottom of the top ten percent and looked for a college in the East because I wanted to be near my then-boyfriend (who is now in jail on Riker's Island for selling cocaine). I graduated from Barnard finally. Looking back on it, that was a great period of life—an apartment with friends on Riverside Drive, roaming in and out of bookstores and shops on Broadway, and working hard at my courses, which I just adored. At first I was an anthropology major, but changed to English. I've always been able to write well, and I really like classical literature.

"Law just surfaced somehow. My Columbia boyfriend and I decided together we should go to law school. The irony of all this is that he scored incredibly high on the LSATs, and I just squeaked by. *I'm* the one who went to law school in the end—he never even applied. My reasons for wanting law were fairly sound, I think. I wanted to be some kind of professional; I wanted power and respect; and I wanted to do something for people. Law seemed to tie it all together. But even though I had a 3.6 average at Barnard, the top-line law schools passed me by. I didn't even try for Harvard or Yale, but Columbia and NYU and Georgetown all said no."

Alyson throws herself at all angles on the big couch. She even does neck stretches. But she keeps talking.

"My boyfriend and I packed off for California. We were fed up with New York. And I got by waitressing, cooking on yachts, and anything else I could do. But after more than a year of that, I remember lying on the deck of a boat on Antigua one day and saying, 'Well, this is great, but something *else* will have to bring ultimate satisfaction.'

"Law school applications went out again, this time to the West Coast. And this time I got in—well, to Loyola, which everybody thought was really the pits. But I went full-time for three years and here I am, a lawyer. Even though I wondered at times, I just kept plugging—there was no way that I was going to bail out before finishing.

"Law school was tough. You're dropped into this big lake and you must sink or swim, all by yourself. And the writing is hardly what I had been accustomed to. In law school, you just have to spit out the facts—no window dressing. But I did okay—dean's list now and then, top third of my class, and I wrote for the *Entertainment Law Journal*. But the big firms seemed to skip Loyola in their recruiting. I had grown close to a professor, and he helped me get the job at my current firm, which, as firms go, is really a good one."

Alyson's law school summers were spent interning with a judge, a tough stint working on forty cases a day in the Superior Court of Los Angeles (and waitressing at night), working with a small firm in Santa Monica, then spending the final summer with her current firm, which then had sixteen lawyers, and now has twenty-five with hundreds more scattered through the nation and in the Chicago main office.

"To my amazement, the firm liked my summer work. All I had done, really, was rifle through stacks of papers in the library, not knowing exactly what I was doing. But I guess my product, when all was said and done, was satisfactory. Although I had thought of joining the public defender's office, my thirty thousand dollars in law school debts loomed heavily in front of me, so the private firm seemed right for the time. The firms seem nearly interchangeable to me, so I was willing to stay where I was. It did occur to me that I would probably be there for only a few years, and then veer off to government or public-interest law if I thought I could afford it."

A big stretch and a yawn . . .

"Now, after two years, I'm making $67,000. But doing what? That's the problem, regardless of salary. Anyway, I have some satisfaction just knowing I've *done it* for a while—big city, big national law firm. It has given me greater self-confidence, no doubt about that.

"What are the pluses and minuses of practicing law in the private sector? Well, all my fears and doubts have been substantiated. Don't get me wrong: Mine is a good firm, so I'm not complaining about the specifics of where I am—my concern is really more generic. There is just so little meaning in what I do almost all day long! The bottom line is in the ledger book, pure and simple. That's okay, I guess—it's a private company. But we in the trenches just never see the end product. In corporate law, the impersonalization of the task is severe. The end result of the case is so far down the line from where I'm sitting. It's *really* frustrating. Well, that's a nutshell summary of what I don't like. What I do like is the money."

Alyson stands, rearranges her denim jacket over her sweats, and continues.

"They don't know it yet, but I'm leaving. I don't know what I'm leaving *for* or *to,* but I'm leaving. I've picked up skills—I know how to approach a problem now, organize it, write it up (writing remains my forte)—and I've learned how to present a case differently, according to the party I'm addressing.

"Where am I going? I don't know. A friend is setting up a law institute in Nicaragua and wants help. That sounds interesting, and I've always wanted to learn to speak Spanish. I may go to journalism school. I've put my résumé out to headhunters, but they keep coming up with firms that look just like mine. And maybe I'll look into the public defender's office—the pay is not great, but L.A.'s salary level is the highest in the nation for this kind of work. I don't know—and remember, I have the big debt.

"Anyway, I can't look many more insurance settlement papers in the face. I'm in a hermetically sealed glass box and I have to break out. Actually, the people at this firm have been good to me, but they're just not my kind of people—their focus is too narrow, their subject too dry. And I'm not living.

"Gender hasn't really been a factor, by the way. I think it *would* be if I stuck it out to try to make partner, but that's not going to happen. Oh, yes, one judge asked if I was the court reporter, and another one had two of us lawyers in front of him and announced, 'We'll just wait a few minutes until the other lawyer makes it in.' I said, 'Sir, I *am* the other lawyer.' He was appropriately embarrassed and said all the right things, but that sort of incident seems to pop up more than it should."

Alyson is flip at times, but it's all surface. She is just struggling to find a place. She is obviously bright, articulate, and ready to commit to something.

"I'd just love to be a part of cause and effect. Can I get that in law? If so, all the respect I'm accorded for my profession will be deserved."

■ ■ ■

"Bright and devious versus bright and principled."

CHRISTOPHER LANE

"In my experience, lawyers seem to fall into one of two categories—boring or intensely exciting and theatrical. The latter, of course, are usually the litigators, but not always.

"I grew up thinking that all lawyers were stand-up-and-argue types. Now that I am one, I know how far from the truth that is—how few of us have the opportunity to argue in front of a judge. And even when it happens, some of the romance is gone for the lawyer because of the scary little black box—the jury. You study your ass off, gather the statistics and other supporting data for the case, rehearse and rehearse, and then perform, and suddenly—zap, it's all over. The jury retires and your whole preparation is down the drain with the verdict in their mysterious hands.

"Well, that's the more interesting group of attorneys—the ones who litigate. They're able not only to think, but also talk, and they seem to get out into the world and stretch their imaginations a little more than the rest."

A long pause and a look around the room at the young, professional crowd holding drinks and talking quietly.

"But most lawyers fall into my category of boring. Really boring. Too many of them talk mostly about themselves—what could be more boring? If they do reach out beyond themselves in conversation, they switch to talking about law. Oh, joy . . . That's why most of my friends are not lawyers, but old college buddies who have gone in a wild variety of directions professionally. Unlike lawyers, they don't spend all their time at parties just sizing each other up."

Christopher Lane, a prematurely salt-and-peppered thirty-six-year-old, could probably consider modeling if all else failed. As we walked into this hotel lounge, more than a few women's eyes appeared to be nowhere else.

And lo, he *is* from Beverly Hills, but now works and lives in

■

Manhattan. Christopher's father, who did not finish grade school, became chairman of one of the most profitable department store chains on the West Coast. His mother did not get far with her education either, and now oversees the family manse near Los Angeles.

Christopher is an only child. He is extremely serious, speaks slowly—almost grinding to a complete halt at times—and is not exactly the happy optimist. But he is the realist.

"To be a good lawyer, at least in my area of specialization—litigation—you have to be articulate, and it probably even helps to be glib. One must persuade and be able to shuffle a lot.

"The best lawyers are incredibly bright. I don't see how you could make it otherwise. And the best lawyers also are not driven by the dollar. But far too many are. That's why you find so many fine attorneys in government and public service—they're not individuals who are in this to become wealthy. In my view, the lawyers in private practice are, on the whole, bright and devious. The lawyers in the public sector are, on the whole, bright and principled."

But Lane feels that he was more or less kept from private practice and "assigned" to government work—he's a litigator for the City of New York, making fifty thousand dollars—by not ranking higher in his law school class. He'd like to have the option of considering the private sector of law, but his résumé and law school record, he feels, disallow it. The headhunters just won't talk to him.

Christopher thinks he has always had the makings of a lawyer, although he wasn't aware of it until rather late. At his well-regarded day school in Hollywood Hills, he was, by his definition, Joe College.

"I was preppy as hell, president of the senior class, always middle of the road politically, and did well academically—actually, I *thought* more than I performed in the classroom (and I'm not certain you could say that for a good many who ranked above me). The Northeast was always full of mystique—I really liked that *Catcher in the Rye* stuff—so I headed off to one of the Little Four in New England for college where, once again, I was quite academic without being much of a student. I avoided the Greek

■

crowd and hung out with the 'Union Building group'—better students, a little offbeat."

Lane eyes the chatty after-work crowd carefully. But he does not wear a happy face.

"I liked liberal arts. But I didn't really know what I'd do next, following college. I headed to New York and became a sales rep for a paperback book company. Soon after, I no longer idealized those who are successful in business as I once had. And I quickly learned one has the challenge in most any endeavor of life to *generate* excitement.

"I decided to try law school—you know, the continuation of liberal arts. And it really did seem right—I had always done research well. If my best grades were on research papers, wouldn't I be good at legal writing? Also, I'm thoughtful—ponderous, perhaps—and I love to argue. And I've always been intrigued by broad social issues. It did seem to add up to law, and I remembered that my old prep school college adviser told me that he thought I'd end up in law someday, that I seemed a 'natural.'

"But deciding to go was easier than getting in. I wanted to stay in New York—the better places shot me down, but I got into New York Law and enrolled as a full-time student. It was a fairly depressing place—grubby study carrels and other signs of midcity tawdry—and I was scared at entry, having been out of school for a while. I was really risking a lot on this move!

"Actually, it turned out that I was pretty good at the Socratic method; my papers were good too, but my exams were awful. I ended up middle of the class and doomed to not being considered by the big firms in Manhattan, which every student at every law school—particularly those in New York—seemed to want. If the truth be known, I felt a little left out at law school when everyone in the top tenth of the class started heading out for firm interviews.

"My job now with the city is okay—I dig into interesting stuff, and I'm in front of the judge enough to make it romantic and somewhat colorful. But this is an extraordinary bureaucracy, so complicated that I usually only see the very small group of people in my little specialty division. We get on each other's nerves a lot. And there is considerable sameness in what we do from day to day. I don't know—I don't seem to spend much time 'fighting for right' anymore—or is it that I just don't *sense* it? Now that's scary."

Lane is now studying the parquet floor.

"What I'm doing, of course, affects self-esteem and quality of life. My law job isn't one bit sexy or esoteric—no one wants to talk about my area of the law at cocktail parties! Not that that is a great criterion for satisfaction, but it does say something.

"It's funny, you know. You grow up idealizing something like law. And then you get into it and catch on to it fairly quickly, perhaps too quickly. It takes *character*, then, to *make* something of it. And that's exactly where I am at the moment, at something of a crossroads.

"I spend too much time, perhaps, studying role models. At my age I should probably *be* a role model to a few others. But I don't have the nerve or the self-confidence. Trotsky was always a second, always next to Stalin. Maybe there are those of us who were cut out to be only lieutenants. I probably look too often for approval."

A very long pause.

"I know now that there is a difference between being very bright and very effective. I'm very bright. Can I muster the character to become very effective?"

A reluctant smile . . .

∎ ∎ ∎

Goodness above Park Avenue.

STEVE HUDSPETH

If the popular stereotype of the Manhattan big-law-firm partner were completely accurate, you'd have to conclude that Steve Hudspeth was in the wrong place at the wrong time, and perhaps in the wrong trade. But in fact he's very happy where he is, successful where he is, and finds considerable meaning in what he does.

Granted, he shares some of the traits of the big-city law partner: he commutes back and forth from the Connecticut suburbs to a midtown skyscraper, he makes big money, and he works demanding hours—2,000 to 2,200 billable hours per year, which translates typically into a twelve-hour day.

■

But the "typical" ends about there. Hudspeth is a gentle man—it shows in the way he speaks, his rather ministerial manner, his somber-but-not-tweedy look, and the way in which he can bring most any topic around to what is "good for people." His view of the law is from a spiritual point of view—a little unusual for one engaged in antitrust disputes, surely. And he is a Pentecostal Christian.

"Yes, I have a fundamental faith in Christianity and a willingness to use this as a central part of my life, including in my work. This makes me a stronger lawyer. In law, one sees people constantly in extremes—people in agony, people who can't sleep, people who must resolve some kind of very large problem for life to proceed comfortably. It is *trying* to deal with these people and to deal with many of their situations. My faith keeps me on track. I resist the temptation to be angry—anger is very destructive in what we're trying to do, and too many lawyers let anger get the best of them. A calm, reasoned approach is the only approach to keep people from being walked over. And you know, my faith has deepened as I've become a more experienced lawyer. Because there are few definite answers in law, it engages one to be philosophical—or spiritual, you might say. I find the law and the spirit walk hand in hand. Each complements the other if correctly served."

Some Sunday mornings Steve Hudspeth teaches Sunday school to fourth-through-sixth-graders at his Episcopal church in a building shared with the local Presbyterians ("an unusual arrangement, eh?"). He gives dozens of volunteer hours to the Episcopal Diocese of New York and also to the Presbytery of New York to help with stewardship campaigns and senior citizen housing programs. Another pro bono endeavor involves representing a convicted murderer from Indiana. The fellow was working as an administrator in a shelter for the homeless in New York. "He had turned it around, in fact, to become a successful and responsible organization," says Hudspeth, "when a Fox Network *Most Wanted* television segment caused him to be recognized as an escaped convict." Hudspeth is rather certain the fellow was framed in the first place. "I want to help him—he deserves it."

Hudspeth is ready to talk about lawyers in general. Everything is said softly.

"I regret the popular view of lawyers—it seems to be a mix

of some respect with a lot of distrust and confusion added in. But actually, lawyers have probably always had a rather questionable reputation. We are, after all, in business to constrain! And we're obviously an important and necessary part of society. Our role differs from culture to culture, but we are certainly central to the operation of Western society. I guess it's natural that we should be both feared and respected—part of that is because our power is rather elusive, sometimes even mystical.

"Lawyers are aggressive—no doubt about that. We have to be to do our job well. But we're also cautious and careful. And if we're any good, we're compulsive regarding detail. Every step that *might* be taken in resolving a problem *should* be taken by a lawyer. Thoroughness is our mandate and our strength if we're well trained. We can spend hours over a final draft, carefully reviewing it three or four times for missed detail—if that time is not spent, the client is not well served and we're compromising the trust placed in us."

Hudspeth's father was trained as a lawyer, but spent most of his time in business. His mother came from England to Omaha and attended two years of college. Young Steve was sent to an Episcopal day school in the Philadelphia area.

"From early on I was studious, quiet, and liked to sing and debate. Also, in high school I was the valedictorian speaker at commencement. Yale was next [class of '68], and my life in New Haven was about the same: I was in the Yale Glee Club, on the Yale Debate Team, and in ROTC. I was a pretty good student in college—in fact, picked up my master's with my B.A. in four years. My major was economics and for a while I was interested in pursuing the Ph.D. in the field. But law won out.

"I envy the kids today who can *try* law after college in a firm or some other agency as a paralegal for a year or two. That opportunity didn't exist when I was that age. I can't imagine a young person now not benefiting by the experience if there is some question as to whether law is the right field to enter.

"Anyway, I didn't have any role models to look at regarding law except my father, who wasn't really practicing law. But it seemed to me that law school and the profession itself were fairly open to personal development. I had studied a lot of economics and business and was convinced that there was less real structure and hierarchy in the big law firm than in the big corporation. At the same time, it seemed to me that there were strong egos in the law firm and that the place could only work if collegiality overcame individual assertiveness. Now I *know* that's true.

"In a way, I was lucky because just as I came along to study law—I decided to stay at Yale—there was a real effort to apply principles of economics to the law. That movement has grown—it used to be that lawyers distrusted economists and vice versa, but not so much anymore. Today, there are certain economic principles *guiding* factors of the law. That relationship always has, and always will, intrigue me."

Hudspeth is an easy interview, with a good knack of translating fairly difficult law concepts into something understandable for the layman.

"I had some great professors at Yale Law School, one of whom I'm working for here—Gordon Spivack, an antitrust lawyer who came to teach at Yale following a very visible and successful stint in Washington with the Kennedy and Johnson administrations.

"How do I spend my time in this firm's antitrust division? Well, let's take two typical cases. First, a criminal case regarding military procurement in which we're defending a corporation whom the Department of the Army claims rigged bids to defraud the government. Criminal cases tend to move rather quickly, so this case should be over in a year or less. A second typical case would be a civil action suit which will probably move slowly and take two to three years. In this case, we're defending a client who was engaged in a form of special transportation. The claim is that three competitors conspired to monopolize a business by alleged price-fixing.

"I might be involved in twenty-five to thirty cases per year, including about twenty-five percent of my time spent in just counseling—merger counseling, joint venture counseling, etc. Questions like 'What is the risk of an antitrust challenge?' come up in general counseling. Eventually, approximately ten cases per year end up in actual litigation. The advantage of the big firm, of course, is that specialty lawyers from all areas of the practice can cooperate on the same case. From three to thirty lawyers here might be handling one case at a time. To the client, that means a cost of

$110 per hour to just under $400 per hour per lawyer, according to which attorneys are involved."

Hudspeth looks out his huge window, up Park Avenue.

"I have a lunch engagement shortly, so we probably should wrap this up. Let me meander through a few last thoughts. . . .

"There are two important elements in practicing law that I cherish: independence and helping other people. We lawyers have enormous freedom—from scheduling to deciding which approach to take on a case, to what types of case we want and think we can best handle, to how much time we spend on the job or with the family. There are constraints—the courts provide a lot of constraints, for example—but nonetheless, there is considerable autonomy in this work. And there is enormous satisfaction in seeing a problem resolved which puts people at ease—be it a financial threat, a criminal accusation, any number of things that can lead from minor inconvenience to major catastrophe for not just one, but hundreds of individuals. Usually, I really believe in my clients and want to help them. I'm convinced I'm performing a real service.

"The only major problem is the time I spend away from the family. My wife, who teaches at a magnet school for kids needing special education, legitimately complains about the time I spend in the law. But there are those treasured Sundays, and sometimes Saturdays, when we're all together. I *love* my tractor lawnmower, for example, but even more, taking the kids on the weekly arcade or bowling excusion. And we're really involved with the church. In all, life is good, really good, so long as we think and care about others—and I can make a habit of that in the law."

There is a warm smile, a strong handshake, and a walk down the all-gray-flannel hallway where I can hear lawyers raising voices that suddenly sound oddly out of place.

■ ■ ■

"Law: the pleasure, the opportunity, the selfishness, and narrowness of it all . . ."

FREDERICK A. O. SCHWARZ, JR.

The man squirms and tips in his chair almost dangerously, throwing a leg over one side and then the other, shifting from side to side, then pitching his body back toward the wall, and the chair with it, while miraculously staying upright. It is not nervousness or just being fidgety. It is sheer energy at fifty-three mixed with a heavy dose of boyishness, imagination, and real joy in telling a full story, grabbing for articulate phrases to match positive thoughts.

He has a famous name, an advantaged background, has had at least a short stay in all the right places (and a few surprising ones), and has a boundless, contagious enthusiasm for the law and strong opinions about it: why it is perhaps the most important of professions, whom it can serve, and how it can lead to a colorful, meaningful, and varied life if only the individual lawyer will let it happen.

He is F. A. O. Schwarz, Jr., called "Fritz" even by his secretary when inviting an interviewer in from the formal lobby of this large Wall Street firm. He is the great-grandson of the toy giant, educated at Harvard College and Harvard Law, and is now a senior partner of Cravath, Swaine & Moore—perhaps New York City's most prestigious law firm. Along the way he has "stepped out" from his career to undertake a host of tough and varied legal and public service assignments: as assistant commissioner for law revision in Northern Nigeria (1961–62); as chief counsel to the U.S. Senate's "Church committee" to investigate the CIA (1975–76); and, most visibly, as corporation counsel of the City of New York—the city's top legal job, running the second-largest law office in the country (second only to the federal Department of Justice) under Mayor Ed Koch (1982–87). Most recently, when the Supreme Court declared New York City's government illegal, Schwarz seemed the natural choice to head the controversial NYC charter revision commission.

There have been tributes along the way. It is rare that *The New York Times* spends editorial space praising a public official, but they were moved to do so in January 1987, when Fritz Schwarz left the Mayor's office:

GOOD COUNSEL FOR NEW YORK CITY
. . . Mr. Schwarz now returns to private practice, having earned the gratitude of New Yorkers for five years of distinguished service as the city's chief lawyer. . . . He met the challenges of his office

from potholes to human rights. He worked for fair ways to ease the city's liability for citizen injuries and sought more consistent tax policy toward charitable organizations. He defended hiring programs for minorities and victims of bias against homosexuals, sometimes winning in the Legislature what he couldn't win in court. At a time of widespread panic over acquired immune deficiency syndrome he helped design and courageously defended in court a sound, humanitarian policy of including AIDS victims in city classrooms. . . . Fritz Schwarz has raised aspirations and performance in city government and made City Hall cleaner and livelier. It's a contribution to be prized, for its content and example.

Fritz Schwarz finds it easy to talk. He strokes his tousled, short gray hair now and then as he shifts from outrageous posture to outrageous posture in the formal side chair. And he gazes into the long, sweeping view of Manhattan (from his office on the fifty-seventh floor, with a view of both rivers converging on the southern tip of the city) before coming up with a new phrase, always well honed, always positive.

"What are the first few words that come to mind when I'm asked to comment on practicing lawyers? Easy. First, the pleasure of it all; second, the opportunity of it all; third, the selfishness and narrowness and lack of imagination that too many attorneys employ to prevent realizing all the diversity and excitement that actually exists for them in law.

" 'Pleasure' is easy to start with. It is a joy to be in this profession—I love it, and can't imagine doing anything else.

"The word 'opportunity' just has to be developed a bit. Too many lawyers complain about the sameness of their activity, day to day, month to month. I don't see it—there is sameness only if one allows the sameness to settle in. One can be enormously creative in law with what to do and how to do it! Too many associates come into the big firms and feel—or are led to feel—that they are only here to learn a trade. They stop growing spiritually and intellectually, and that's tragic. They get caught up in some kind of humdrum, borne down by pressure, and feel the profession is dull as a consequence. Our best associates simply don't allow that to happen to themselves."

Schwarz throws his body in a different direction.

"Forgive my using a self-example, but it's apt. Before I first came to this very good—and granted, rather conservative—firm, I had developed a real interest in problems resulting from apartheid in South Africa. After the Sharpeville incident, there was a general financial crisis in South Africa, and banks became the target of protest due to some of their policies and social positions. One of the targets happened to be a bank which is a major client of this law firm. I led a little local protest of the bank here in New York as a symbol of my feeling regarding what was going on in South Africa. To the credit of Cravath, no partner ever mentioned or criticized my involvement in that cause, which was, of course, potentially embarrassing to the firm.

"Granted, there seems to be more pressure on the new associates today and they're expected to put in enormous billable hours. But they could, nonetheless, establish priorities and time early on to vary their lives, creating less chance for boredom and burnout. And we in the big firms should encourage it more! We say that more than we do it, but we always seem to notice the associate who is a good lawyer *and* is creating an interesting, lively, varied professional life."

This man causes one to forget all stereotyping of high-level lawyers. He is spirited, does not seem to be on guard, speaks up and speaks out, and has a delightful, disarming manner.

"You know, I get three big kicks from the law: first, the emotional high of arguing a case, *if* I argue it well; second, the stimulation of helping people who are 'in trouble' resolve problems, whether it is Tom Watson and Dr. Lande or Mayor Koch—in other words, private or public involvement—the level of stimulation is the same; and third, helping society improve, which usually comes in practicing law in the public sector.

"I mentioned earlier that selfishness and narrowness get in the way of lawyers' branching out. I really mean that. The selfishness too often relates to making more money—there is plenty of that in our field—and narrowness often results. Too many lawyers, for example, don't bother with outside reading—no wonder we're myopic and often considered dull! In my view, beyond just reading about what the rest of the world is doing, we should *all* manage to do something quite different. We should arrange along the way to work in both the private and the public sectors. Some will move to public-interest or government work first and then join the private firm; others will take a break from private practice and work in government or the public sector. Unfortunately, too many lawyers say they will move from the private to the public sector in time, but don't really grow serious about it until some real disenchantment with their normal life sets in—and then it may be too late. It is tough to switch to government or public-interest law after fifty—some skills, like dealing with the press, just haven't been developed along the way, not to mention the knee-jerk reaction to doing so many things so quickly."

He quickens the pace, with continuing animation.

"I've been lucky in terms of timing. Just when I had been working on a huge, well-publicized monopoly case here long enough—seven years—the Church committee assignment in Washington was offered. It was almost as easy—although it's never easy when you have clients that mean a lot to you and depend on you— to break from my private practice when the New York City corporation counsel offer was made. And these changes in context and assignment challenge us to develop new skills, new responses, and develop new views. My job with the City of New York was particularly rewarding in that regard. I was only going to stay for four years, by the way, but then the corruption scandals broke and also I wanted to argue a case in the Supreme Court, so I stayed another year. It was a lively and wonderful assignment."

Schwarz consents to share a few recollections on how he was lured to the law.

"Well, it was a natural draw, I guess. My father was a lawyer, and one of the best—he was with Davis, Polk, here in the city. He was a great role model—he had even clerked for Oliver Wendell Holmes. And it's funny, I know, to mention this, but I found a photograph of me at three years old in the attic: someone had labeled it 'Judge Schwarz.' There must have been some early indications there . . .

"At high school—Milton Academy outside Boston—I did a little bit of everything: was head monitor (president of the class), played end in football (but they asked me to call the plays), played some basketball and baseball too, was fairly popular, and ranked in about the top fifteen percent of the class. At Harvard I did better academically—ended up in the top six percent—and stroked varsity crew. In college I became more conscious of social issues, and that expanded at law school. I went on to Harvard Law largely because my father had gone there. At the time, there was great social unrest in the South, of course—as blacks protested Woolworth's in Greensboro, North Carolina, for example, I remember organizing a protest at Woolworth's in Cambridge to show support for the cause. Law school, by the way, was okay, but if I headed the place now, I'd sure try to make the third year more of an intellectual challenge rather than just more of the same. Harvard Law was a great place—I'd check out the schism within the faculty there today, though, before signing up."

The phone rings, and it is obviously his wife (who is Mayor Koch's coordinator of youth services and as such, the liaison between the mayor's office and the Board of Education). Schwarz says, "Did you get hold of what's-his-name?" A long silence. And then there is an apology to the interviewer, as Schwarz hangs up, that he will have to cut this off soon, as he has to introduce Senator Moynihan shortly at a dinner.

While Fritz Schwarz is on the telephone, I can't resist reading his résumé again, hoping to catch a comment on each of his major interests. But the list was impossibly lengthy. He is *currently* director or trustee of: the Fund for the City of New York, the Vera Institute for Justice (a program dealing with criminal justice and the special needs of the disadvantaged), the NAACP Legal Defense Fund, the Natural Resources Defense Council, the City Bar Committees on the Bicentennial of the Constitution, the New York / New Jersey AIDS Commission, and other organizations; he was *formerly* director or trustee of Harvard University, the Manhattan Bowery Association, the Experiment in International Living, the New York City Criminal Justice Agency, and many more.

"How do I balance the formal lawyering with the pro bono work and other outside responsibilities? Well, I probably give at least fifteen percent of my time to pro bono involvements, sometimes more. But if the big case of a client calls, I'm there. Usually, with good planning, it all works out. Both 'careers' balance each other."

The sun is beginning to set over Manhattan, never more impressively than from this view-of-views which Schwarz honors by having next to no furniture in his office. One large Nigerian hammered tin piece controls the wall across from the view.

"Oh, *that*. Yes, it's from Nigeria. But I can't tell you much more. I don't know if I should be embarrassed or proud to tell you that I retrieved it from the trash barrel downstairs. I have no idea who was pitching it out, but I'm very pleased to have it."

A huge smile with a tinge of the guilty look . . .

The secretary comes bustling in to tell "Fritz" that time is slipping and he does have the Senator Moynihan commitment . . .

He shakes my hand and wishes me well. (And calls the next day to make certain that I haven't misunderstood professional, law-firm commitments versus pro bono commitments. "They're equally important and they both fit in . . .")

FIVE

■

STEPPING OUT:

A View of Lawyers by Nonpracticing Lawyers

■ ■ ■

There are those who have left the law—some smiling and content, some full of anger or frustration.

Why did they leave? Was it more difficult to leave than it had been to enter? Does law serve them well in alternative careers? Is there a moral to their stories?

Those who "step out" often allude to the euphoria of escape. And in looking back they find it easy to articulate the elements of lawyering that provoked their need to get away: the materialism that compromises loyalty to the client or to the firm or to the profession; the rigidity that restrains the mind, the manner, and the person; the arrogance that too often develops; the "arcane pursuit" of technicality; the predisposition to follow rather than to lead; and the sacrifice for work of one's time for family and other loves.

In chorus, those who have left the practice of law proclaim their *use* of the law in their lives today, but also seem to speak as one in echoing this refrain: "Lawyers are pretty sharp and pretty dull."

■

■ ■ ■

"It's tragic . . . but the majority just drudge on."

STEVE YANDLE

The associate dean of the Yale Law School, tilting backward toward the heavily leaded windows in his office inside this Collegiate Gothic full-city-block enclave of dark classrooms, moot courts, and old tile, tactfully refuses to play the interviewer's game of "What are the first words that come to mind when I say 'lawyer'?"

He leans forward a bit and flashes his always ready, huge smile.

"Well, first, let's limit the question to practicing lawyers. Then let's forget adjectives, the simple way out. And let's say, lawyers are a competent group of professionals who fall far short of reaching their potential in terms of contributing to economic growth and/or creating greater social justice in our country. They have a good record, but it could be far better."

He stops. And seems satisfied. Next question, quick response.

"Well, I guess everything I'm going to say will fall under the umbrella of lawyers not reaching their potential. Let's take, for example, attorneys to small businesses. Almost all of them make certain the owner gets his or her taxes filed and is up-to-date on the new tax laws. The lawyer will inevitably check the contracts and a few other essentials. Too often, you see, attorneys just follow a checklist. The service could be so much broader and more creative, not to mention more helpful! The lawyer *could* look at the entire project, for starters, as simply a prospectively interesting business. The first question asked the client should be, then, 'How can I help you prosper?' All the checklist elements would be covered, but a much more comprehensive and inventive process would ensue, and both parties would gain and be more satisfied with the relationship."

Big smile again. And a tilt backward.

Steve Yandle has a law degree from the University of Virginia (a B.A. in economics from there as well) and has been admitted to the bar of Virginia. But he just doesn't want to be a lawyer.

"I have no aversion to it. I just have never had a burning desire to practice law. Quite frankly, I think my current job is more interesting."

Yandle is a company man.

"If there is any group of lawyers who could change the world, they'd probably come from here. Yale is different in training for the law, and that's why none of my work is drudgery."

A pause and a glance at the cemetery across the street.

"But different as we are, and try as we do to make this training intellectually stimulating and help students grasp a genuine sense of public responsibility, we seem to fall short in converting them fully.

"All of our students, you see, have competed heavily and have *won* academically. So they constantly seem to say to themselves, 'Give me a new goal and I'll reach it.' And they do. They're obsessed with winning and think they can figure out how to do it. Unfortunately, the goal of their national peer group today comes with huge dollar signs attached. 'Who can make the most?' seems to be the key question. Even in the late sixties, of course, there was a lot of interest in joining the big firm in the big city. But now that seems to have become almost exclusively the goal, and there is genuine competition among these kids to beat each other and the rest of the world in starting salaries. We've not succeeded in changing that much, regrettably.

"God knows we've tried. We've beefed up the loan assistance program, knowing the average kid who received some financial aid here—two-thirds of the student body—leaves with a debt of $35,000 to $40,000. We've worked out a number of creative ways to postpone or relieve that debt so making big money immediately *can* become a secondary goal. Also to increase interest in public responsibility, we have really beefed up the forums, the clinical experiences, and the relevant lectures and workshops. Also, we think the more student-generated activity in the public sector that we can help initiate, the more that kind of work will be taken seriously.

"But at the end of the line, the great majority run off to the private sector—even those who initially take clerkships for a couple of years. What worries me is that so many of these students are setting themselves up for failure. They head to big firms in the big cities saying 'I don't really want to do this, but I will temporarily, just to see what it is like and to prove to myself and everybody else that I can catch the big reward following all that hard work and achievement of college and law school. I know I'm really above this sort of rat race, but . . .' Then the competition inside the firm gets to them and they're on a treadmill they don't like— trying to compile impressive billable hours, trying to beat out the competition to make partner, still trying to prove to themselves once again that they're the best. It's just tragic. A few wise ones drop out after about three years, but the majority just drudge on."

Now and then, clerks tap on Yandle's door and enter or leave with huge stacks of paper. He says he does a little bit of everything here, and always has in his law school jobs. After getting his own J.D. at Virginia ("I grew up in the tiny town of Petersburg, Virginia, and finally chose U Va for college and law school because to a straightlaced small-town kid, it suggested being worldly and a little naughty"), he worked in admissions and placement and became dean of students at Northwestern University School of Law. He came to Yale in 1985 and, although his responsibilities relate most often to budgetary matters (including the tricky business of overseeing apportionment to student organizations and activities), Yandle "dabbles" and enjoys it all.

"Yale has, for years, been identified with something called 'legal realism.' I guess you might say it is a relatively modern approach to studying the law. It responds pragmatically to great principles in the sky. It brings social science and the law together. It suggests what law *can* be, that it can be bigger than what is conventionally imagined. Law schools, you see, are more alike than they are different. But what this law school wants to avoid at all cost is the reputation of being a 'black-letter' law establishment, a school that primarily prepares students for the law boards.

"When our students finish they won't be dramatically different from all the rest that graduate from other schools. But my hunch is that, after Yale training, they'll be a *little* different and it will show up at their firms in subtle but important ways. They will not dare belong to all-male clubs; they will approve wholeheartedly of their bar associations getting involved with homelessness; they'll take risks; and although they might be sucked into becoming Republicans, they'll be on the liberal fringe of that party.

"Yeah, I make about half of what I'd probably make as a partner in a reasonably respectable firm. But law is key to our society. And Yale is key to changing the way law is perceived and practiced in our society. That beats money every time."

The big smile.

■ ■ ■

The law, the piano, the stock market, and Mr. Nixon.

DAVID BOTTOMS

"You know, if it hadn't been for that agonizing divorce in 1980, I'd probably still be a law partner commuting by train from Darien to Wall Street every day. What good things come, surprisingly, from the trials of life . . . Here I am in euphoria—an altered career, doing what I have dreamed of doing for years in money management, close to owning my own company. Granted, there is risk, but sudden vitality! Too many lawyers get caught on a treadmill and can't muster the courage to jump off. Life is too short to get stuck anywhere."

David Bottoms arrived twenty minutes late for an 8:30 a.m. interview at his office in midtown Manhattan, eleven stories up from one of those showpiece Art Deco skyscraper lobbies. He apologized for being late, but his heart didn't seem to be in it.

"I hate to keep anyone waiting for anything," says this soft-spoken man with graying hair, French cuffs, and monogrammed shirt. "But my commute these days—just downtown from the Upper West Side—is so great that I hate to see it end. I'm using my car in Manhattan now. That allows me about forty minutes a day to listen to the Mendelssohn and Schubert tapes of the pieces I'm rehearsing on piano. Anyway, sorry to be tardy."

Bottoms—trite as it may sound—is one of those Renaissance types: successful lawyer; successful financier; successful politician in minor excursions (enough to convince him not to pursue greater heights); concert-level pianist; outstanding high school and college athlete; nice, balanced, and respected person. He left Manhattan's oldest law firm, where he had been for nineteen years—a partner for fourteen—to concentrate on money management. He still practices law a portion of his time (most of his trust and estate clients stayed with him when he departed the law firm), but the world of finance has captured his enthusiasm and "about eighty percent of my time." He seems comfortable in his classy-but-warm new office with green marble window ledges, family art, antique clock, cardboard boxes of law files stuffed neatly under a conference table, original World War I posters in the hallway (AND THEY THOUGHT WE COULDN'T FIGHT!), and desk monitor flashing current market prices as he attempts to concentrate on telling his life-and-values story, reflecting particularly on the law.

"How was I lured to the law? Well, I just drifted toward it because everyone said I should. I don't mean to sound self-serving, but I ran nearly everything in high school and college, so people said I was bound to be a governor or senator someday. The way to get ready for that, I was told, was law school.

"Although my father was associate professor of agricultural education at Auburn University in Alabama, I was really part of a farmer's family and had an extremely sheltered childhood. At public high school, I probably looked ambitious in the political arena—was president of my class nearly every year—athletic and musical. The only trauma I can remember from those days was related to my interest in piano. If boys didn't concentrate on football in Alabama, you see, they were sissies. At least I had the baseball and basketball ability to counter my 'musician' image, but there was wrenching pressure for a boy to hide any artistic dimension."

It is past nine a.m. now, so Bottoms keeps one eye on the stock market indicator as he continues reminiscing. His warm stare bounces back and forth from the monitor to me.

"At William and Mary College in Virginia I had a great time—that means I wasn't a hardworking student, enjoyed the Kappa Sig house, and dated heavily. My grades were moderate. I was president of my class every year except the last year when I was president of the student body. I worked my butt off in basketball and stayed on the varsity—in fact, did well. And late at night, I'd often drift over to the music division's rehearsal rooms and practice the piano. Music was acceptable in college, and I loved the piano more and more. Also, I got to know the dean of the law school at W and M, and he encouraged my interest in law—again, with a political future in mind."

Bottoms continues in measured tones.

"All of a sudden, at the University of Virginia Law School (which I got into, admittedly, with pull), I came alive as a student—I remember the ecstasy of getting a 4.0 on my first big exam. Part of the new seriousness was that I had married right after college, and part of it was real joy in what I was studying. Law school, regardless of what the critics say, prepared me wonderfully well for the practice of law and applying critical thought to most anything."

Suddenly this seemingly controlled man jumps from his desk chair and looks like an umpire calling a strike.

"Zow! Zayre is finally taking off. I told a bunch of my clients to buy in at nineteen. It just hit twenty-two!" He smiles broadly, nearly skips around the room, and returns to his desk. "I'm sorry. Where were we?"

He sits down, tries to concentrate, and takes one last gulp from his cardboard coffee cup with I LOVE NEW YORK emblazoned on the side.

"After law school, between 1964 and 1966, I went into the army and ended up in Europe as a captain in the artillery. The best part of that experience was the piano I rented and played religiously during off-time.

"My wife and I headed to Atlanta from the army, since both of us considered ourselves Southerners. I worked at a good law firm there for a while and my wife taught English in high school. But Atlanta wasn't the urban wonder it is today. We both yearned for a little more in the cultural zone, and I knew New York was the nation's hub for law. We headed north."

For the moment, his eyes avoid the monitor. They always do when he starts to talk piano.

"In New York, I couldn't help but seek out professional coaching, or at least some appraisals of my musical ability. And that was very encouraging. A prominent pianist at Juilliard was kind enough to listen to me, *after* telling me that I should concentrate on law and forget the piano. When I finished playing for her, she paused for a long time and then said, 'You must quit the law. You have something in music that one cannot be taught.'

■

"Well, I didn't quit the law, of course, but later I did find my current piano teacher—a wonderful woman and pianist. She gives me an hour once a week. Usually I rehearse at least six hours during the weekend and when I'm not too tired, one hour each weeknight. She encourages small recitals, so each spring I do one in her or my apartment for friends and musicians. I have the piano in proper perspective now and it really gives me a boost."

Eyes back to the monitor . . .

"Let's talk more about the law. Lawyers, to me, are interesting, curious, intelligent, and cussedly rigid—rigid of mind, rigid of manner, rigid of person. Unfortunately, at least in the big cities, there is a certain way lawyers are supposed to behave—they accept it, and *become* it. That's really tragic because so many lawyers I know have broad interests—more lawyers than you might guess can talk about almost anything. But often they don't, because they're not supposed to. Sad . . .

"But my years at the law firm here were good years. I left, finally, because I sensed the firm was only willing to plan for the short term—the management was not willing to take risks for the long haul. It happens so often in these large firms that one individual with limited vision somehow is allowed to take control—in my firm's case, that individual's tenure was long and hurtful. But also, I had dreamed of having my own investment business for at least a decade. It was time to risk change. But damn, that's hard to do after nineteen years in one chair.

"In law, you get, now and then, the case of a lifetime. And mine came as a grand finale at the firm. The great movie producer, Sam Spiegel, was interviewing a few trust and estate lawyers to handle his will. He was eighty-four at the time, and died six months after I met him. I was lucky to be one of the interviewees—someone had mentioned my name to him. We had a good chat and I was about to leave when he said, 'I hear that you play the piano.' He pointed at the beautiful grand in his Manhattan apartment and said, 'Horowitz played on this piano. Let's see how you do.' I was thrilled, and jumped into one of my favorite Liszt sonatas. He listened intently. At the end there was an embarrassing silence when I thought he might be disapproving, but instead he rose and said, 'Well, you're my lawyer.' Several years later now, I'm still working on Mr. Spiegel's will—it takes me and several of my

■

associates at the law firm all over the world. It's been a fabulous experience, one rarely available."

A flash at the monitor, a flash back to the story.

"My greatest joy as a lawyer was making partner. My greatest sorrow was my wife's accusing me of 'marrying the firm.' Knowing this was her view, I started leaving work early, homework in hand, and getting home by seven p.m. (Trust and estate lawyers can do this—others, not so easily.) She was not convinced, and we finally split. The girls have lived with me. Their mother pursued her Ph.D. in English and now teaches college."

This time, a long look at the monitor. Not to study market prices, it seems.

"Life is so full. Somehow, back in 1971, the White House got hold of my name. They were looking for someone to be an advance man for President Nixon as he toured foreign nations. The law firm gave me time off to do it. Those were good times, but I quickly learned that the political arena was not for me. [An elected stint in Pelham only added to that hunch.] Much as I enjoyed the White House job, Mr. Haldeman and a few others I met gave me the edgy feeling that there were important happenings somewhere under the table. I felt uneasy about the whole business and wanted to return to the law firm. But one incident was memorable. While touring the Kremlin in advance of Mr. Nixon's historic 1972 visit, I spotted a magnificent piano in the old tsar's quarters, which are perfectly maintained inside the Kremlin. Interestingly, my Russian escorts had somehow learned that I played classical piano—curious, because I don't think any of Nixon's people knew that. Anyway, they invited me to play. It gave me a chance to celebrate Scriabin's hundredth birthday in his homeland. I've never enjoyed a piano performance more."

It is time to pull this interview to a close. Bottoms takes the lead in his usual gracious but monotoned manner.

"You've caught me at a good time. I feel I'm in the real world now. My years in the law were good, but I took few if any risks. Now I'm risking almost everything—my money (which lawyers rarely do), my reputation, my lifestyle. And I've learned more in the last year than I learned in my last fifteen years at the law firm. Why? Because I'm stretching now, really stretching. God, I wish everyone could muster the courage, or just find the wherewithal

∎

somehow, to make changes. Too many lawyers dull out. I was on the verge . . ."

He walks me past the World War I poster gallery to the Deco elevator and rushes back the moment the door closes—to see how Zayre is doing, I trust.

∎ ∎ ∎

The Second Lady wants to practice law.

MARILYN QUAYLE

"I want to step back into the arena of formally practicing law. And soon. I realize that what I do must be very carefully chosen. Everyone is watching, particularly women. It will just *have* to work."

Marilyn Quayle does not waste words. She looks at her interviewer steadily, and her determination is clear. She is fully at ease in her ice-blue-and-white, formal but comfortable quarters in the Executive Office Building, down the hall a bit from her husband's Vice Presidential suite, and next door to the White House. She is far more attractive than her pictures—and stylish, even in red, white, and blue. There is a touch of the Hoosier in her accent, but her voice is controlled. Both her charm and her seriousness are worn on the surface.

"I'm seeking a lot of advice to find my niche for practicing law in Washington. But contrary to public perception, no one is telling me I *can't* practice law as the Vice President's wife. Actually, I'm getting encouragement from a lot of people, including the President and Mrs. Bush, as well as Richard Thornburgh. Obviously I'm limited by potential conflicts of interest due to the parameters of my husband's work—I'm well aware of that, but I'm becoming equally aware of some of the possibilities that do exist."

At the end of softly, rather slowly stated, no-embellishment sentences, Marilyn Quayle always places a period. And then is silent.

After a pause, she repeats: "Whatever I do with law, it has to work. I know that a lot of people are watching and hoping it will work."

Marilyn and Dan Quayle are Indiana, through and through. He went to DePauw University in Greencastle, and then Indiana University Law School. She was born in Indianapolis, attended Broad Ripple High School ("the Ripple Rockets!"), then Purdue University in West Lafayette, followed by the night division of the Indiana University Law School in Indianapolis. While growing up she lived in a large, traditional home in the most established neighborhood of Indianapolis. Her parents were both medical doctors.

"My lure to the law?—Well, I cannot remember *not* wanting to be a lawyer. First, I was determined to do something that my mother had not done. Second, I was always impressed by my two uncles and grandfather, three small-town lawyers. They were smart, well respected in their communities, and seemed to have enough time left over from professional responsibilities to pay attention to their families and enjoy life. One of my uncles became a Supreme Court justice; and at the other extreme my grandfather was an itinerant circuit court judge, traveling between two little towns, Salem and Paoli.

"My brother is continuing the family country-lawyer tradition. He is still in Paoli—a litigator—and although he is often invited to consider large firms in large cities, he wants to remain where he is. He's a symbol of why I respect the small-town lawyer: he's a superb attorney, a devoted family man, and even has time for a curious hobby—he's a muzzle-loader and shoots 'long boards' competitively in tournaments around the world."

Mrs. Quayle smiles demurely. Her smile is often there, but rarely spirited.

"My brother thinks I should be a litigator, and I guess he has convinced me. Time will tell."

A long pause . . .

"You know, I think anyone who is intelligent, community-minded, serious, and willing to work hard should consider law school. The training law school provides can be helpful in almost any profession. Granted, these very characteristics *can* add up to a person who is potentially dull, but I think lawyers, on the whole, end up being positive and vibrant people. Every profession has its rotten apples, and law is no exception—it's too bad that some of the sour, greedy attorneys get more than their share of the press.

"Law school helped me to think differently. I was forced to

■

organize my mind. The first year of law school was jarring, but by the second year I had learned, as they say, to 'think like a lawyer.' I guess the heart of law training is just becoming mentally organized. We all could profit from that, of course. The training benefited me in reading, in planning a daily schedule, in setting goals—well, in most everything I do."

Mrs. Quayle does not complicate. There are few subtleties. But there is certainty and credibility.

"My so-called career in law has been disjointed. I law-clerked for the attorney general in Indianapolis and did some work for the Indiana Supreme Court. But it wasn't until 1974, when Dan and I moved to Huntington, Indiana, that we decided to hang out our shingles—together. But Dan was working for the family newspaper, so his law career was limited—he probably made it to court only a couple of times, and soon he was involved in a full congressional campaign. I spent more time with the law, along with family, in a general, small practice. And then, suddenly we moved to Washington in 1976. I did limited work for Indiana firms here, but my legal/family/political selves remained separate and—well, disjointed."

Marilyn Quayle suddenly becomes animated . . .

"I can't tell you the excitement small-town lawyers feel in coming to Washington, the heart of our government. For us, there was so much room for growth, so much room for contribution! It was a very vibrant period for both Dan and me.

"Have I been frustrated not practicing law here? Well, actually, I've been Dan's lawyer, spending full-time in research. I did a lot of legal research for him when he served in the House, and kept with it as he moved to the Senate. So although it appears that my legal work has been very limited, I've actually been very active, although my involvement has been quiet and behind-the-scenes."

Another pause.

"Another relevant point to all this is that I'm a voracious reader. I'm the type of person who reads every tiny sign on an airplane. So researching the law, looking for the fine points, gives me great pleasure—it's a rather natural thing for me to do."

There was another minor stirring in the light blue damask wing chair.

"We *have* to have lawyers, you know. There are so many

regulations on the books now, and almost all of them can be interpreted ambiguously. The subtleties can only be resolved case by case. And there are ethical concerns which make the law so important to our society. We all wish the law could be simplified, of course, and that is a great challenge for both the lawyers and the politicians. After all, we do not have a risk-free democracy, so the laws become particularly important here."

After a quick look at her gold watch, Marilyn Quayle's smile clicks on.

"I do have another appointment now, and I'm running a bit behind . . .

"Advice for the young people, the potential prelaw students? Well, I think they should know that training in law can be used in many segments of life. Whether you're working with charities or corporations or whatever, law school training proves to be a wonderful tool. Mental acuity is important, wherever one travels."

Mrs. Quayle stands, slowly and gracefully.

Despite the amenities and protocol and restraint dictated by her position on the ice-blue-and-white stage of the Executive Office Building, one just knows that this Second Lady is smart, assertive, and willful, just like most of the other lawyers. And she wants to be one of them.

■ ■ ■

From football to law and back again . . .

ED WOODSUM

Eddie Woodsum has always been bigger than life. For starters, he's just *big*: big person, big voice, big manner. And he has built on that—football player of note, lawyer of note, Yalie of note. Nothing he does is minor league. Everything works out big.

Some who are large in visibility consistently bring large criticism. Not Eddie. Everyone seems to know him and say nice things about him. But the latest reaction is envy, particularly among the Northeastern lawyer set. For Ed Woodsum, at fifty-seven, has stepped out of his successful and lucrative law practice (a firm that bears his name in the alphabetical lineup) to do what many would surely yearn to do: return to alma mater as the director of athletics.

■

"Molloy to Woodsum" is a well-worn phrase among Yale alumni of the early-fifties era. It meant Ed Molloy, quarterback, passing to Ed Woodsum, split end, for a nearly certain big yardage gain. ("It's a hell of a lot more difficult to throw it than to catch it," says big Ed generously.) In their senior year, the Bulldogs powered by Harvard and everyone else except Princeton and Navy, for a 7–2 record. After being drafted for Korea and serving his time, Woodsum was drafted by the Chicago (then St. Louis, now Phoenix) Cardinals.

Football was Eddie Woodsum's way out—or way in, one might say. From South Portland High School in Maine, where he was captain of football and basketball and led two baseball teams to state titles, he had planned on the good life of a fisherman, emulating the men on his mother's side. That sounded okay to Ed's father, a maintenance man with the local gas company.

But big young men with hustle, speed, and agility have a way of being noticed as they prepare to leave high school by Old Blues and college alums of many other colors. They all converged on Woodsum. Since he was batting a ninety-three-ish academic average (although most of his courses were in the business track), a competitive college did indeed seem a possibility. He was attracted by the fishing and climbing scenes in the Dartmouth catalogue, and the strong reputation of nearby Bowdoin, but it was his high school physician who begged him to talk to a Yale alumnus, "to get the guy off my back." And that alumnus helped seal the deal. Woodsum was off to New Haven. He says now that Yale was just the path of least resistance, given the zealous attention of their graduates.

"I knew Yale would be tough, and it was. But I was never in any academic trouble and my friends would probably describe me as 'conscientious' in college. Early on, history courses were intriguing, but somehow I had this feeling I'd end up in business school. I had worked hard every summer since I was eleven, and there was an entrepreneurial streak in me. I just didn't know what was out there to do after college. The question, quite frankly, did not become 'Will I succeed?'—it became 'What will I succeed in?' "

Woodsum is munching on a sandwich in a collegiate-looking hangout close to his new office at Yale. He has just rolled in from a weekend of packing moving crates at his house on the ocean in

Cape Elizabeth, Maine. His well-worn green polo shirt has a large rip under one arm, and white hair can also be seen on an unshaven face. He has big glasses, a big smile, and needs a wide booth for big gestures.

"In the service, I met an impressive guy who had just passed the Massachusetts bar exam. I liked what he had to say about law as vocation, and all the diverse possibilities a law degree introduced. That came at about the time the Harvard Business School sent me their application, the *fattest* set of forms I had ever seen . . . too fat!"

A pause and a smirk.

"Suddenly law school looked very interesting. I applied to the law schools in the Chicago area, since I'd be there with the Cardinals right after leaving the service. But Columbia, Harvard, and Yale were of interest too. The more I thought about it, the less I felt drawn to New York, and the Harvard Law School seemed too darn big. And I was a bit influenced, I must admit, by a slogan that was everywhere: 'Go to Harvard if you want to enter corporate private practice; go to Yale if you want to be a judge.' That made Yale sound like the more interesting of the two, the more intellectual of the two. Having been admitted to Yale, and being frustrated in not getting a clear answer from the Cardinals as to whether I'd survive their final cuts for the traveling squad, I headed, once again, to school in New Haven and said goodbye to football.

"But was I happy for the football mentality when I encountered my first law professors! You had to have real stamina to withstand their assaults. All the students surrounding me were bright as hell, although one could have asked, perhaps, for a little more on the personality side. Nonetheless, it was a new game for me, and tougher than the Cardinal scramble would ever have been.

"Like so many others, I learned in law school that the perceived pinnacle of success was getting a bid from the big firm in the big city—I guess that's even more true today, but it was current in my class way back in the late fifties. After my 2L year, I headed off to White and Case in New York and stayed there for about six years. My wife and I both liked New York, surprisingly, and I really liked White and Case—the people and the work. We commuted into the city from Brooklyn Heights, which felt almost like a rural neighborhood. But we treasured the returns to Maine in the summer."

Woodsum speaks with force and knows exactly where he's headed, but there is a gentle quality to it all. He doesn't speak like he looks.

"Out of the blue, two fellows from Portland, Maine, who had just started their own firm up there, called to ask if I'd be interested in joining them. We doubted if we wanted to make that kind of move, but Joan and I flew up to talk to them for a couple of hours and ended up talking an entire day. I was tempted, and Joan said, 'Let's give it a go for three years and see what happens.'

"We three partners started out in 1965, and by 1987 the firm had grown to over forty lawyers. We were extremely busy from the start. For me, having been exposed to a large firm of specialists in New York City, it was fun to be forced into the generalist role and all the learning that is necessary to carry that off. As the practice grew, I ultimately did more and more corporate work, but having to start from scratch with a broad-range practice was a great experience."

Woodsum snaps out of his autobiographical mode.

"Times have changed. There is more concern about the bottom line these days. The young lawyers, along with everybody else in the country, seem extraordinarily materialistic. That atmosphere fosters less loyalty to clients, to the firm itself, and to the profession of law. The climate of big mergers has colored the atmosphere too—the whole enterprise is less personal, and a little sticky, since lawyers can get nailed so easily for malpractice. Still, some of the old rules pertain: the commitment to detail remains paramount for a lawyer's success, and getting the work out quickly. The workplace is the same in some ways, very different in others. I guess there are a lot of people who, somewhat cynical about the route law is taking these days, are a little envious of my stepping into another kind of arena, something that appears to be a bit more laid-back and fun."

Woodsum shakes his head . . .

"I may be in for a lot of big surprises. I'm told being director of athletics at a sophisticated place like Yale is similar to being president of a little college. All I know is that they wanted someone to kick a little ass here. And I'll probably have to do that. I inherited a staff of over twenty-five coaches, and over two hundred full-time employees. Yale wants and deserves the best, and we intend to have it. Part of the job will be the long-overdue refurbishing of some of the major sports facilities, and that will take tons of money. Our Payne-Whitney gym, built in the thirties, was for decades the showpiece of the nation, but now it's far behind what comparable institutions, like Harvard, have built. And look at the Yale Bowl—it's falling apart, and is never filled. What do you do with a huge white elephant like that? And with thirty-five varsity sports, equally divided among men and women, there is bound to be internal competition for resources and attention. Chances are that my skills in law will come in handy."

Woodsum knows Yale well. He was appointed to the Yale Corporation twelve years ago, and has held such important offices as chair of the Investiture Responsibility Committee, which has, of course, dealt with the sensitive South Africa issues. Beyond Yale, he has done his stint back in Maine as head of United Way, served as president of the Portland Symphony Board for two years, and was elected for three terms to the Cape Elizabeth Town Council. One of his great pleasures is serving as national treasurer of the National Audubon Society.

Given the whole story, Ed Woodsum would seem the natural politician, the sure vote getter. The athlete-with-mind, dutiful to community service and quietly dependable and honest, sells well if one considers the Bill Bradleys and the Jack Kemps.

"Politics? Absolutely not for me . . . When you run for office you inevitably have to compromise your standards to make certain your appeal becomes universal. I have never found it necessary to equivocate and don't intend to start now."

He rises and, with a warm handshake, stalks out of the restaurant as though he's heading from the huddle to the front line. There is no missing the fellow and he moves with sure direction. But life and profession don't appear to have subtleties for this team player. Woodsum always seems to want to go for the big play and the win.

It works.

■ ■ ■

■

*"Without the booze I could do anything, and so could a lot of lawyers
who have drinking problems and just get by."*

DERMOT MEAGHER

"Well, to tell the truth, I'm nosy and gossipy and love to know
what's going on in people's lives. So that's why I'm well cast here
at 'BoBo' (Board of Bar Overseers). Also, I like to resolve things
quickly and positively—what lawyer doesn't? At BoBo, we rarely
lose a case. Given the fact that I didn't give a damn about law
school, this is a good situation. And very lucky for me . . ."

The spokesman is forty-seven, heavyset, and has a happy Irish
face, unruly curly hair, unruly tie, unruly shirt, and a very unruly
office highlighted by a paper bag full of pencils and ballpoints,
askew original art, and a stained carpet with hospital-green walls
surrounding.

Dermot Meagher is first assistant bar counsel at the Board
of Bar Overseers in Boston, a statewide agency set up by the
commonwealth's Supreme Judicial Court to "monitor" lawyers
throughout Massachusetts. The organization was founded in 1974
over the objection of the Massachusetts Bar Association, who correctly saw the court's action as a criticism of their own ability to
monitor lawyers, as bar associations are expected to do. (Massachusetts is not the only state where such an agency has been
established in recognition of the bar association's inability to patrol
and discipline its own.)

BoBo follows up on complaints on individual lawyers that
are submitted by clients, other lawyers, or any responsible source.
After appropriate investigation ("we basically are a little court,"
says Meagher), prosecutions are made if warranted, with ultimate
penalties ranging from informal admonition to public censure or
disbarment. Approximately two thousand complaints are formally
acknowledged annually (there are 30,000 practicing lawyers in the
Commonwealth of Massachusetts). Of this number, approximately half are multiple complaints about the same lawyers. Although many lawyers are found guilty of some lesser degree of
malfeasance and are appropriately notified and penalized, only 10
to 15 attorneys per year are disbarred within Massachusetts for
major infractions such as stealing when handling an estate. The

two most common complaints about lawyers submitted to the Board of Bar Overseers relate to neglect and fees.

"Part of the heart of our activity is far from visible to the lawyers and the public. I'd guess that sixty-five to seventy percent of the lawyers whom we find guilty of some type of infraction, large or small, have an alcohol or drug abuse problem. We're dealing with complaints regarding legal practice, yes, but we're also dealing with a much deeper, perplexing issue. We're talking about human frailty among normally serious and able people—and how they, as individuals, and how we, as a profession, should cope while concurrently serving the public responsibly."

There was a long moment of silence and the happy-faced lawyer turned somber.

"They hired the right guy for this job. I am an alcoholic, although I haven't had a drink in thirteen years now. But for a long time, I didn't know I was a drunk. I don't know if I was fully competent or not, but I damn well know I was scared in the later years of that period. And just spending time and effort on *being scared* probably compromised my performance."

Meagher's family tradition, on his father's side, is law. His grandfather was one of the first Irish lawyers in Worcester, Mass. He concentrated on representing non-Protestant immigrants and was a trial lawyer during Prohibition days. Dermot's father is now a judge in Worcester and is known to some as Blackjack for being so tough on lawyers in the courtroom. Meagher's mother's heritage includes an Irish contractor who built Holy Cross College. Of the six Meagher children, two are now lawyers. The whole clan attended either Harvard (three) or Catholic colleges—Fairfield and Georgetown.

"I was the number-two kid. And because I was so sweet, Mom and Dad kept their hands off and trusted me. I was, of course, sent to a Catholic day school. I wanted Harvard after that not only because I was a little snob, but also because I heard there were a lot of interesting oddballs there. But one night at a deb party, shortly after I received my admit letter from Harvard, I got pissy drunk and passed out in front of everyone. Dad then wondered if I had the willpower to make the most of Harvard—a family friend had to talk him into finally letting me go. But even

∎

after that close call, Dad stayed his distance. I don't think he even knew what I was majoring in at college.

"At Harvard I guess I was intimidated, finally. But still I didn't hustle. I tried government courses but found them boring, so my degree finally came in English. In short, I didn't work very hard at college. And part of the reason is that Harvard never challenged my values. They should have . . ."

A secretary pops in to say that a lawyer insists on talking with Meagher immediately by phone. He wheels around on his tawdry rug and picks up the phone. His entire demeanor changes from the nonchalant Irishman to a tough cop.

"Look, everything you want to know is written plainly in D.R.2-106A. Have you read it? A lawyer, pure and simple, cannot charge excessive fees. Read D.R.2-106A—it's talking to you! And what's the urgency of this call at this moment? What you need is what you can read, and lawyers are supposed to be good at that. Read 2-106 and call me back later if anything needs clarification. I don't think it will."

A big, contagious smile, and back to the interview . . .

"After Harvard I couldn't think of anything to do. Law school of course, because of the family tradition, was a possibility. But an unexciting one. Some college buddies of mine were going to trek off to Mexico to find their souls and mystical truths by tackling social work. Although the idea had some Lana Turner kind of appeal, it seemed to me to represent hedging our bets, but I did join them for several summer stays. Law school was inevitable, even though I had hurt my chances some by getting drunk the night before the Law Boards."

Meagher refuses phone call after phone call from his buzzing secretary to continue the story.

"I ended up going to Boston College Law School, a solid Catholic training ground. And I hated it—hated it. I plugged along in the middle of the class, and toward the end of it all, really started boozing. But I graduated and took a job with a law firm in Worcester, admittedly through family connections. The beginning of real trouble was flunking the bar exam and receiving, in turn, a reduced salary from my firm. On the next round, I really studied for the bar, was sober, and passed with flying colors. You see, there's a message here: Without the booze, I could do anything, and so could a lot of lawyers who have a chemical problem and just get by.

"The next few years were really good, I guess you might say. I worked for a fellow who is now Governor Dukakis's chief fundraiser, doing legal writing. Then my dad called to say that the district attorney's office in Worcester had a vacancy, and I should try for it. I got the job, of course—probably with a little quiet influence from the old man. I lived in Boston and commuted to Worcester. The job provided a wonderful experience. But some big names told me my success as a lawyer would be ultimately hurt if I stayed longer than three years in the D.A.'s office. So at the end of the three, I quit, which was okay, because I wanted to work more with systems."

Meagher keeps right on talking while gazing out the window at a busy Boston street in the neighborhood of the State House and a grand old federal home housing the Massachusetts Bar Association.

"But then the booze started hitting hard, and I got really scared. I did fairly well in a string of interesting jobs, none of which lasted very long. I worked for the city manager of Worcester (and helped write a treatise on drugs and youth!), and then won a fellowship at the Harvard Center for Criminal Justice and really blew it. At this point, I was really into booze and getting more scared. Then I nailed a job with the National Center for State Courts—it was great! I was to visit all the chief justices east of the Mississippi. But I knew I had a drinking problem now. Before every chief justice's interview, I'd booze up. And soon thereafter a series of other problems popped up—my lover took off, for example, with one of my best friends. And now I was heavy into Valium, a substitute for the liquor. I needed Valium so bad that I couldn't read or write without it."

The stare out the window remains constant. The story is coming now without emotional tone.

"Then everything hit the fan. My boss told me to leave, and I went crazy. I probably seemed in control, but I wasn't. I didn't know what to do—so I slept and shopped a lot. I tried a few interviews, but didn't really get to first base. Then I started modeling because I was still thin then. Although it provided a few

■

bucks—but not enough to keep me from selling my house—I knew I was without a profession at this stage, and it frightened the hell out of me.

"Then a miracle walked in. A friend told me about this job in 1976. I walked into the waiting room of the Board of Bar Overseers to report for the interview, and bumped into a recovering alcoholic friend of mine, one of the crazy ones. I relaxed then. The director of the program liked me—and he hired me without (thank God) exhaustive contacts to references.

"I like the controlled day here. I start at 8:30 and quit at 6:30. I like the fact that we start a process and finish a process, and the fact that we're doing damned serious work. One of my great joys is the organization I helped to start called Lawyers Concerned with Lawyers, for attorneys with a chemical addiction problem. Granted, I make half as much here as I might with a law firm, but the work is important and I'm satisfied. And I don't mind saying that moving to a firm would worry me in terms of pressure. I have everything under control here—with my job and with my life.

"What might I do in the long run? I don't know, but I'm applying for a judgeship. Since that is the work I'm doing currently at the agency, why not do it from the bench?"*

There is a long pause, a look at the watch (6:25 p.m.), and a quick departure. "This is my weekly night for a massage. I need it and, more often than not, I think I deserve it."

■ ■ ■

"Once in law school, my light bulb popped on."

RICHARD THORNBURGH

"Quite frankly, I was never much of a student. At prep school, my friends probably would have described me as happy-go-lucky and fairly bright. Then I went on to Yale and majored in engineering, which was the family trade. But I was uneasy about going into the family trade.

---

* In May 1989, Dermot Meagher was sworn in as a judge of the Boston Municipal Court.

"One day I audited classes with a friend at the Harvard Law School. The Socratic method really appealed to me, so I decided then and there law school was for me. Since my college record and the family means didn't allow consideration of a Yale or a Harvard, I headed home to the University of Pittsburgh. Once in law school, my light bulb popped on. I knew I was in the right place."

The Attorney General of the United States appears comfortable indeed behind his huge desk inside a vast maze of sterile hallways and uninviting office entries at the Department of Justice in Washington. But even the grand floor-to-ceiling gold brocade drapes cannot set this head-of-U.S.-law up for formalities. In shirtsleeves, sporting a winter tan, and with a leisurely tilt of the leather chair, he is fully at ease and makes others feel the same. (Thornburgh said in his inaugural address, on becoming governor of Pennsylvania, "I promise a simplicity that knows the real greatness of Pennsylvania cannot be enhanced but only debased by the pretensions of its leaders.") Pretentious he is not. And "simplicity" does describe the Attorney General's style and demeanor.

"You must forgive my glow. I just argued a drugs-related case in front of the Supreme Court. It proved to me (and a few others, perhaps) that I'm still a lawyer. Even those fortunate enough to be named to high office must find it honorable to get back into the trenches."

Dick Thornburgh has a way of talking and nodding as though you're over at the house for dinner.

"What traits do I think lawyers have in common? Well, to succeed, they have to be precise; and they have to be persistent. They have to be tendentious and have real purpose. At their best, lawyers have a sense of proportion and a sense of humor. And they must be well versed in the society and culture they are a part of—and nothing contributes to that more than habitual general reading."

A pause and a twist of the big chair.

"In fact, 'well read' just has to be a priority criterion for good lawyering. I was lucky—my mom influenced us all to be strong readers."

One can't help but notice a number of family pictures placed

around the office. The Attorney General alludes to "family" often
as he discusses a number of topics.

"Law school was just as I had been warned. You know the
old saying—'The first year they scare you to death, the second
year they work you to death, and the third year they bore you to
death.' I didn't really know what I'd do coming *out* of law school—
I wish there had been more clinical experience there—but I did
know that having a wife and three kids (in three years) meant I
had to do something substantial quickly. So I went to work for
the legal department of Alcoa Aluminum. But it didn't take long
for me to know that I wanted to be a *real* lawyer. Soon after, I
joined a Pittsburgh firm."

Then Dick Thornburgh's face quickly turns solemn. And, in
a moment, his eyes mist.

"But my perspective changed overnight. My wife was killed
in a tragic automobile accident on July 1, 1960, that also left one
of my sons brain-damaged."

Silence . . .

"Although the formality of the firm practice was interesting,
I was suddenly drawn to public-interest law: pro bono projects in
civil rights at the community and state levels, my neighborhood
legal sentinel group, ACLU projects and others."

Thornburgh has jumped from one law-related assignment to
another. In 1967, he was an elected delegate to Pennsylvania's
Constitutional Convention, whose goal was to reform the state's
judicial system and strengthen local government. Then, for six
years, he served as U.S. Attorney for Western Pennsylvania,
prosecuting drug traffickers, corrupt public officials, and major
organized-crime leaders. In 1975, President Ford appointed him
Assistant Attorney General of the United States, heading up the
Criminal Division. Then came two terms as Governor of Pennsylvania, during which his fellow governors (in a *Newsweek* poll)
named him "the nation's most effective big-state governor." And
The Wall Street Journal noted: "Thornburgh has kept his promise
to run a clean, efficient and economical state government."

"What was my legacy as Governor of Pennsylvania?"

Uncharacteristically, the response seems rehearsed.

"First, I tried to restore people's confidence in government.

Just prior to my term, there had been an epidemic of corruption. I wanted the people to view me as an ally in cleaning all that up.

"Second—and my toughest challenge—was to get the state's economy back on track. We created 500,000 new jobs. Our unemployment rate moved from one of the ten highest states in the nation to one of the ten lowest.

"Third, we had to teach everyone to do more with less. And that meant management reforms. We got 15,000 jobs out of government and were able to cut taxes.

"Finally, Pennsylvania had a crime-and-drugs problem that had to be addressed quickly. During my years in office, the state's serious-crime rate dropped by more than seventeen percent and was consistently the lowest of any large state. We instituted programs to assist crime victims, put in place mandatory jail sentences for violent and repeat offenders, and undertook the largest prison expansion in Pennsylvania's history."

The Attorney General continues in a relaxed manner. The speech seems to be over and spontaneity resurfaces.

"The big question, I guess, is what I hope my legacy will be as Attorney General. I'll take my lead, of course, from the President—but I know already that the drug problem is at the top of the list. My biggest surprise in coming back to this office after ten years is the explosion in international-related crimes—drugs, money-laundering, and a host of others. There is an international umbrella now to almost everything we do. American crime can no longer be addressed just within American borders.

"White-collar crime is another area of major concern. There is just too much public corruption in the U.S.A. now."

There is a pause, a long pause.

"I only hope we can convey to the people that every individual *counts*—that is the key in applying the law. It begins right here in the office place—people are people, not just résumés.

"Also, I'm well aware that the Department of Justice has traditionally been very generously funded. Ironically, that can be a problem. When an operation is flush, people are not as attentive as they might be, and perhaps not as innovative as they ought to be.

"I've been lucky in my pattern of work. The management experience of being a governor was important to my running a federal department this big and complicated. I'm thankful that I didn't move directly from assistant attorney general to the top post without that breather—it was a very different experience. I advise others to 'keep their options open' and my own path has profited from just that. I have pity for people, lawyers or others, who feel they must follow a precise game plan. Life is less interesting if one does that, and probably less effective, too."

The Attorney General, in the company of his assistant, gives the impression that he is open to chatting at length. At one point he pops out of his chair to show me a recent portrait of the family, describing each member. His spunky second wife, Ginny, heads Harvard's program for the disabled although she is phasing out there to join her husband in Washington. Peter, the boy disabled in the car accident, is in the picture, as is the youngest son, now a Seabee, and the two older boys and their wives.

"Yes, I have a few words of wisdom for those thinking about going to law school. First, I think that a student heading for law school should be sure that he or she wants to be a *lawyer*—although the training is general, the great majority of graduates head to the law, so we are talking about career training. Law school should not be treated as a crutch or a fallback—it should represent commitment to a profession. On the other side of the coin, the danger now is that law is becoming *too* professional—a business, if you will, with less a service orientation."

A pause, and the voice intonation of a Conclusion.

"Law is not the priesthood; lawyers are not protected. Lawyers must be prepared to undergo scrutiny and be held accountable for whatever they do. Accountability is consistent with the station. A lawyer must be prepared, must always be at his or her best, in court or out. But like the priesthood, I think law *is* something of a calling."

The nation's legal business has to be addressed, so I am thanked for writing about my interest in "the importance of law and lawyers" by the uncomplicated, direct, rather homespun attorney in charge of them all.

■ ■ ■

■

*"As I looked around it seemed to me that ninety percent of the
decent-paying lawyers' jobs were to help the rich keep their money.
. . . As they move along professionally, the great majority
of attorneys just don't stand for much."*

CHARLES BAKER

It's difficult to decide if Charlie Baker, forty-two, just found his
way out of a Wyoming mountain range or is caught in a late-
sixties time capsule. The scuzzy untrimmed beard, the thick silver-
trimmed spectacles, and his near-weightlessness set him apart in
any crowd, even in Laramie, Wyoming, where he is stationed as
a reporter for the *Casper Star-Tribune*.

Charlie Baker is also a member of the Wyoming State Bar
who graduated sixth in a class of thirty-five from the University
of Wyoming Law School. But he has never grossed over eighteen
thousand dollars a year.

Charlie didn't always walk to a different drummer. But he
believes in his drummer, and thinks most others are out of step.

"Everybody has heroes or heroines," says Charlie. "My hero
was close at hand. I originally wanted to do everything just like
my father did it: above all, go to the University of Wyoming and
attend football games with the ATOs, and maybe even be a lawyer
like he was. Dad was city attorney of Cheyenne for a while, but
died early of a heart attack after an unsuccessful run for judge
against a real incompetent.

"Our Cheyenne family has nine degrees from UW, so there
really wasn't much choice for me, although my mother remort-
gaged the house to send one maverick brother to Pratt Institute in
New York—he wanted the arts. I majored in American history,
and later passed up a scholarship to Georgetown Law and an
invitation to be a congressional intern just to stay in Wyoming.
But, thanks to—good? bad?—timing and a chance trip to San
Francisco in 1969, my life took a different turn."

This lawyer-turned-journalist speaks softly, calmly. He recalls
every morsel of his story and recounts it with restrained pride—
but a bit defensively, as though the audience is expected to express
disapproval. Being on the calm defensive is part of Charlie's demeanor now.

■

Charlie saw all the UW Cowboy games as a kid, and once in college, set himself the goal of being sports editor of the campus paper. He met his goal, and then some. Not only did he become sports editor of the campus paper and the Laramie city paper simultaneously; later he was named editor in chief of the UW paper.

"The beginning of my real enlightenment was in the late sixties. I started reading other universities' newspapers and was stunned to find how provincial we were in Wyoming. Then UPI sent me to Houston for a summer job. I met my first hippies there and liked them, liked their music, liked their style. The next summer, UPI put me in San Francisco. I did the whole thing: lived in a boardinghouse commune, soaked up *Soul on Ice* by Cleaver and *The Autobiography of Malcolm X,* and was intrigued by Black Panther marches. I was struck by racial inequality, yearned for more education and experience regarding minorities in America, and returned to Wyoming eager to share my newfound sensitivities with the people who meant so very much to me.

"I started a column in the campus paper called 'Racism Is . . .' with a different twist each week—like the All-American high school black quarterback who was recruited by Wyoming, then placed immediately for some strange reason at tight end. Our only visible blacks then were jocks; they all quietly wondered if they could seek the highest station in Wyoming's all-white milieu. Or just be themselves, for that matter.

"The big test came in the fall when I returned from California. The Wyoming Cowboys were riding high in football—were ranked fifth in the country, and had been to the Sugar Bowl the preceding year. Then came the 'Black Fourteen' incident. Our black ballplayers wanted to make some small acknowledgment of what was going on in the nation—and like some other teams, came up with the idea of wearing black armbands against one of our big rivals, Brigham Young. On hearing about the plan, the coach called the blacks into the stadium the day before the game and fired them from the team. To many of us, this was unfathomable. But it sure proved football was king."

The quiet Charlie can't stop talking now.

"The Black Fourteen incident shook my faith in everything. Did *anybody* in my milieu have any understanding of racial justice, of the need for black power? How distant could my own people be? My family? I was thrown off rudder—my faith in the University of Wyoming was shattered. And quietly, I delighted in the fact that the Cowboys started losing games without the key players. They lost almost all the next season's games.

"Meanwhile, my campus paper was falling apart. I decided not to put out a special homecoming issue and my sports editor cried. As I grew more bold on issues of Vietnam and race, my staff started to bail out. Eventually, just four of us were trying to get the paper out. And having started the first semesters of law school as number one and number three in my class (I was editor-in-chief of the UW paper while at law school), I suddenly found my grades were falling apart due to all the pressure and time with campus politics. So I quit as editor. And the damn paper popped right back to emphasizing Greeks and fashion, sports and fun.

"It must be said at this point that I loved law school—loved it. Synthesizing, analyzing, tackling tough intellectual exercises, and just the emphasis on *reasoning* put me in heaven. Plus that, my law class became a new kind of fraternity for me—there were dramatic moments as we worked together. It didn't dawn on me— my naïveté, I guess—that for most of my friends law school was a means to an end. For me it *was* the end—true intellectual exercise and stimulation.

"But then graduation came, all too soon. I made the terrible mistake of returning home to Cheyenne to practice law. I organized political protests, but also got two appointments from federal crim- inal courts. You can guess what they were: a Mexican arrested for marijuana and a conscientious objector case. I won the latter at jury. But the Black Fourteen case was coming to trial. And my period of disenchantment with the judicial system was peaking. The only [Wyoming] U.S. district judge found no trace of racism in what happened to the black UW players—and he had to say, of course, that he'd seen no instances of racism in Wyoming for thirty-five years. After all, the fact that the athletes were recruited indicated that Wyoming *really* wanted those blacks to participate at UW.

"Suddenly I felt like a real pariah. I couldn't see around me any legal victories for social justice, for the environment. Mean- while, I married a woman who really supported me. But the big

■

incident was about to happen. It eclipsed a period of extreme embarrassment for my mother, who had made her way to a prominent position in Cheyenne society, just at the time I was playing the unpopular maverick. In retrospect, I know I really wasn't fair to her.

"A black student at Cheyenne High School was expelled for not saying the Pledge of Allegiance. He came to me and I told him his rights, and represented same to his principal. But the principal went straight to the newspaper and talked about me publicly as a 'rabble-rouser,' said I was agitating the town's youth—he never commented on my points regarding the constitutional rights of all citizens."

Charlie's head drops as he talks on.

"I was tired of everything at this point, including my hometown of Cheyenne. And I had really hurt my mother. The law that was fun to learn was not rewarding to apply—and I'm not, of course, speaking of money.

"As my dad might have done after a big set of disappointments, I turned to the outdoors, and spent a lot of time in our wilderness cabin. I love birds, plants, the mountains, and the forests. Then, so my wife could finish college, we moved to Laramie. I was, quite literally, digging ditches. And I did yoga, a lot of yoga. For a while, I was paid a little to be student attorney at UW on the condition that I wouldn't take anyone to court and wouldn't sue the university—instead, I played with tenants' rights and that sort of thing. I still wanted to be a lawyer, deeply. But as I looked around, it seemed to me that ninety percent of the decent-paying lawyers' jobs were to help the rich keep their money—through taxes or estates or helping corporations find twists to compound or keep large reserves. And that wasn't me.

"After a while, I started writing again, even won an award for an environmental article in the *High Country News*. And then came a string of environmental jobs—a research assistant for a forest project, a four-month fire tower lookout position with a 360-degree vista of wheatlands. I even went back to school to beef up again on math and astronomy and computers—the latter to prove to myself that we weren't giving up all our individuality in America. An article on an endangered toad species west of Laramie—a toad whose closest relative seemed to be in Manitoba—

∎

landed me a spot, ultimately, with the *Casper Star-Tribune* as a general news reporter, stationed in Laramie. My wife is a special-ed instructor now. Someday we'll probably just be subsistence farmers."

Our dinner, in a rural Wyoming diner, has long since disappeared.

"It's late, isn't it? So what are the common threads of my story? A love of Wyoming and the refusal to leave. And a special view of lawyers: So many have a good heart and are brilliant and courageous. But arrogance, and with it, inconsistent priorities, set in. As they move along professionally, the great majority of attorneys just don't stand for much. And that's not what Dad set as a goal for me. I'm not strong enough to go it alone in the law."

As we shake hands to depart, Charlie says: "You going to be around this weekend? My brother and I are going backpacking and would love to show you the real Wyoming."

∎ ∎ ∎

*"Luck plays a part in success, but not so large a part
as whom you choose to travel with."*

THOMAS KARSTEN

Everybody talks about the diversity of life a law degree can foster, but too few exemplify the idea.

And too few, surely, are as spry as Thomas Karsten after half a century of using law as a springboard to hop from one colorful and substantial assignment to another: from the governor of Puerto Rico's naval aide to associate prosecutor at the Nuremburg trials, to member of a youthful group of Manhattan Democrats hell-bent on upsetting Tammany Hall, to member of a Wall Street law firm, to, finally, entrepreneur extraordinaire as a result of aligning with the right autocrats with the right money who needed the right advice at the right time.

At seventy-three, Thomas Loren Karsten has done it all. And he didn't even graduate top-of-the-class at the University of Chicago Law School.

Moral: "Do the best job you can and if you're lucky, lightning will strike. Your luck will improve if you have sought out people of extraordinary ability to be next to."

Given the turbulence in Karstein's early life, it is rather amazing that he talks about luck at all.

"We're all from complex backgrounds. Who knows how it all relates to what happens later? Life is funny. . . . But one thing I have learned is never to harbor a regret for longer than two or three days. If we spend much time regretting, we lose precious time moving on. And let us remember that whatever happens, it is the result of our own doing."

Karsten's parents were children of immigrants. His mother was "an insecure Jewish woman who arrived in WASPish Minnesota to face considerable anti-Semitism." His father was the son of Russian immigrants, one of six children who struggled to keep their parents going.

"Through sheer perseverance, Dad became a lawyer at the University of Minnesota. He was a buoyant man and seemed to have a good start as a lawyer. But there was something about him that was troubling—he always craved money quickly. Anyway, through a number of slips, he got into trouble and was disbarred. The family in Minnesota was disgraced and urged us to move away. We were off shortly thereafter to Chicago—I was six at the time.

"Dad just couldn't align with the right people. He was a gifted man, but had a propensity for falling into bad associations. In Chicago, after some years, he became involved in a bank/insurance company embezzlement scheme. At this point, I was an undergraduate at the nearby University of Chicago—so I was still young, but it fell to me as the oldest of the two boys to find bail, find a lawyer, to manage the whole unseemly thing. Bad led to worse . . . the long and short of it, obviously, is that Dad kept us on a constant roller coaster. To make matters worse, we had to put Mom in a sanitarium about this time.

"I can't tell you how many times I told Dad we'd happily, as a family, settle for less money. We begged him to 'get a regular job.' But no, after he got out of the navy, he became involved with someone named Tucker (yes—this story is a movie now) in a new frenzy to make money. I helped force him out of the situation, but as you possibly know, there were arrests for violating security laws in attempts to finance the operation.

"Well, the bottom line was constant turbulence at home. I knew I had to move on. Now, this was at a time when Jewish parents really thought there was only one choice for a bright son to make: between medicine and law. For me, the choice was easy. It was law.

"It's not that I had been an outstanding student in science *or* humanities and social sciences. I had been sort of a nice guy, not a very serious student in college—and actually, that description fit me in law school too. Once out of Chicago's law school, I really didn't feel ready to do *anything,* including law. Law school sharpened my mind, but I didn't feel prepared to practice."

Karsten does not look seventy-three. Not at all. He is trim, tan, and freckled, with a full head of brown hair. He is lively, articulate, and on top of every nuance of the conversation. He appears a rather humble man; but he expends considerable effort telling his full story. If a question is asked, a lengthy—often extraordinarily personal—answer is given. "Am I moving too slowly for you? Well, we all like talking about ourselves, you know. But I don't want to give you more than you need."

A soft smile through a Hemingwayesque beard . . .

"Even if I had done better in law school, it would have been hard to find a decent job. This was 1938, Depression years. Anything I found was at terribly low pay—and anyway, I wanted out of Chicago in the worst way.

"These were Franklin Roosevelt years, and many good lawyers were finding their way to Washington. With a hundred dollars in my pocket, I decided to head to the capital. I fell in love with the place, but as the federal government was in retrenchment, I couldn't find a job in law. So I became a shoe salesman in a department store that had a predominantly black clientele. But in moving around the capital, I happened to meet a lawyer in the Department of Agriculture who was general counsel to the food-stamp program. He was very busy and once he was groaning that he had to prepare a difficult brief overnight and didn't know how he could possibly get it done. I pleaded with him to let me do it, and in desperation, he consented.

"I worked all night long on that goddamn brief with a bottle

■

of bourbon at my side—and guess what, it turned the case around. Well, my friend was now beholden to me for some kind of big favor, so he introduced me to another fellow who was an assistant in Consumer Standards. And this was a big break—I helped him do several sections of *The Handbook on Federal Indian Law,* which remains an important treatise to this day. But let me tell you—I took on all these free-lance assignments with great anxiety, given my less than outstanding record in law school. But I *really* worked hard on them—they represented my best effort, and provided a possible avenue out of selling shoes."

Tom Karsten crosses his legs and relaxes even more in a big easy chair. He is enjoying recounting this story. And his memory seems clear as crystal.

"Then I actually got a job using the law. Hired! They called me 'executive assistant to the undersecretary of the interior.' I was asked to research and write some briefs—for example, an important one on whether reservation Indians could be subjected to state income tax. You know, I hadn't thought my work would be of consequence, but a number of times, my opinion became the opinion of my authorities and, in several cases, law. Also, I became close to Abe Fortas who taught me a great deal."

As the story proceeds, I continue to ask the "moral" for those starting out in the law.

"Well, I can't state strongly enough how important it is for young people to try their damnedest to stand next to the best minds, the best mentors they can find. At the same time, one must avoid being manipulative. You can move intelligently and strategically without manipulation. *Exposure* is the key, and one should aggressively manage to find it.

"In the early forties, predecessors of Joe McCarthy were snooping around trying to spot Communists in government. It was a horrible time, and so many mistakes where made—some *wonderful* federal employees were forced out. Some of us started trying to help the victims undercover—in my case, for example, a Japanese woman who was just superb and no threat to anyone. We gave friends legal advice, found legal help.

"I guess it was during this period that a few people noticed me and liked what I was doing. The long and short of it is that the governor of Puerto Rico, then appointed by the president, took me along as his naval aide. (Strange, yes—but I was 1A for the draft, and this naval commission proved timely and strategic.) Actually, the governor needed legal help and advice, and I was there to give it.

"And then a big opportunity came, evolving through a series of connections in Washington. A staff of about twenty lawyers was needed to do research in preparation for the Nuremburg trials. I left for this assignment in 1945, did most of my work in London for the trials of 1946. I was just thirty, you see. A great opportunity . . ."

Karsten waltzes through one "great opportunity" after another. Could all this happen today? "Probably," he says.

"Then one of my colleagues wanted to start his own firm and asked me to join the effort. And somewhere along the way I had read Eric Sevareid's book, *Not So Wild a Dream,* in which he proclaims that every young professional owes it to himself to spend at least one year in New York City. Having grown fairly pessimistic at the Department of the Interior about getting departmentally sponsored legislation through Congress, I decided it was indeed time to try private practice. So a group of us young turks started out to conquer New York in private practice, although all of us were also intrigued with politics. The 'private firm' did get off the ground, but we really wanted to take over the Young Democrats Club, and did. We organized an army of followers, and succeeded in knocking off the president of Tammany Hall. That was a fun and heady period.

"Just about then I met my wife, who, coincidentally, had also gone to the University of Chicago. This was in 1950, when the U.S. was involved in the Korean War. Soon after I had a call from the Truman administration to come back to Washington to head price control in the Director of Consumer Goods Division, an independent agency. And soon after that, I was flirting with the private sector once again."

Karsten shifts in his seat to signal a new era.

"I became close to a father and son who founded what became a large oil company that was bogged in litigation for about eighteen years. The case would rise to the Supreme Court, then move back down, then up again. When all the litigation was said and done, the family profited handsomely. And they needed research on how

∎

to diversify their assets. They gave me the assignment. Skirting around almost insurmountable egos, I helped them diversify with some very successful starts in real estate. And that, in a way, is where I've been ever since—with different individual mega-investors, granted, but with a real estate development emphasis throughout. These adventures have kept me largely in either Baltimore or California.

"Through this stage I was reminded again and again of my father—I met and worked with strong individuals with great capacity but with near-disastrous flaws. My friend back in Washington, Abe Fortas, was a good counselor more than once during this time.

"I was also reminded time and again of what I said early on: Luck plays a part in success, but not so large a part as whom you choose to travel with."

It is obvious that Karsten oversees something of an empire today. His firm has five offices scattered about the nation, employing eighty-five professionals. Karsten Realty Advisors consults on the development of headquarter high-rises and multi-use centers; they deal in cooperative pension trusts, where real estate is an accepted medium now; and they creatively salvage, on behalf of banks or other large investors, real estate investment trusts and other gone-astray investment phenonena.

"Do I do much of my own legal work? No, it's beyond me. Here in the Los Angeles office, for example, we have hired two in-house legal counsels, both from Yale Law (one of whom had a baby yesterday). But I am able to watch over their shoulders and more or less know what is going on. It's on the money side of things that I must surround myself with good advisers. I'm not sorry I didn't go to business school, but I know I should keep close to those who did."

Tom Karsten sits up straight now, as though there is a windup message en route. Sure enough . . .

"But that reminds me to circle this back to law. I can't say enough for law education, looking back on it all. Law school not only drives clear and persuasive writing and reading home to all students who succeed there; as important, I learned at law school to cut through all the extraneous material to the core of the problem. I may not always know the answer, but I know the real problem and what the answer *shouldn't* be. I don't know of any other scholastic preparation that is so thorough in building these crucial skills of communication and analysis.

"I can spot a good lawyer almost intuitively—he or she will display damn good intellect, will be cautious and methodical, will be creative, and will employ good people skills as a counselor.

"But one thing concerns me. Law seems to be more of a business these days. It used to be that the lawyer and his client would become very close, very good friends. I'm not certain that is allowed to happen much anymore with all the specialization and obsession for the bottom-line profit. Law firms are less congenial than they used to be. Part of the problem, I guess, is that the young attorneys display less loyalty to their mentors and to the firm. They'll jump from firm to firm if there is a bit of financial profit to be found. This mobility is clearly conveyed to the clients. It is no longer a joy for many of us to deal with many of the law firms—a sense of kinship has disappeared.

"Nonetheless, law sets one up for anything. For everything. I think it is the best preparation a sharp young person can have."

■ ■ ■

Wrong record, right place, right time.

PATRICK MULHEARN

Pat Mulhearn didn't graduate Phi Beta Kappa from college. On the first round, he didn't even get admitted to law school. Once in law school—at what was hardly a first- or even second-rung institution—he didn't make journal, or graduate top-of-the-class. But he makes a good case for having the best job in law that a thirty-eight-year-old could possibly have. Despite this, however, he is about to "step out" . . .

Mulhearn is counsel to the Mayor of New York City. Having gained Ed Koch's confidence over a six-year stay as counsel, he is part of the Mayor's informal "inner circle" of five or six (according to who is counting). He writes many of the Mayor's speeches; he tried his first case in court after two months on the job; he has been in court, among others, with the "Son of Sam" trial, the garbage collection union, and a Brooklyn College professor denied

■

tenure because of an alleged relationship to the CIA; he accompanies the Mayor on trips around the country and abroad; he deals officially with Albany and Washington, D.C.; he chairs the Mayor's managerial Task Force; he keeps an eye on Off-Track Betting on behalf of City Hall; he chairs the New York Banking Commission; and "above all, I take considerable joy in the fact that I can wake up and read in *The New York Times* something that happened the day before that *might* have happened differently if I hadn't been in the room expressing an opinion. I wouldn't take anything away from the importance of the Mayor's opinions or actions, but there are plenty of times when we underlings give him an idea that sticks."

There was a time, not long ago, when Pat Mulhearn thought lawyers came in just two classes: Perry Mason and Others.

"As I left college, I still felt that way—lawyers that I knew anything about talked, talked, talked, and were pretty sharp and pretty dull. And then there was Perry Mason's group (I learned later that that group was labeled 'litigators'). They were different, and I had a hunch I wanted to be part of them."

Mulhearn is comfortably lounging on a small couch in his small, plain office in City Hall which is enlivened slightly by his own prints and posters, most of them depicting something in New York—the harbor, the zoo, the apple. He has something of the Boy Scout about him—the well-scrubbed look, baby-faced, fresh with dark tidy clothes, and with an air of the Irish about him. He talks openly, calmly, and with great warmth.

"My dad was with AT&T, so we hopped everywhere: New Hampshire, Minnesota, Iowa, New Jersey, Nebraska, and more. My parents sent me to the Christian Brothers Academy in Albany, and from there I headed to Boston College largely because Boston the city seemed irresistible. In college I was social—was even social chairman of student government—and dabbled in forensics. My grades were somewhere between 3.0 and 3.5, hardly outstanding, but good enough for dean's list now and then. On the whole, it was a typical Joe College undergraduate career.

"What to do next? Well, that was a problem. I thought maybe the forensics pointed in the direction of law. And my uncle was on criminal court in New York City. He was a real gentleman, and bright, so that was it—I decided to try for law school. But the law schools weren't cordial—not even my own Boston College! Harvard turned me down too—I wanted their joint business and law program—so I was stuck. Somehow I landed a job in concert promotion and it appeared I could work up the scale in that 'profession' quickly. But my dad really opposed it. So I made late applications to law schools nearby my home in Bronxville. New York Law took me—that's not NYU Law, that's NY Law. The public thinks there is a very big difference, you see, and there probably is . . ."

The Mayor's counsel just sat and delivered as though he were on a talk show. He was poised and boyish but self-confident.

"I really started digging in. *Dutiful* is a word that has always applied to me. Happily, New York Law is located very close to City Hall, and I was able to get fieldwork jobs here with ease. My clinical program at school hooked me into the corporation counsel here (it is, essentially, the largest public law office in the country outside of the federal Justice Department). I worked with the Paternity Section of the Family Court Division—the city, at great expense, goes after a lot of negligent fathers. After a few hectic months I moved to where all the action was, the General Litigation Division, and loved it. On one hand, I was out serving papers on wildcat sanitation workers, trying to look mean, while they were asking me how to get their kids into law school."

This man is calm. He just moves along with his story at a comfortable clip . . .

"I've never been really interested in making the big buck. So I was wary of falling into the big-firm trap in New York City. 'Law school is supposed to be a broadening experience,' I kept telling myself. I really didn't want the same goal that everyone around me seemed to have: big firm, big city, and big money. I did try the big firm for one summer and all my negative presuppositions were confirmed.

"Actually, I hated law school. Looking back on it, it was just a holding pattern for me. Moot court and the clinical program were interesting, but on the whole, law school had no punch to it. I stuck with it, as always, got decent grades, and passed the bar.

"One lucky stroke—and there have been a number—changed my life. The New York City Corporation Counsel addressed my third-year class one day. I guess he liked some of the things I asked or said, and later pulled me aside and asked if I would like to go to work for him. I did. The city was in a fiscal crisis then and all kinds of cases and emergencies popped up. I was in the front lines immediately, and often found myself in court arguing against senior partners from New York's biggest firms. It was a heady beginning. I can't imagine that *anybody* could have had better exposure to the excitement of the law. The salary wasn't too great—I started out at thirteen thousand dollars in 1977 and worked up to forty thousand dollars by 1982—but the top-level involvement was fabulous.

"While doing some litigation work with the New York City Board of Elections in 1981, I met Mayor Koch. He noticed me on a couple of assignments; soon after, he asked me to be counsel. Once again I was immediately on the front lines, preparing drafts of executive orders, writing speeches, etc.

"I really like Ed Koch. I guess that's obvious, or I wouldn't have been here this long. He is honest and hardworking and has probably reshaped American politics to some degree. He was the first, or one of the first, to announce publicly his taxes and salary and net worth each year—he started that when he was first elected to Congress. He is interesting to watch in foreign countries, some of which receive him as a head of state. You should see the reception he gets in Central America, for example! There are more Dominicans in New York, you know, than there are in Santo Domingo. And he, of course, relishes the popularity (which is usually more assured abroad than it is at home). Also, the man has an incredible memory—he can remember minutiae that will dazzle any audience, political or legal or otherwise. And he's generous of spirit—for example, he knows he needs advice from others and he actively seeks it. No good lawyer or politician can move ahead without advice, although plenty try. Not Mayor Koch. He knows his limitations."

Mulhearn switches from the Mayor to himself, as if on cue.

"What aspects of my work here am I most proud of? Well, just having a responsible say in almost everything that goes on would have to head the list. But some rather personal things rank up high also. For example, I've always felt a little odd that I didn't serve in Vietnam. So I've spent a lot of time organizing activities and all the accompanying fund-raising initiatives to honor those who served. I guess you might say I was one of the driving forces behind the Vietnam Veterans Memorial Commission. It is in New York City, but clearly carries national importance. We hosted the largest ticker tape parade in the history of New York for the Viet veterans in 1985, created a fund for unemployed veterans, constructed the superb Vietnam Veterans Memorial near here on the East River, and published a book of 'letters home' that has raised millions of dollars for our activities. I'm really proud of that. And then there are particular pet projects that the Mayor has let me oversee—modernizing aspects of the New York City Board of Elections, for example.

"But even with all this, I've been wondering about change. And it's about to happen. You might guess that this job has provided a lot of exposure to *other* jobs and to a lot of people in influential positions, public and private. My interest in combining business with the law has finally gotten the best of me. And so has the need for a little more money. My wife and I live in Riverdale now, with kids who are six, four, and two. I need six thousand dollars per year just for kindergartens! Two years ago, the president of New York Telephone, now chairman of NYNEX, had occasion to spend a lot of time here and liked my work in one rather public victory. He offered me a job then, and again recently, so I'm heading off to the private sector. I'll be in management, overseeing one thousand workers in Business Marketing Operations, an important job that still puts me in the arena of public policy, and isn't a lot different from many of the things I've been doing here—I've been sort of a hybrid in the mayor's office between manager and lawyer. How will I like corporate headquarters? Time will tell. . . .

"But I'll miss the Mayor. There have only been three three-term mayors of New York, you know—LaGuardia, Wagner, and Koch. He deserves a fourth. As for me, no job could have been as good as this job, but we just all move on and I'm intrigued by management in the private sector. Will most of those people be cold and profiteering? Maybe, but I won't be guilty of either. Who knows? I may use the law more formally again soon, and may even head back to government. In the interim, I'll certainly be doing some pro bono work for government. But the private sector calls. I think we all need to get recharged now and then, and change often forces it."

The obvious parting question is asked.

"What—me run for office? I can't imagine it. Being mayor is Ed Koch's entire life. I have a family and am happy putting them in a priority time slot."

As I leave, three City Hall workers are lined up outside Mulhearn's door with papers for approval. He nods and asks the first one in.

"Proud to be a lawyer . . . but not a parasite."

ED KOCH

"How was I lured to the law? Jewish syndrome—nothing more, nothing less. *Every* Jewish boy, in the view of my family and their friends, would eventually become a doctor or a lawyer. For me, considering my talents, it was law, pure and simple. There was no other choice."

Ed Koch, mayor of New York, is sitting in a big red easy chair in his office at City Hall, sipping coffee from a plastic container. A tiny tape recorder with its red light aglow is at his side on the table. He is tan, chubby, and relaxed. (In fact, everyone in public view at City Hall seemed relaxed. The receptionist in bold red and white stripes immediately outside the Mayor's quarters, framed by a portal decorated with Big Apple cards and a picture of herself with the boss, was exclaiming to a hidden professional companion, "I don't care! I just don't see any point in being rich. There are too many problems associated with having too much money. I'm happy the way I am—well, a *little* more would be nice, but . . .")

The Mayor looks at the interviewer with squinting, somewhat suspicious eyes. His press secretary has warned that if the Mayor doesn't like the way the questioning is proceeding, the whole thing could be over in minutes. On the other hand, if the Mayor gets caught up in the proceedings, the session could continue until the interviewer is satisfied, within reason, of course. The press secretary himself is quietly monitoring the affair, seated on a nearby loveseat.

■

"So, you see, I just assumed I'd be a lawyer from childhood on. At Southside High in Newark—my parents had emigrated there from Poland in the thirties—I was in debating, kept up with current events, was fairly social, a less than mediocre athlete, and a decent student . . ."

The big Koch smile suddenly warms up.

". . . and I had a lightning-rod personality. I have *never* been a pussycat."

The Mayor explains that during the high school years life was not easy. He worked at the deli counter of a grocery store afternoons, helped his father run a hat-check concession in a catering hall at night, and created opportunities for making money during school vacations—one summer, he organized a baby-sitters' cooperative.

It is obvious that the Mayor is settling into this conversation. It is also obvious that the Mayor has the ability to listen well and concentrate on the subject at hand. The swirl of activity and the customary controversy surrounding him—the morning paper is full of it—are set aside.

"As my family moved to Brooklyn, I started college at CCNY, supporting myself as a shoe salesman in a department store. My college career was lackluster at best. And two years after I began, I was off to the army.

"After the war—and I saw my share of it in northern France and the Rhineland—it was time to investigate the long-held goal of law school. I was admitted to NYU Law by a real fluke. (Where would I be if that hadn't happened?!) I wandered over there one day to see what I had to do to eventually get in. Now, bear in mind that I had had only two formal years of college at this point, although I'd had some quasi-academic training in the army. The professor I was assigned to talk to gave me the expected: go back to CCNY, pull my grades up from the current B range, and come back to see him.

"Just then a senior professor walked by and overheard our conversation. He interrupted to say, 'Listen, B's at CCNY are worth B-plus to A anywhere else; add to that some war experience, and this fellow deserves a slot here right now!' The man had influence, I guess, because I was admitted pronto. To make a long story short, I passed through NYU law in two years—they had an accelerated program then—so college and law school took me only a total of four years. That makes me sound brighter than I am. Right? . . ."

Giggles from the chair. Laughter from the loveseat.

"Actually, I was quite average in law school. But I was a *good* lawyer soon thereafter. There is no doubt about it—law school sharpens the mind and sets you up for a variety of careers beyond the law itself."

The Mayor grows reminiscent and no longer needs the questions laid out.

"I remember the first day of law school. I was apprehensive, to say the least. One professor put a sizable list of readings on the board. I dutifully copied them down. But I made one big mistake. I thought the assigned reading was for the next day. Instead, the list was for the whole semester! . . . Anyway, I stayed up all night reading, wondering how the hell I could finish all that stuff. It really knocked me out. I went to class the next morning exasperated, thinking I'd flunk out quickly, although I had actually read a lot and understood a lot. Then I learned of my error and grinned from ear to ear. I knew I was going to be okay from that moment on."

A warm grin and a pensive look out the window . . .

"The case method was good, although I would have benefited from more lecturing. One superb lecturer—a real raconteur—always had me on the edge of my seat. But one day he strayed from the law and said something I would never forget. He said that when *he* was in law school the son of the cloakmaker, the son of the butcher, and the son of the shoemaker could not go. He went on to announce that he questioned the current demographics of the law school's entering class. Given the fact that my class of around eighty-five had a noticeably increased number of Jews and Italians (but not many women or blacks), we knew exactly what he was addressing. And we didn't—well, *I* didn't like it one bit.

"Later, when I became mayor, NYU Law asked me to give their commencement address. And guess who was on the front row—that same professor. I introduced myself as the proud 'son of a cloakmaker,' the kind of student one of my law school professors had questioned as suitable for NYU Law when I attended.

That professor on the front row knew exactly whom I was talking to. Later in the receiving line—the professor did not show up, by the way—a little Jewish lady kissed my hand and tears were in her eyes as she thanked me for identifying who I really was, quietly acknowledging the change in NYU Law. I'll never forget it."

The Mayor is leading his own story along now.

"Next, I flunked half of the bar exam—the procedures part. I passed it on the next round. But law school left me with my own set of procedures. Ask any one of my staff members. The classroom procedure of law school is the staff meeting procedure now at City Hall. We employ the Socratic method. I state the issue or the problem and present some searching questions. Everyone around the table—sometimes called upon—offers an opinion, supported by the best evidence that he or she can come up with. After it appears to me that we have heard enough, I either clap my hands— it's now my warning that a decision is at hand—or we agree to meet again (and sometimes again and again) until there is over-riding evidence to support one action or another. With some issues, the discussion goes on meeting after meeting with no obvious conclusion in sight—settling on a location for more prison space in New York, for example."

His little tape recorder bleeps, and he signals to the loveseat. The press secretary rushes to turn the tape, the Mayor glances at his watch, and nods to me to ask the next question. But before I have it out, he continues, sticking with the topic, forgoing political histories and commentaries along the way.

"When I entered Congress in 1969 [the Mayor was on the New York City Council at the time he was elected to the U.S. House of Representatives from Manhattan's "silk stocking" district], I left my law practice, which I really liked. I just can't imagine how you can give yourself to full-time congressional work and maintain a law practice. To me, it just invites conflict of interest."

He switches to the future.

"At some point, I will no longer be mayor. What will I do? Will I go back into law? Doubtful. Law these days strikes me as too parasitic. Lawyers just hang on, often unnecessarily. Why can't they decide to put caps on things rather than just hoping and pushing forever for more? There are all kinds of examples of what

■

I mean, including right here in the city. Too often we're treated in litigation or negotiation like we're a private business with unlimited hidden resources. Well, we don't have unlimited resources and often when you pay excessively for one thing you take money from something more important, something all the people really need. Yes, we'll have our little share of incompetence and corruption like any government or private industry. But we can't afford to pay endlessly for our mistakes and be prevented from going on with the business of running government as responsibly as we possibly can.

"On the other hand, lawyers today strike me as good people. They're more interested than disinterested in pro bono work—we profit from a lot of that generous spirit here in the city—and they're genuinely interested in working full-time for government, even though we pay considerably less than the private sector. I make $130,000 per year as mayor—some kids make close to that several years after law school in the big firms here in New York. But look at the influence I and others working for this great city have! Ours is the fourth-largest budget in the United States—following the budgets of the U.S. itself, the State of California, and the State of New York—so we have incredibly important decisions to make on behalf of millions of people."

The Mayor veers toward a list of political accomplishments in office to prove his point. But he catches himself.

"You asked me what I'll do when I'm no longer mayor. I don't know—the law, all by itself, is too confining for me now. I've learned other skills. One of my best has been further honed in office—the knack of translating a very complicated issue or concept to a short, concise definition so it is readily understood by the layman, by the people. Somehow I want to build on that very skill. Succeed Dan Rather? Well, there could be worse fates."

It is time to call this discussion to a halt. Happily, that is the interviewer's task. But first comes a word of advice for prelaw students.

"If a bright young person doesn't have an enormous gut desire to enter some other profession, then law school is the place he or she should go. It quickens and sharpens the mind and prepares you to head out anywhere."

The Mayor is quickly silent and smiling. He is finished. And so is the coffee. And, as the bleep signals, so is the tape.

■　■　■

"Attorneys are just good followers. . . . The lawyer mentality is to follow the rules and make a big pile doing it."

HARRY PALMER

"Lawyers are full of shit. They have an opinion on everything, whether asked or not. Worse, they think they *know* everything. The lawyers in the big firms are the worst—they waste countless hours just in-fighting. Only rarely does the public get a whiff of that, when a noteworthy firm falls apart. But, believe me, the clients are paying for all those lost hours of internal warfare. And every lawyer who is part of it thinks *he* has the answer to the firm's woes."

Curiously, the speaker, a fiftyish man in Los Angeles with a Cary Grant look accompanied by all the right alligators and tassles, fits his own depiction of the "other guys" rather well. He seems to be a poor listener, and has a ready, firm opinion on any topic— whether in his frame of familiarity or not—but claims one important point of departure from the rest.

"I never became a legal groupie. And I guess that is best documented by the fact that three years ago I left, I got out. Fatigue and disenchantment and anger just caught up with me."

Harry Palmer has top-drawer credentials. He attended one of the best high schools in L.A., picked up his B.A. and master's at Stanford in English, and then entered Stanford Law, one of the nation's most selective law schools.

"Why did I go? Well, what else was there to do? I used the language well, and law school seemed to lead to the right career for that. But I hated it. *Hated* it. This was just after the Korean War—most of my classmates had tried a little business and then veered off to law school. Our class was only around one hundred, with not more than two or three women. Everyone talked career, career, career. And I guess I did too.

"My first shot at law as career was in a big California firm— 120 lawyers. My worst suspicions were honored: they expected

■

me to marry the right woman, join the right clubs, pull in the right clients, and pick up the right money. I lasted six months."

"I needed something a lot more broadminded. And one reason was—or rather is—that I'm gay. I didn't, of course, breathe a word of that. It is the rare lawyer, even today, who can 'come out,' at least while working for a firm."

Harry moved to a small firm in the suburbs of L.A., lived his own life with less pressure, and became a specialist in real estate law, which he liked. He worked up to charging two hundred dollars an hour. And he worked quite a few eighteen-hour days when big zoning projects hit his desk.

"But as the years passed, I grew tired of living by all the rules. That is, after all, what a lawyer advises people to do, and must do himself. Does a time sheet tell you anything about the quality of one's work? There is a lot of time-sheet mentality in the law.

"I guess the thing that most got to me as a 'regular lawyer' was the realization that attorneys are just good followers, good advice-givers. They lack imagination, and they rarely become leaders. Sure, there is the rare lawyer-politician who makes a difference, but on the whole, the lawyer mentality is to carefully follow the rules and make a big pile doing it. And in the process, attorneys pick up this air of great authority. Most of them are just a pain in the ass."

This handsome, outspoken man, dressed so carefully in his casuals, nods to several groups of men entering a Santa Monica brunch palace.

"At the moment my life is very full. I've found some incredibly constructive projects to dig into. They don't pay, but happily, I saved enough money early on to put that concern largely to rest."

I order a Bloody Mary. He passes up the complimentary drink with brunch and orders seltzer. This is hardly a man at ease. He may have left the formal legal race, but he speaks earnestly about his current work.

"I'm called on now and then by my old firm-mates to step in when a well-contained project seems to have my name written all over it. I'm working on one now at a bank—it won't last for more than several weeks, but I'm putting in twelve-to-fourteen-hour days. But my heart is in other projects where my knowledge can really make a difference. The AIDS Project of Los Angeles desperately needs lawyers, particularly related to housing discrimination. A lot of AIDS-diagnosed guys are thrown out of housing or lose jobs and can't pay for decent housing. There's no one around to help them. I've been a part of setting up pro bono programs to address the issue. This service is catching on around the nation. The National Gay Rights Advocates organization in San Francisco is doing a hell of a job in this arena. But God, there are some terrible problems out there related to this plague, and many more lawyers are going to have to come forward."

A few more barbs toward lawyers accompany dessert, and Palmer is off with a handshake and a hint of a smile.

SIX

·

CONCLUSION

· · ·

It is a little depressing to reach the conclusion. Why? Because those just stepping in and those who have stepped out of the law are more buoyant and optimistic, on the whole, than those who are now practicing law.

Scott Turow, America's celebrated author/lawyer, helps point out why: "The law remains in some manner a troubled profession. In spite of the prominence of law, lawyers themselves aren't entirely well regarded. Many lay people do not like lawyers. And to a surprising extent, lawyers often do not like themselves."*

It appears that throughout history lawyers have rarely been "liked" by laypeople, although a grudging respect may be accorded. And the anecdotal testimony in this book makes it clear that lawyers often do not hold their own in high regard. Consider this sampling of adjectives used by our profiled now-or-former lawyers to describe those in their profession: *parasitic, greedy, boring, myopic, intense, manipulative, aggressive, driven, workaholic, alcoholic, anxious, lonely.* Yes, some positive, or at least neutral, words crept in—*professional, analytical, problem-solvers, craftsmen*—but the negative labels have predominated.

As a postscript to the interview, each lawyer was asked to spontaneously rank five professional groups—doctors, lawyers, religionists (formally accredited ministers, priests, and rabbis), educators, and businessmen/entrepreneurs—in terms of overall respectability, including honesty, commitment to duty, hard work, and concern for others. A few demurred. As Peter Britell said, "No, I can't rate your five professional groups on overall respectability. They all make different contributions. Stereotyping them would be like stereotyping ethnic groups—it's both risky and wrong." The majority of the lawyers jumped right in, however, responding without much pause.

Educators and religionists were almost always named first (sometimes in reverse order). Tom Allen said, "Educators and

* "Law School v. Reality," *New York Times Magazine*, September 18, 1988.

religionists don't seem to define victory by what they make or whether they win. I have great respect for that." Doctors and lawyers almost always vied for third position. And usually the businessmen/entrepreneurs ranked last. Alyson Singer said: "The businessmen, unfortunately, have no code of ethics, like all the others—that means there is no restraint, and they show it."

Fritz Schwarz probably speaks for the majority in his assessment of the professional groups (which he declined to rank): "The educators are wonderful in terms of what they aspire to do and aspire to be, but they too frequently grow complacent. Also, I wish they regarded teaching as important as research. The religionists are not as important as they should be. Some are awful, some wonderful. The doctors disappoint me constantly. They do some great things; on the other hand, they seem the most selfish and too often, careless. The businessmen seem to have great angst, like corporate lawyers, in taking someone else's ideas or money and making something of it. But their emphasis is on financial success, and that is very limiting to a worldview. The lawyers are incredibly important to society. But we too often, as a group, settle cases with half-truths and we too rarely step back and ask, 'Whom are we serving?' Also, we are too often guilty of a 'we versus they' attitude as it affects our profession, and too often, our lives."

Tom Karsten echoes other respondents in adding, "The lawyers rank high on commitment to clients, but they have slipped considerably in commitment to public service."

Sol M. Linowitz, an international negotiator and former ambassador and, at seventy-four, the senior counsel of Coudert Brothers law firm in Washington, thinks Karsten's point is the key to personal lawyer dissatisfaction and, more important, to society's dissatisfaction with the law as currently practiced.

In addressing the Cornell Law School Centennial in April 1988, Linowitz lamented the dehumanization of the practice of law, due largely to the growing influence of huge firms.

> It is . . . disquieting to realize how things have changed in the fifty years since I was graduated from law school. . . . I am talking about the changes in our profession, in the practice of law. . . . When I graduated from law school, the law was an esteemed and honored calling. . . . Lawyers regarded themselves

■

as charged with a public trust. . . . Over the years, however, something seriously disturbing has been happening to the legal profession. We have become a business, dominated by "bottom line" perspectives. In too many of our firms, the computer has become the Managing Partner as we are ruled by hourly rates, time sheets and electronic devices. . . . We are making more and achieving less, and in the process, I am afraid, we have lost a great deal of what we were meant to be.

Linowitz cites the existence of more than 700,000 practicing lawyers today (one for every 354 citizens)—twice as many as there were in 1970. He says that in 1960 there were only four firms in America that had over one hundred attorneys; today, more than two hundred firms have at least one hundred lawyers, some over five hundred. And to keep such megafirms ("these business enterprises") alive requires an enormous national billing, close to forty billion dollars a year.

These escalating numbers disguise an even more pervasive problem facing the profession. The individual attorney has become increasingly distanced from the human client. Associates at our large firms spend years writing research memos before they ever meet a client. And they may never encounter individual clients who need the counsel of lawyers to deal with their personal problems. We have been witnessing the dehumanization of the law, and this has been accompanied by a widespread distrust and suspicion of lawyers. The public impression that the practice of law has become a money-making, profit-maximizing undertaking has brought into question the intention, the integrity and the value of lawyers generally.

Sol Linowitz documents the decline of "human relations—the stuff of which law is made." His favorite target is always the big firm, the very arena to which most high-ranking law students aspire. In an April 1988 *New York Times* interview, he said: "The quid pro quo at large firms is dazzling. We attract them, we lure them, we bribe them, and in the process we don't tell them that they're going to be giving up a decent way of life."

And there is the rub. So many lawyers—particularly the

young, so recently initiated but now on track and, at the other
end of the spectrum, the fiftyish, now reflective attorneys—anxiously (and more and more publicly) question whether lawyering
provides "a decent way of life."

Didn't they *know* what they were getting themselves into,
one might ask?

No. Their reasons for entering law were naïve and obscure
at the outset, and law school does not seem to sharpen the perspective. As Scott Turow observes, "Law school is about training
legal scholars. Despite the persistence of the timeworn phrase, law
school does *not* teach students to think like lawyers. It teaches
them to think like law professors. . . . While they [the students]
learn about the capacity of all arguments to be undermined, they
are taught nothing about the ends to which that skill is meant to
be applied."

Law school becomes a leading suspect, then, when hunting
for the source of confusion over what one is *expected* to do in the
profession of law versus the disappointment that so often surfaces,
once one finds out.

So we come to a key question: Who should go to law school—
and what should they expect to learn there? A hint of the confusion
in finding an answer comes in a comment from Francis Beytagh,
the dean of the Ohio State University College of Law: "We law
school deans constantly fight a single battle on a number of fronts:
is the law school part of The Profession or part of The Academy?
We rather prefer the latter."

But many unsuspecting students enroll thinking it is the former. The current, standard curriculum of law schools is questionable as an appropriate and effective introduction to serving the
common good as a lawyer. Turow suggests a more thorough
grounding in professional ethics, and Linowitz suggests a broader,
more classical curriculum: "A good lawyer . . . has a grasp of what
yesterday teaches us about today and tomorrow, and knows that
the real meaning of words like 'freedom' or 'justice' can only be
found in the tapestry of history."

Do all agree with Linowitz in defining what perspective a
good lawyer should have? Should such esoteric qualities influence
the law school admissions committee?

■

The director of admissions at one of the Ivy League law schools, who vented such frustration that he chose to remain anonymous, said flatly, "We can't answer those questions—or rather, our faculty doesn't seem very interested in debating those questions. Meanwhile, we're looking for the incisive, analytical mind and the person who enjoys the intellectual exercise of logic, careful reading, and clear writing. We're *not* looking for career definition. We're looking for intellectual horsepower as indicated by a good academic track record and high LSATs, plus some vague 'enrichment factor'—the potential of an individual's willingness and enthusiasm to contribute. The problem is, however, that we're risk-averse, so we usually end up moving in favor of the highest scores and grades."

A more numbing confession comes from a member of the Test Development and Research Committee of the Law School Admission Council, the outfit in Pennsylvania that oversees the content and administration of the all-important Law School Admission Test (LSAT): "We know so little about legal education. We continue to do what we've done for the last 80 years without really knowing whether what we do is sensible or effective. We ought to try to find out about that. . . . We're finally taking steps to try to help law students receive a better education. It's about time."*

Beth Cobb O'Neil, director of services and programs of the Law School Admissions Services, says there is a very disappointing correlation between LSAT scores and early law school performance. "So many factors that should be considered for law school admission—imagination and perseverance, for example—cannot be objectified, of course. So the criteria become rigidly numerical. The real source of the problem is the law school faculties who, almost always, set admission standards and policy. They're such elitists. Everyone but Yale wants to be Harvard and each faculty thinks the better their school's entering profile of LSATs and college GPAs, the shinier their prestige badge will be.

"What is lawyering, anyway? It surely goes beyond demon-

* *Law Services Report*, Law School Admissions Services, March 1988.

strated intelligence. But neither the academy nor the profession seems ready to acknowledge that, despite some fairly convincing evidence out there."

There is not silence everywhere regarding the relevance of schooling to problems that must be resolved in the workplace. Former Dean James Vorenberg of the Harvard Law School shows signs of interest in relating the academy to the profession:

> The President of my university has advised us that too many of the best young people are going into law. While I think he is wrong (and we will continue to compete for students), his point raises issues that we should be exposing our students to. . . . To what extent is the work of lawyers in various settings directed too much to fighting, when the interests of society would be and could be better served by heavier reliance on mediation and negotiation? In a period when much of the apparatus that was assembled in the past 25 years to meet legal needs of poor people seems to be in danger, are we at law schools taking the responsibility we should to maintain the present system or seek a better one?*

Meanwhile, the law schools continue to pump out grade-grubbing survivors of the Socratic and case-study methods to practice law, appropriately trained or not.

Then without paying much heed to the "diversity" the law degree is thought to promise, most of the soon-to-be graduates line up ("like pink-eyed rats," says Gerry Spence) in their dark clothes to nab the most prestigious firm offers available. (The University of Wisconsin's law school placement office handbook advises its students who are about to undertake firm interviews to "Present a good appearance. One law firm recruiter suggested a man should look like an off-duty minister and women should look as if they are going to a funeral.") Although some plan to stay "temporarily," to sample firm life and, just as important, to pay off the financial debts accumulated through the stages of education, most tend to linger. And to doubt . . . but linger, anxiously,

* *Harvard Law School Bulletin*, Winter 1986.

■

nonetheless. Scott Turow, in his *New York Times Magazine* article, describes what often happens next:

[What evolves is] the legal malaise. Many lawyers do not like to practice; they regard themselves as imprisoned in gilded cages—highly paid, well regarded, and unhappy. The fact is that life at the bar is hard. The nuts-and-bolts work can be frustratingly detailed or numbingly routine—and the environment sometimes dismal. On one side stands the adversary, of dubious ethics and limitless zeal; on the other, the client waiting hungrily for favorable results. Together, they make for a stressed-out existence of economic pressure and ceaseless competition, a parade of deadlines, obdurate judges, unreturned phone messages, lost weekends and evenings, a Sisyphean struggle to catch up.

As the backlog of work piles up, the treadmill continues to roll and the tired runners try to go the distance. Newcomer Alyson Singer captured it: "When I think of lawyers now, I think of legions of dark-suited people marching in a line, not looking to the right or to the left, but straight ahead."

Why can't attorneys hop off the treadmill if the "fit" is wrong? Remember what Steve Yandle, watching his young Yale Law alums moving into the professional world, observed: "They head to the big firms in the big cities saying 'I don't really want to do this, but I will temporarily, just to see what it is like and to prove to myself and everybody else that I can catch the big reward following all that hard work and achievement of college and law school. I know I'm really above this sort of rat race, but . . .' Then the competition inside the firm gets to them and they're on a treadmill they don't like—trying to compile impressive billable hours, trying to beat out the competition to make partner, still trying to prove to themselves once again that they're the best. It's just tragic. A few wise ones drop out after about three years, but the majority just drudge on."

"I'm spending most of my hours in a firm like this benefiting corporate America, aiding accretion of capital. I'm a tool of management!" says Russ Li, an agonized product of an "emancipated" generation.

*So why can't bright, independent young people move out,
move on?*

Mark Saunders: "No, I'm not certain it was wise to fall to
law. But here I am. Law today needs people who love gamesmanship, who enjoy scheming. I just don't. One always hopes there
might be something more. But, dammit, there hardly is."

*So why can't bright, independent middle-aged people move
out, move on?*

But let us remember the Judge Rymers, the Fritz Schwarzes,
the Peter Britells, the Richard Reyeses, the Gerry Spences, the
Lesley Martins, the Robert Johnsons, the Steve Hudspeths—even
the Chandler Cumminses, the Barbara Smithes, and the James
Thomases—who, although regretful of some elements within their
professional environment and critical of some of their fellow practitioners, have nonetheless carved out a niche that "fits." These
individuals seem fulfilled in pursuing law with energy and determination and are convinced they are making a positive contribution.

And yet, there are so many of the lonely and disillusioned,
frustrated but hanging on while young, while old. Some are profiled in these pages. There are undoubtedly thousands more in the
halls of government agencies, corporations, public services, and,
of course, in the law firms.

No one point of view can fairly represent the enormous variety of lawyers out there, nor their diverse points of view. But
Wyoming's Charlie Baker, who tried the law and tried the city
and tried to keep his conscience intact but kept running back to
solitude in the woods, offers a haunting summary:

"So many [lawyers] have a good heart and are brilliant and
courageous. But arrogance, and, with it, inconsistent priorities, set
in. As they move along professionally, the great majority of attorneys just don't stand for much."

. . . A somber warning to those stepping in; a sad and ironic
consolation to those stepping out; and a challenge to those in step.

We who watch remain hopeful. The law is all of us.

FOR THE BEST IN PAPERBACKS, LOOK FOR THE

In every corner of the world, on every subject under the sun, Penguin represents quality and variety—the very best in publishing today.

For complete information about books available from Penguin—including Pelicans, Puffins, Peregrines, and Penguin Classics—and how to order them, write to us at the appropriate address below. Please note that for copyright reasons the selection of books varies from country to country.

In the United Kingdom: For a complete list of books available from Penguin in the U.K., please write to *Dept E.P., Penguin Books Ltd, Harmondsworth, Middlesex, UB7 0DA*.

In the United States: For a complete list of books available from Penguin in the U.S., please write to *Dept BA, Penguin*, Box 120, Bergenfield, New Jersey 07621-0120.

In Canada: For a complete list of books available from Penguin in Canada, please write to *Penguin Books Ltd, 2801 John Street, Markham, Ontario L3R 1B4*.

In Australia: For a complete list of books available from Penguin in Australia, please write to the *Marketing Department, Penguin Books Ltd, P.O. Box 257, Ringwood, Victoria 3134*.

In New Zealand: For a complete list of books available from Penguin in New Zealand, please write to the *Marketing Department, Penguin Books (NZ) Ltd, Private Bag, Takapuna, Auckland 9*.

In India: For a complete list of books available from Penguin, please write to *Penguin Overseas Ltd, 706 Eros Apartments, 56 Nehru Place, New Delhi, 110019*.

In Holland: For a complete list of books available from Penguin in Holland, please write to *Penguin Books Nederland B.V., Postbus 195, NL-1380AD Weesp, Netherlands*.

In Germany: For a complete list of books available from Penguin, please write to *Penguin Books Ltd, Friedrichstrasse 10-12, D-6000 Frankfurt Main I, Federal Republic of Germany*.

In Spain: For a complete list of books available from Penguin in Spain, please write to *Longman, Penguin España, Calle San Nicolas 15, E-28013 Madrid, Spain*.

In Japan: For a complete list of books available from Penguin in Japan, please write to *Longman Penguin Japan Co Ltd, Yamaguchi Building, 2-12-9 Kanda Jimbocho, Chiyoda-Ku, Tokyo 101, Japan*.

FOR THE BEST IN EDUCATION, LOOK FOR THE

☐ **TALES OUT OF SCHOOL**
A Teacher's Candid Account from the Front Lines of the American High School Today
Patrick Welsh

A veteran teacher at a large, diverse public high school recounts his experiences in and out of the classroom and outlines the ways in which many students and teachers have already pointed the way to truly successful education.

"Courageous and optimistic"—*Washington Post Book World*
220 pages   ISBN: 0-14-009442-3   **$6.95**

☐ **GUIDE TO AMERICAN GRADUATE SCHOOLS, FIFTH EDITION**
Harold R. Doughty

The first comprehensive guide to graduate and professional study in the United States contains vital, up-to-date information on fields of study offered, admissions requirements, financial aid possibilities, housing situations, and much more for more than 900 accredited institutions.
582 pages   ISBN: 0-14-046725-4   **$15.95**

☐ **THE PLUG-IN DRUG**
Revised Edition
Marie Winn

The revised edition of the groundbreaking study on TV addiction in children includes new material on video games and computers, and a new chapter, "Television and the School."

"Extremely important . . . ought to be read by every parent"
—*Los Angeles Times*
288 pages   ISBN: 0-14-007698-0   **$6.95**

You can find all these books at your local bookstore, or use this handy coupon for ordering:

Penguin Books By Mail
Dept. BA Box 999
Bergenfield, NJ 07621-0999

Please send me the above title(s). I am enclosing _____ (please add sales tax if appropriate and $1.50 to cover postage and handling). Send check or money order—no CODs. Please allow four weeks for shipping. We cannot ship to post office boxes or addresses outside the USA. *Prices subject to change without notice.*

Ms./Mrs./Mr. _____

Address _____

City/State _____ Zip _____